THE STRUGGLE FOR
POLICE REFORMS IN INDIA

Also by the author:

Kohima to Kashmir: On the Terrorist Trail

The Naxalite Movement in India

THE STRUGGLE FOR POLICE REFORMS IN INDIA

RULER'S POLICE TO PEOPLE'S POLICE

Prakash Singh

RUPA

First published by
Rupa Publications India Pvt. Ltd 2022
7/16, Ansari Road, Daryaganj
New Delhi 110002

Sales Centres:

Allahabad Bengaluru Chennai
Hyderabad Jaipur Kathmandu
Kolkata Mumbai

ISBN: 978-93-5520-247-5

First impression 2022

10 9 8 7 6 5 4 3 2 1

The moral right of the author has been asserted.

CONTENTS

PREFACE

At the end of my 35 years of police service, I was convinced that its working required a complete overhaul. Police should be people-friendly and it should inspire confidence among all sections of society as the protector of their lives, property and honour. Unfortunately, however, we continue to be saddled with a colonial structure which was created by the British, who wanted a police force which should be at their beck and call and which would uphold the interests of the Empire. As such, they created a 'politically useful' police which would obey their orders—right or wrong, legal or unlawful. With the dawn of Independence, it was expected that the police's role would be redefined and it would reflect the democratic aspirations of the people. However, that did not happen. Not that the founding fathers of the Constitution did not have foresight; it is just that they were optimistic about both the politicians and the policemen working in harmony in the overall interests of the country. They could not foresee that politics of the country would take a nosedive and that a symbiotic relationship would develop between the politicians and policemen wherein the politicians would use, misuse and abuse the police for their partisan ends.

It is a sad commentary on our governance that whatever was recorded more than a century back about its flaws and shortcomings is true *a fortiori* even today. The Fraser Commission (1902) recorded that the police is 'generally regarded as corrupt and oppressive, and it has utterly failed to secure the confidence and cordial cooperation of the people'. The Commission interestingly recorded that 'radical reforms are urgently necessary? It appears that time has stood still for the police in India. Nothing has changed in the last more than a hundred years. In fact, whatever changes have taken place, apart from the cosmetic improvements in resources, has been for the worse. There has been politicization of crime and criminalization of politics.

While in service, I raised my voice to the extent I could, but was discouraged and silenced by well-meaning senior officers. The home secretary of Uttar Pradesh (UP), during one of our interactions, when I was quite worked up, chided me, saying, 'Prakash, who wants an honest policeman?' I was stunned by his observation and had no answer. The All India Services (Conduct) Rules of 1968 imposed constraints on what I could do beyond a limit for systemic reforms in the police. After superannuation, these constraints were gone, and I decided to knock at the doors of the Supreme Court, having exhausted all other options.

I filed a public interest litigation (PIL) in the Supreme Court in 1996. My assessment at that time was that the struggle would last for four to five years. Had I known that it was going to be a long, long struggle, I would perhaps not have embarked on this exercise. However, having initiated it, my nature being what it is, I could not give up half way either. I was convinced about the need, relevance and urgency of reforms, and so there was no question of abandoning the cause. Tagore's lyric 'Ekla chalo re' (Walk Alone) sustained and motivated me in this prolonged struggle.

It took 10 years to get a favourable judgment from the Supreme Court. Surprisingly and disappointingly, it has already taken 15 years to get the directions implemented— and the end is not in sight!

I am now in my mid-80s and do not think I shall see the fulfilment of my dream of a ruler's police transforming into a people's police in my lifetime. However, that does not bother me. I am convinced that the efforts to bring about reforms in the police are a historical process and, therefore, there could be no stopping them. The vested interests may delay it, dilute the judicial directions or even try to subvert them, but the wheel that has been set in motion will continue to move on.

The idea to write this book came to my mind because I felt that I must document all that has gone into the effort to bring about police reforms, especially through the judiciary. Whoever takes over the baton should find this documentation useful. Besides, it should educate the public on a subject which is very vital for their security and well-being, and make them aware of the relevance and urgency of police reforms in the country.

Police reforms are absolutely necessary for India to emerge as a progressive, modern state. I have faith in the destiny of India and am therefore convinced that transformational changes in the police shall happen in the country in the not-too-distant future.

I would like to record my appreciation of all those who helped me in writing this book. Dr Madhurima Sen, archivist in the West Bengal State Archives, provided me documents and photographs of police during the colonial rule. Dr Vipul Mudgal, director, Common Cause, was of great help in preparing graphics for the book. My two sons, Pankaj and Piyush, also contributed. Pankaj Kumar Singh, director general, Border Security Force (BSF), painstakingly went through the text and made valuable suggestions. Piyush Kumar Singh, CEO, Terrene Labs (USA), advised me on the technological challenges which police are likely to face in the future. George Thampi Kutty laboriously typed the manuscript. And, on a lighter note, I must thank the government also for the lockdown during the pandemic, which restricted my movements and thereby enabled me to concentrate on this project.

1

HISTORY OF POLICE IN INDIA

EARLY HISTORY

The concept of rule of law and administration of justice was known to the earliest Indian lawgivers. There are references to policing functions in the scriptures. The *Āpastamba Dharmasutra* (600 to 300 BC) mentions that the King should see that there is 'no danger from thieves in villages and forests' and that he should 'appoint in towns and villages officers and their subordinates who are pure and truthful for the protection of the subjects'. The *Dharmasutra* goes on to say that 'if the King does not punish the guilty, he incurs sin', that the 'judges should be men of learning, clever and fulfilling their duties' and that the 'witnesses should tell the truth and be punished if they are untruthful'.[1] The great lawgiver Manu ordained that a king must have spies or agents who should investigate the thieves who steal properties and officials who swindle the state coffers. *Manu-smriti* classified crime under 18 heads, which included assault, theft, robbery, violence, gambling and defamation.[2]

The scriptures mandated that the State was ultimately responsible to compensate for all articles lost or stolen. This was first laid down in the *Vishnu Purana*. 'Having recovered

---

[1]Giriraj Shah, *The Indian Police: A Retrospect*, Himalaya Publishing House, 1992, p. 10.

[2]Anupam Sharma, 'Police in Ancient India,' *Indian Journal of Political Science*, Vol. 65, No.1, January–March, 2004.

goods stolen by thieves, let him (the King) restore them entirely to their owners, to whatever caste they may belong. If he has been unable to recover them, he must pay (their value) out of his own treasury.'[3]

In Mohenjo-daro, one of the two centres of the Indus Valley Civilization, archaeologists have excavated images indicating the presence of policemen who looked after the safety of people. Harappa, the other centre of the civilization, has also thrown up evidence of police presence in those days. Archaeologists have found a seal portraying a man with a stick showing, in all likelihood, the earliest image of a policeman.

THE MAURYAS

The Mauryas (321–185 BC) established a good administrative structure. The provinces were placed under officers designated as Pradesikas, who were entrusted with revenue and police functions. The towns were placed under Nagaraks, whose responsibilities included keeping a watch over inns, sarais (resting place) and places of entertainment, especially to track the arrival of foreigners and persons of bad character and also to detect thieves. The villages were placed under a gramani, who was assisted by a council of village elders. He had the power to try minor offences, impose fines in certain cases and even expel thieves from the village. The State had an elaborate system of espionage. Criminal law was severe and stringent. The King would ensure that the officers were not corrupt, oppressive or partial. According to Megasthenes, the ancient Greek historian and diplomat, Indians were remarkably law-abiding and crime was very rare.[4]

---

[3]Giriraj Shah, *The Indian Police: A Retrospect*, Himalaya Publishing House, 1992, pp.10–11.

[4]Anandswarup Gupta, *Crime and Police in India* (upto 1861), Sahitya Bhawan, 1974, p. 3.

Kautilya's Arthashastra

Kautilya's *Arthashastra* is India's most comprehensive book on governance, which throws light on the criminal justice system of those days. Kautilya was an erudite Brahmin who received his education in the University of Taxila. He had moved to Pataliputra but was humiliated by its King, whereupon he vowed to destroy the ruling Nanda dynasty. He mentored Chandragupta, a child of royal family but brought up by a cowherd, and helped him become the King of Magadha, defeating its King, Dhana Nanda. The *Arthashastra* states that only the rule of law can guarantee security of life and the welfare of people. The following aphorisms from the *Arthashastra* are illuminating:

> The maintenance of law and order by the use of punishment is the science of government (*dand-niti*).
>
> It is the power of punishment alone, when exercised impartially in proportion to guilt and irrespective of whether the person punished is the king's son or the enemy that protects this world and the next.
>
> A severe king (meting out unjust punishment) is hated by the people he terrorises, while one who is too lenient is held in contempt by his own people. Whoever imposes just and deserved punishment is respected and honoured.
>
> An innocent man who does not deserve to be penalized shall not be punished, for the sin of inflicting unjust punishment is visited on the king.[5]

An essential duty of government, according to Kautilya, is maintaining order. This includes both maintenance of social order as well as order in the sense of preventing and

---

[5]L.N. Rangarajan, *Kautilya: The Arthashastra*, Penguin Books India, 1992, pp. 492–93.

punishing criminal activity. A judge is called a dharmastha or the upholder of dharma. It implied that the ultimate source of all law was dharma.

The State is responsible for any failure resulting in loss of money or property by its subjects. If a thief could not be apprehended and the stolen property not recovered, the victim must be reimbursed by the king from his own resources.

Arthashastra mentions three kinds of arrests: on suspicion, for possession and for crime such as murder.

Torture appears to have been fairly common in the Kautilyan state. However, only those against whom there was a strong presumption of guilt were to be tortured to elicit a confession. The following categories of people were not to be tortured: those suspected of minor offences, minors, aged, sick, insane, suffering from hunger, thirst or fatigue after a long journey, etc. Torture must not result in death; if it does, the person responsible shall be punished.

The creation of a secret service with spies, secret agents and specialists such as assassins, is a task of high priority for the king. Such a service is necessary for the security of the kingdom and to further the objective of expansion by conquests.

There is a chapter on foreign policy too. The *Arthashastra* supports an 'active' foreign policy. It says that 'the enemy, however strong he may be, becomes vulnerable to harassment and destruction when he is squeezed between the conqueror and his allies.'[6] Elsewhere, it says that 'an enemy's destruction shall be brought about even at the cost of great losses in men, material and wealth.'

A king should be guided by the following principle: 'In the happiness of his subjects lies the king's happiness; in their

---

[6]Ibid. 541.

welfare his welfare. He shall not consider as good only that which pleases him but treat as beneficial to him whatever pleases his subjects.[7]

THE GUPTAS

The Gupta period (320 to 540 CE) was also marked by good administration. Towns were placed under the authority of Purapals, who maintained law and order with the help of the police, secret agents and troops. Villages were placed under a gramadhyaksha, who was assisted by a council. Fa-hien, a Chinese Buddhist who stayed in India for about six years during the reign of Chandragupta Vikramaditya (376–415 CE), has written about the peaceful conditions prevailing in India, the rarity of serious crimes and the effectiveness of administration, and observed that one could travel from one part of the country to another without any apprehension:

> The people are numerous and happy. They have not to register their households, or to attend to any magistrates and their rules. The king governs without any decapitation or other corporal punishment. People of various sects set up houses of charity where rooms, couches, beds, food and drink are supplied to travellers.[8]

There was a difference between the administrative systems of the Mauryas and the Guptas. The Mauryan kings had a centralized administrative system, while the Gupta kings had a comparatively decentralized administrative structure.

---

[7]Ibid. 149.

[8]R.C. Majumdar, H.C. Raychaudhuri and Kalikinkar Datta, *An Advanced History of India*, Macmillan and Co., London, 1953, p.197.

HARSHAVARDHANA

The empire of Harshavardhana (606–647 CE) stretched from the Brahmaputra delta in the east to Kathiawar in the west and from Punjab in the north to Narmada river in the south. His system of administration has been outlined in *Harshacharita* written by the court poet, Banabhatta. Law and order was enforced by dandikas. Punishment for offences included fines and imprisonment. The worst crime was treachery, for which a person could be imprisoned for life or even be punished by amputation of a limb. According to Hiuen Tsang, another Chinese traveller, the country, in general, observed the benefits of a good government. Taxes were light and people were not subjected to any arbitrary punishment. Labour was generally paid, though there were instances of forced service. A great seat of learning had come up at Nalanda during his period. Regarding the character of the people, Hiuen Tsang recorded that they observed moral principles and would not wrongfully take anything. Cheating was unknown and people kept their promise. It was a kingdom 'oozing art, culture, learning, religion and spirituality'.[9]

VIJAYANAGAR EMPIRE

Literature and history throw light on policing in South India. *Thirukkural*, a Tamil treatise written in early Common Era (CE) by Saint Thiruvalluvar, mandates that the punishment should be proportional to the severity of the offence and act as deterrent to crime.

The Vijayanagar Empire (founded 1336 CE) believed in expanding its frontiers. As such, there was a great deal of military build-up. The regions were guarded by military

---

[9]Ashwin Sanghi, *Where is Harsha? Kumbh Kahani*, Government of Uttar Pradesh, 2014.

chieftains called nayaks or poligars, who were selected by the king and entrusted with building forts, employing soldiers and raising cavalry. They had a dual role: maintaining law and order during peacetime and fighting during war. Their peacetime duties included acquainting themselves with 'all the events and accidents that happened within the seven walls and recover everything that is lost.'[10]

Persian and European visitors to Vijayanagar have left behind vivid descriptions of life at the capital during the fifteenth and first half of the sixteenth century. Their accounts of the spectacular ceremonies of the nine-day Mahanavami festival are particularly very detailed. They have written about the bazaars, temples and palaces of the city. 'Their reports on the precious stones, including diamonds, textiles and other luxury goods on sale in the markets testify to the role of the capital as one of the greatest emporia in South India.'[11]

The Portuguese traveller Domingo Paes was at Vijayanagar in about 1520–22 during the reign of Krishnadevaraya. He has given invaluable information on the walls, gates, streets and markets of the city as well as the major temples of the city including the Virupaksha at Hampi together with a colonnaded bazaar. Paes has described the Mahanavami festival in some length; it included 'processions of animals, warriors and courtly women, as well as wrestling matches, fireworks and other entertainments.'[12] The high point was the review of troops which was held at some distance from the city.

---

[10]Giriraj Shah, *The Indian Police: A Retrospect,* Himalaya Publishing House, 1992, p. 19.

[11]Robert Sewell's *A Forgotten Empire (Vijayanagar)* gives translations of these accounts of travel.

[12]Vijayanagara Research Project, https://www.penn.museum/sites/VRP/html/Forin_Visitors.html, accessed on 20 November 2021.

SHER SHAH SURI

Sher Shah was the 'architect of a brilliant administrative system'.[13] It is said that his reign, even though it lasted just five years (1540–45), was marked by the introduction of wise and salutary changes in every branch of administration. According to Keene, 'No government, not even the British has shown so much wisdom as this Pathan.'[14] The principle of local responsibility for local crimes was enforced and the village headman was made responsible for the detection of criminals and maintenance of peace in the rural areas. The efficiency of the system is testified by all the contemporary writers. Nizamuddin recorded that 'such was the safety of the highways that if anyone carried a purse full of gold (pieces) and slept in the desert (deserted places) for nights, there was no need for keeping watch'.[15]

THE MUGHAL PERIOD

Babur did not have the time and Humayun had neither the inclination nor the ability to set up an elaborate system of government. Akbar (1556–1605) organized an administrative framework which was actually a 'centralized autarchy' in which the King's power was unlimited. 'He was the supreme authority of the state, the commander of the state forces, the fountain of justice and the chief legislator.'[16] Each province or suba was placed under a governor or subedar and it was his duty to administer criminal justice and maintain law and order. In the cities and towns, police duties were entrusted to

---

[13]R.C. Majumdar, H.C. Raychaudhuri and Kalikinkar Datta, *An Advanced History of India*, Macmillan and Co., London, 1953, p.439.
[14]Ibid. 439.
[15]Ibid. 441.
[16]Ibid. 554.

the kotwal[17] whose duties, as enumerated in the *Ain-i-Akbari* were multifarious. These included (i) detecting thieves, (ii) regulating prices and checking weights and measures, (iii) keeping watch at night and patrolling the city, (iv) keeping watch over the movements of strangers, (v) employing spies to gather information, (vi) preparing an inventory and taking charge of the property of deceased or missing persons who left no heirs, (vii) preventing the slaughter of oxen, buffaloes, horses or camels, and (viii) preventing the burning of women against their will.[18] According to prominent Indian historian J.N. Sarkar, this long list represented the 'ideal' and not the actual state of things.[19] The Venetian writer and traveller Niccolao Manucci also gives an exhaustive account of the kotwal's duties.[20] It is obvious that the kotwal was a very important functionary in the administrative structure. In the districts, law and order was maintained by officers called faujdars. He was actually the commander of the military force stationed in the area and had to take cognizance of violent crimes, put down smaller rebellions and make demonstration of force to overawe any opposition to the revenue authorities.

Abul Fazal, minister in the court of Akbar, has recorded as follows:

> The *Kotwals* of cities, *kusbahs,* towns and villages, in conjunction with the royal clerks, shall prepare a register of the houses and buildings of the same, which shall include a particular description of the inhabitants of each habitation. One house shall become security for

---

[17]The first kotwal of Delhi was Malik-ul-Umra Fakhruddin, who was appointed in 1237, with headquarters at Qila Rai Pithora (today's Mehrauli). The last kotwal was Gangadhar Nehru (father of Pandit Motilal Nehru).
[18]R.C. Majumdar, H.C. Raychaudhuri and Kalikinkar Datta, *An Advanced History of India*, Macmillan and Co., London, 1953, p.558.
[19]Ibid.
[20]Ibid.

another; so that they shall all be reciprocally pledged and bound each for the other. They shall be divided into districts, each having a chief or prefect, to whose superintendence the district shall be subject. Secret intelligence officers or spies shall be appointed to each district, who shall keep a journal of local occurrences, arrivals and departures, happening either by day or night. When any theft, fire or other misfortune may happen, the neighbours shall render immediate assistance, especially the prefect and public informers, who failing to attend on such occasions, unless unavoidably prevented, shall be held responsible for the omission. No person shall be permitted to travel beyond, or to arrive within the limits of the district, without the knowledge of the prefect, the neighbours or public informers. Those who cannot provide security shall reside in a separate place or abode to be allotted to them by the prefect of the district and the public informers. A certain number of persons in each district shall be appointed to patrol by night the several streets and environs of the several cities, towns, village etc., taking care that no strangers infest them, and especially exerting themselves to discover, pursue and apprehend robbers, thieves, cut-purses, etc. If any articles be stolen or plundered, the police must restore the articles, produce the criminal, or, failing to do so, become responsible for the equivalent.[21]

There was no written code of laws. During Jahangir's reign, however, 12 ordinances were issued and, during Aurangzeb's reign (1658–1707), a digest of Muslim law, *Fatwa-i-Alamgiri*, was promulgated. The judges generally followed the Quranic

---

[21]India Police Commission, *History of Police Organization in India and Indian Village Police, Being Select Chapters of the Report of the Indian Police Commission, 1902–1903*, General Books, 2010.

injunctions or interpretations of the Holy Book by eminent jurists and any rules or directions issued by the emperors. Customary laws were given due recognition. The Mughal emperors laid emphasis on speedy administration of justice. Peruschi wrote about Akbar that 'as to the administration of justice he is most zealous and watchful.'[22]

THE MARATHAS

Shivaji adopted the Mughal system of administration; however, he found Sanskrit equivalents for Persian names. He also dispensed with the hereditary system of recruitment for officials and instead appointed persons on the basis of merit and transferred them from one place to another. Shivaji also employed spies and had a good intelligence network.

The village headman and the village watchman were the backbone of the police machinery in India during this period. The headman occupied the position of a police magistrate and the watchman worked under his orders. The latter's functions were graphically described by Mountstuart Elphinstone in his report (1819) on the territories conquered from the Peshwa:

> His (the watchman's) duties are to keep watch at night, to find out all arrivals and departures, observe all strangers, and report all suspicious persons to the *pātel* (headman). He is likewise bound to know the character of every man in the village; and in the event of a theft committed within the village bounds, it is his business to detect the thief. He is enabled to do this by his early habits of inquisitiveness and observation, as well as by the nature of his allowance, which being partly a small

---

[22]R.C. Majumdar, H.C. Raychaudhuri and Kalikinkar Datta, *An Advanced History of India*, Macmillan and Co., London,1953, p. 559.

share of the grain and similar property belonging to each house, he is kept always on the watch to ascertain his fees, and always in motion to collect them. When a theft or robbery happens, the watchman commences his inquiries and researches. It is very common for him to track a thief by his footsteps; and if he does this to another village, so as to satisfy the watchman there, or if he otherwise traces the property to an adjoining village, his responsibility ends, and it is the duty of the watchman of the new village to take up the pursuit. The last village to which the thief has been clearly traced becomes answerable for the property stolen, which would otherwise fall on the village where the robbery was committed. The watchman is obliged to make up this amount as far as his means go, and the remainder is levied on the whole village.[23]

DECAY OF THE TRADITIONAL POLICE

Sir Thomas Munro, who was an ardent supporter of the indigenous police, described the institution as it existed in the Madras Presidency in the following words:

There is already an ancient system of police in India which answers every useful purpose. In every village there are hereditary watchmen whose business it is to guard the property of the inhabitants and travellers from depredation, and to exert themselves in recovering it when lost or stolen; and there is, perhaps no race of men in the world equally dexterous in discovering the thieves. They are maintained by the produce of an *inam*

---

[23]*The Imperial Gazetteer of India*, Vol. IV, Oxford at the Clarendon Press, 1909, pp 384–85.

(free grant) land, by a trifling tax on each house, and by a small allowance from travellers when they watch their property at night. No war or calamity can make them abandon their heritage.[24]

In his testimony before the House of Lords in 1853, Sir George Clerk, who had been the governor of the Bombay Presidency, emphasized that the police system which had prevailed in India from time immemorial was far more efficient than anything the Company had substituted for it and that the native institutions of the police were neglected and had fallen into disuse because the officers of the British government favoured the more expensive police set up after their own form. Sir George also stated that they had lost much by disregarding the ancient institutions of the people.[25]

This traditional police structure, which had so far withstood the test of time, started developing cracks due to a combination of factors: the infighting among the local chieftains, the buffeting of foreign invasions and the British's preference for their own systems.

Aurangzeb's death in 1707 marked the beginning of the disintegration of the Mughal Empire. The state of law and order, when the British arrived in India, has been graphically described in the following words:

> Extortion and oppression flourished unchecked through all gradations of the officials responsible for the maintenance of peace and order. Both village watchman and the heads of villages, and even higher officials, connived at crime and harboured offenders in return for a share of the booty. Their liability to restore the stolen property or make good its value was disregarded;

---

[24]Ibid. 385.
[25]Anandswarup Gupta, *Crime and Police in India (Upto 1861)*, Sahitya Bhawan, Agra, 1974, p. 302.

or if this obligation was enforced, neither the property nor its value was restored to the owner. Fines were imposed when a more severe punishment was called for; and offenders who were possessed of any property could always purchase their liberty. Many offenders are taken, but great numbers also escaped. They (*zamindars*) abused the authority entrusted to them (and) extorted and amassed wealth, which was dissipated in a jealous rivalry of magnificent pageantry. The weapons which were intended for the enemies only of the State were turned against [the] State itself and against each other, and were used for plans of personal aggrandisement or public plunder. It was sometimes with difficulty that the regular or standing army of the State could restrain the insolence, or subdue the insubordination, of these intestine rebels and robbers.[26]

RISE OF REGIONAL POWERS

A brief panoramic view of the political landscape would be necessary to understand the law-and-order situation during the eighteenth century.

There was political turbulence across the country marked by the rise of regional powers—the Jats, the Marathas, the Rajputs and the Sikhs—and repeated invasions from across the north-western frontiers. The scattered units of Jats were united by Badan Singh. The Marathas were the most formidable group, who pursued the ideal of *Hindu-Pad-Padshahi* or the ideal of establishment of an independent Hindu Empire. The Rajput princes, who had been alienated, disowned their

---

[26]*History of Police Organization in India and Indian Village Police: Being Select Chapters of the Report of the Indian Police Commission, 1902-1903*, University of Calcutta.

allegiance to the Mughal Empire. The Sikhs had consolidated their power in the Punjab.

The invasions of Nadir Shah from Persia and Ahmad Shah Abdali from Afghanistan sounded the death knell for the Mughal Empire. Nadir Shah invaded India in AD 1739; he routed the Mughal army, plundered Delhi and massacred its inhabitants. The ruthless conqueror carried away all the crown jewels, including the priceless Peacock Throne of Shah Jahan and the famous Koh-i-Noor diamond. Abdali led several expeditions into India; his most decisive campaign was in 1761, when he vanquished the Marathas in the battle of Panipat.

ADVENT OF THE BRITISH

Meanwhile, certain European powers—the Portuguese, the Dutch, the French and the English—had come to India essentially for trade, but they were all tempted to fill the political vacuum in the absence of a strong central authority in the country. In the long run, the East India Company was able to establish its dominance, defeating its European rivals and winning over or subjugating one by one, the Indian kings and princes. The British victory at Plassey (1757) laid the foundations of the empire in India even though, as stated by noted statesman K.M. Panikkar, it was not a battle but 'a transaction in which the rich bankers of Bengal and Mir Jafar sold out the Nawab to the English'. A major part of Nawab Siraj-ud-Daulah's army 'stood still' during the battle. According to historians, 'Clive won the battle of Plassey in spite of himself.'[27] The English henceforth became the de facto rulers of Bengal and they utilized the resources of the state to enhance their financial and political interests.

---

[27]R.C. Majumdar, H.C. Raychaudhuri and Kalikinkar Datta, *An Advanced History of India*, MacMillan and Co., London, 1953, p. 665.

Robert Clive, the 'first white Mughal'[28], established in Bengal a system which came to be known as Dual Government, in which power was vested in the Company, while responsibility, in the Nawab. It was an unworkable arrangement, which had a deleterious effect on law and order. In a letter written on 24 May 1769 addressed to the Court of Directors, Richard Becher, a servant of the company, made the following observation:

> It must give pain to an Englishman to have reason to think that since the accession of the Company to the Diwani[29], the condition of the people of this country has been worse than it was before; yet I am afraid the fact is undoubted... This fine country, which flourished under the most despotic and arbitrary government, is verging towards ruin.[30]

THE GREAT FAMINE OF 1770

The Chhiyattarer Manvantar or the Great Famine of 1770, sparked off by crop failures in two successive seasons, 1768 and 1769, and aggravated by the 'ruthless exploitation of the economy of Bengal'[31] caused great distress to the people. In a letter to the Court of Directors (May 1770), the Bengal government estimated the loss of about one-third of the

---

[28]Manimugdha S. Sharma, 'Robert Clive was an 18th-century nouveau riche dream come true...To downplay Plassey is to downplay history', *The Times of India*, 24 June 2020.

[29]Emperor Shah Alam II formally granted, through a *firman* (a grant or permit), the Diwani of Bengal, Bihar and Orissa to the East India Company on 12 August 1765.

[30]R.C. Majumdar, H.C. Raychaudhuri and Kalikinkar Datta, *An Advanced History of India*, MacMillan and Co., London, 1953, p. 675.

[31]Basudeb Chattopadhyay, *Crime and Control in Early Bengal 1770-1860*, KP Bagchi & Company, Calcutta, 2000, p. 2.

population.[32] According to Charles Grant of the East India Company, who was then living in Murshidabad, three million would be a moderate estimate of famine mortality in Bengal.

The relief measures undertaken by the Company were not enough to alleviate the misery of the people. The situation, in fact, became worse when it decided to corner nearly 120,000 maunds of rice for the use of the army. The situation was further aggravated by the Company's servants and their Indian agents, who tried to take advantage of the situation by hoarding food grains.

'In the aftermath of the famine of 1770 rural violence covered a wide area and manifested itself in various forms. These ranged from numerous instances of dacoity and smuggling to rebellions and insurgencies like Sannyasi and Fakir revolts, Rangpur *dhing* or Chuar uprisings.'[33] It is true that the deterioration in the law-and-order situation during the eighteenth century was mainly due to the political strife in different regions and the absence of a strong central authority. However, it is also a fact that the situation was aggravated by the rapacity of the Company's officials, for whom exploiting the resources of the country for their imperial masters was always an important consideration.

EARLY BRITISH RULE

Warren Hastings (1772-74)[34], soon after his arrival, admitted having received 'repeated complaints from all parts of the province of the multitude of dacoits who have infested it for some years past and have been guilty of the most daring and

---

[32]Binay Bhushan Chaudhuri, *Agricultural Growth in Bengal and Bihar, 1770-1860*, p. 295.

[33]Basudeb Chattopadhyay, *Crime and Control in Early Bengal 1770-1860*, KP Bagchi & Company, Calcutta, 2000, p. 8.

[34]It refers to the period Hastings was the Governor General of India.

alarming excesses.[35] Hastings issued a set of 37 Regulations on 21 August 1772 to streamline the administration of criminal justice. There was however no improvement in the situation. Hastings had limited resources and was hamstrung by opposition within the Council. His changes amounted to merely rearranging the old pieces which had already lost their relevance.[36]

Lord Cornwallis (1786–93)[37] found that the criminal administration was in a state of chaos and that 'murders, dacoity and other serious crimes were daily committed with impunity and there was a general feeling that life and property were very inadequately protected.'[38] On 7 December 1792, he passed the 'Regulations for the Police of the Collectorships in Bengal, Bihar and Orissa'. The police powers were vested in the magistrates, who were directed to divide the districts into police jurisdictions. Each police jurisdiction was placed under the charge of a darogah, who was nominated by the magistrates in the first instance, while the future vacancies were filled up on their giving a security for an amount of ₹1,000. Interestingly, no darogah could be removed from office except upon proof of misconduct to the satisfaction of the governor general in Council. In view of the widespread complaints against zamindars of their having a nexus with criminals, they were divested of their executive responsibility, though in practice they retained the power of punishing their tenants through fines and corporal punishments.

The new police station set-up has been beautifully

[35]M.E. Monckton Jones, *Warren Hastings in Bengal, 1772–1774*, Forgotten Books, 2019, pp. 207–08.

[36]Basudeb Chattopadhyay, *Crime and Control in Early Bengal 1770–1860*, KP Bagchi & Company, Calcutta, 2000, p. 20.

[37]It refers to period when Cornwallis was the Governor General of India.

[38]Anandswarup Gupta, *Crime and Police in India (Upto 1861)*, Sahitya Bhawan, Agra, 1974, p. 31.

described by Basudeb Chattopadhyay in the following words:

> The *darogah* was the first officer of the thana. He was authorised to exercise a general control over the *mohurer, jamadar* and *barkandazes* attached to his thana. He was enjoined to preserve peace within the limits of his jurisdiction; to report to the Magistrate all occurrences connected with the police which came to his knowledge; to prevent, as far as possible, the commission of all offenses; to discover and apprehend offenders; to execute process and obey all orders transmitted to him by the Magistrate and perform such other duties as were prescribed in the Regulations.
>
> The *mohurer* was second officer of the thana and, in the absence of the *darogah* from his station, exercised the powers vested in that officer by the Regulations. It was the particular duty of the *mohurer* to preserve the thana records, to write reports and prepare other papers under the direction of the *darogah*.
>
> The *jamadar* was considered the third officer of the thana. In the absence of the first two from the thana, he was authorised to exercise the same powers as were vested in the *darogah*. The *jamadar*, whether stationed at a thana or at outposts, was to act under the orders of the *darogah* and was to see that the *barkandazes* were in attendance at their posts and that their arms and accoutrements were kept in a state of efficiency and that prisoners and property brought to the thana were duly guarded during the time they remained under the custody of *barkandazes* attached to the station.[39]

---

[39]Basudeb Chattopadhyay, *Crime and Control in Early Bengal 1770–1860*, KP Bagchi & Company, Calcutta, 2000, pp. 64–65.

There was however no marked improvement in law and order. Cornwallis admitted that crime was not under control because of collusion between the darogas and the zamindars. Besides, the majority of collectors were 'deeply engaged in commerce' under the name of some relative or friends. In 1793, Cornwallis therefore again reorganized the revenue, judicial and police administration. Every district was to have two administrative officers: the collector, who was entrusted with the collection of public dues and a magistrate with civil and limited criminal jurisdiction. Every magistrate was bound by an oath to perform 'to the best of his ability, to act with impartially and with integrity and not to accept any fee or reward or any emolument beyond what government authorized'. Their main duty was to 'apprehend murderers, robbers, thieves, house-breakers, all disturbers of the peace, and persons charged with crimes and misdemeanours'.[40]

Anandswarup Gupta credits Cornwallis with having 'substituted the chaos created by the Company's misrule of 29 years since Plassey and 21 (years) since the assumption of Dewani by a well-defined system of administration with a hierarchy of district and controlling officers and a body of definite laws and procedures'.[41]

The law-and-order situation nevertheless continued to cause concern. Lord Wellesley instituted enquiries in 1801 to ascertain the causes for the deterioration in Bengal, while in Madras (now Chennai) another committee was appointed in 1806 by Lord William Bentinck for the same purpose. The Regulation IX of 1808 created the office of the Superintendent of Police. The primary object of this appointment was 'apprehension of public offenders guilty of the commission

---

[40]Anandswarup Gupta, *Crime and Police in India (Upto 1861)*, Sahitya Bhawan, Agra, 1974, p. 43.
[41]Ibid. 46.

of robberies and other crimes by open violence.'[42]

The Select Committee of the British Parliament, appointed in 1812 to examine the affairs of the Company prior to the renewal of its charter for another 20 years, found that the Supreme Government had been 'least successful' in establishing an efficient police and ascribed the difficulty to the nature of the country which is 'intersected by rivers and abounding in woods and wastes', which afforded a 'ready means of escape to robbers' and to 'the depravity of certain classes of the natives'.[43] A new Regulation was passed in October 1813, which abolished the office of the kotwal in the cities of Dacca (now Dhaka), Patna and Murshidabad as 'unnecessary and in some respects prejudicial to the maintenance of an efficient police in those cities'.[44]

Another set of Regulations passed in 1829 provided for the appointment of Commissioners of Revenue and Circuit in 11 divisions of Bengal, Bihar and Orissa (now Odisha) and nine in the Western Provinces. The preamble to the Regulations stated:

> The system in operations for superintending the magistracy and the police, and for controlling and directing the executive revenue officers...has been found to be defective. For the correction of the above defects, it has appeared to be expedient and necessary to place the magistracy and police, and the collectors and other executive revenue officers under the superintendence and control of commissioners of revenue and circuit, each vested with the charge of a moderate track of

---

[42]Basudeb Chattopadhyay, *Crime and Control in Early Bengal 1770-1860*, KP Bagchi & Company, Calcutta, 2000, p.131.
[43]Anandswarup Gupta, *Crime and Police in India (Upto 1861)*, Sahitya Bhawan, Agra, 1974, p. 96.
[44]Ibid. 106.

country as may enable them to be easy of access to the people...and it has been deemed proper to abolish the office of the superintendent of police.[45]

It was an extraordinary coincidence of history, as stated by Anandswarup Gupta, that 'these retrograde steps were taken in the police administration of India by its British Rulers in the very year in which the British Parliament passed the Metropolitan Police Act to set up, for the first time, a whole time paid police force in their own country under the independent control of two Commissioners of Police'.[46]

Another Select Committee of Parliament, which inquired into the affairs of the Company in 1832, found that changes introduced in Bengal in 1829 and earlier in Madras in 1816 had both led to adverse consequences, that the subordinates were low paid, corrupt, inefficient and oppressive and that the supervision of commissioners and collectors was ineffective. The Act of 1833, which renewed the Company's Charter for another 20 years, made important changes. The governor general of Bengal became the governor general of India and he was vested with the superintendence, direction and control of the whole of civil and military government of all the territories in India. The Act added a legal member to the Council of the governor general of India. Lord Macaulay was the first legal member. He was entrusted with drafting the Penal Code. The first draft of the Code was submitted by him to Lord Auckland in May 1837. The draft was sent to England and was received back with critical observations. The Penal Code was revised in 1848 and again in 1850. (Macaulay had relinquished office in 1838.)

The Act XXIV of 1837 empowered the Government of Bengal Presidency to appoint Superintendents of Police for

---

[45]Ibid. 222.
[46]Ibid. 223.

their respective territories or any part thereof and laid down that the Commissioners of Revenue were to cease to exercise any powers in regard to the magistracy. In 1838, a committee presided over by W.W. Bird was appointed to draw up a plan for the reform of police in Bengal. The committee admitted 'extreme unpopularity of our system, and the grievous oppressions connected with its operations.'[47] It made a number of recommendations but the only one which was acted upon was the disunion of the offices of the collector and magistrate. The senior officer was made the collector of the district.

THUGGEE

It was around this time that thuggee had become a problem in the country. The thugs lurked in jungles and desolate places and they preyed on travellers, strangling them with a silk cord, which they used with great precision. The early British administrators described them as detestable race of 'monsters' and abominable pests of society.[48] As mentioned by Kim A. Wagner, 'a sensational and almost hysterical terminology was used right from the beginning and this was to remain a key element in the colonial representation of thuggee.'[49]

Sir William Henry Sleeman was placed in charge of the thuggee department in 1835. He developed a system of informers, enlisting several convicts for the purpose and took effective action to put down the crime. He was greatly helped by the Act XXX of 1836 which provided that whoever shall

[47]Basudeb Chattopadhyay, *Crime and Control in Early Bengal 1770–1860*, KP Bagchi & Company, Calcutta, 2000, p. 140.
[48]S. Bhattacharya, 'Monsters in the dark: the discovery of Thuggee and demographic knowledge in colonial India (2020),' Palgrave Communications, 6 (1), Art. no. 78, https://bit.ly/3GZZfiR, accessed on 21 February 2022.
[49]Kim A. Wagner, *Thuggee: Banditry and the British in Early Nineteenth-Century India*, Palgrave, MacMillan, 2007, p. 224.

be proved to have belonged to any gang of thugs shall be punished with imprisonment for life with hard labour. It is estimated that Sleeman collated the details and identities of 200 gangs in India, creating a database of 4,000 names with family trees as well as Hindu and Muslim aliases, and that each thug was assigned a unique number.[50] The results were startling: 504 of the 4,500 thugs were tried between 1826 and 1848 and sentenced to death, and more than 3,000 were sentenced to life imprisonment.

Wagner's comments on Sleeman's role in the eradication of thuggee are illuminating:

> Right from his first report in May 1830, Sleeman consistently emphasized the more exotic and sensational aspects of thuggee and though he may have acted with the best of intentions, his own opportunism and self-serving agenda overshadows this. Thus the information that Sleeman collected from the approvers was, to use a contemporary phrase, 'sexed up' in order to promote a sense of urgency concerning the threat posed by thuggee... Sleeman tried to present thuggee as a religious practice, which would resonate with the Evangelical sentiments of the day.[51]

The following observations of Tom Lloyd of the University of Edinburgh regarding the methods adopted by Sleeman and his team of officers are also revealing:

> Early colonial efforts to suppress banditry in India—and particularly the ATC (Anti-Thug Campaign)—relied upon the creation of a zone of sovereign power that was justified

---

[50]Vappala Balachandran, *Keeping India Safe: The Dilemma of Internal Security*, HarperCollins, 2017, p. 119.

[51]Kim A. Wagner, *Thuggee: Banditry and the British in Early Nineteenth-Century India*, Palgrave, MacMillan, 2007, p. 225.

as a means to ends that conventional, judicial power allegedly could not reach. This functioned as an excess of conventional, judicial power, through procedural and punitive innovations such as indefinite detention without trial, the use of denunciations from proven criminals, and the criminalization of a subject-position (Thug), rather than the establishment of individual guilt for particular acts... British colonial officials abrogated for themselves the right to produce specific definitions of criminality that located the accused in a realm beyond what was defined as ordinary legal procedure—a 'state of exception'—in which multifarious forms of violence against them were deemed acceptable.[52]

The highway robberies were certainly a problem. However, these were, to an extent, due to the breakdown of the traditional system of policing in the country for which the East India Company was primarily responsible. There is reason to believe that the thugs were eliminated by processes which were, at best, extrajudicial. According to Chattopadhyay, the repressive shortcuts adopted by Sleeman curtailed the already limited protection for the accused and 'made mockery of the rule of law.'[53]

In 1839, the task of dealing with dacoity was added to the duties of the Thagi and Dakaiti Department, which had been created in 1830. When the police were reorganized in the early sixties of the nineteenth century, the department became mainly concerned with the suppression of organized dacoity in Hyderabad, Central India and Rajputana, and the capture of dacoits who had fled from British to native territories.

---

[52]Tom Lloyd, *Thuggee and the Margins of the State in Early Nineteenth-Century Colonial India*, University of Edinburgh.
[53]Basudeb Chattopadhyay, *Crime and Control in Early Bengal 1770-1860*, KP Bagchi & Company, Calcutta, 2000, p. 150.

CENTRAL CRIMINAL INTELLIGENCE

Later, in 1877, during Lord Lytton's Viceroyalty, the department was reorganized as a Central Agency for the collection and dissemination of criminal and political intelligence. In explaining the scheme to local governments, the Viceroy said:

> It is by no means desirable to create an extensive system of secret police, but it is certainly expedient to pay great attention to all secret sources of information regarding foreign emissaries, intrigues or unusual political or social phenomena.
>
> By requiring the submission of regular news reports to the Supreme Government and by establishing there a Central Office for the collection of such reports, there is no intention of exercising any interference with Local Governments or encroaching on the powers hitherto exercised by them within their own limits. The main object of the new scheme is to establish, under the direct orders of the several I.G.Ps in India, an organization, hitherto wanting, by means of which Local Governments may systematically obtain both from their own and other provinces, information necessary and desirable in their own interests, and may communicate so much of their local information to the Government of India and other Provincial Governments as may be of advantage for the latter to know. It is clearly of importance that intelligence of more than merely local interest should be communicated inter-provincially and also furnished to the Supreme Government, so that the authorities responsible for the maintenance of law and order may be enabled to exercise a watchful control over the movements of the criminal classes, the conditions which predispose to crime and important

political, religious, or other movements throughout the Empire.[54]

Administrative approval was given by the Secretary of State on 25 March 1887. In 1904, the Thagi and Dakaiti Department was abolished. Its establishment in Hyderabad was merged with the police of that state while the establishments in Rajputana and Central India were transferred to the control of the agents to the governor general. The former Central Agency was replaced by the department of Central Criminal Intelligence working under the Home Department of Government of India. Harold A. Stuart, ICS, Inspector General of Police, Madras Presidency, was appointed as the director of the Central Criminal Intelligence.

The object of this new department was 'to collect and communicate information regarding such forms of organized crime as are committed by offenders operating along the railway system, and by criminal tribes, wandering gangs, organized dacoits, professional poisoners, forgers, coiners and the like whose operations extend beyond the limits of a single Province.'[55] It was felt that the railways, posts and telegraphs had enabled astute criminals to disperse or concentrate in a manner that baffled purely local authorities, and therefore a central agency had become necessary 'to procure the knowledge and cooperation requisite for dealing with them, and it will work in connection with the police of Native States as well as those of British Provinces.'[56] The department was rechristened Central Intelligence Department in 1918 and finally Intelligence Bureau in 1920.

---

[54]Ibid. 79–80.
[55]*The Imperial Gazetteer of India*, Volume IV, p. 395.
[56]Ibid.

IRISH CONSTABULARY MODEL

Sindh was annexed by the British in 1843. One of the first measures undertaken by General Sir Charles Napier was the organization of a regular police force in the province. Napier took as his model the Irish Constabulary because he found that the newly conquered province needed a semi-military rather than a civil force. An important feature of the new force, which distinguished it from police in the rest of the country, was that it was a separate, self-contained organization and its officers were not given any other responsibilities.

Sir Charles had observed:

> To secure the peace of the country, and avoid disseminating the troops, which would render them familiar with the people, and possibly diminish the wholesome fear of our power, I established a police of 2,400 men, well-armed, drilled, and divided into three classes—one for the towns, two for the country, the first of all Infantry, the two last Infantry and Cavalry, called the Rural Police. They assist the Collectors, but form a distinct body under their own officers.[57]

This system attracted the attention of Sir George Clerk, the governor of Bombay, who reorganized the Bombay Police on similar lines in 1853. A superintendent was appointed in every district who, while being generally subordinate to the magistrate, had exclusive control over the police.

In Punjab also, which was annexed in 1849, the police were organized on the pattern of Sindh. It consisted of two branches: a military preventive police and a civil detective police.

Madras was the next province to adopt the new police model. The Irish Constabulary model was found relevant

---

[57]Anandswarup Gupta, *Crime and Police in India (upto 1861)*, Sahitya Bhawan, Agra, 1974, pp. 289-90.

to the colonial needs of the Empire. As stated by Basudeb Chattopadhyay, apart from the overriding consideration of maintaining internal order, 'this model met two other needs of the colonial state: it was the least costly and more suited to a repressive role than the civil constabulary of the London Metropolitan pattern.'[58]

The Torture Commission Report of 1855 brought to light great abuses in the working of the police. The commission recommended the separation of revenue and police functions and the placing of the police establishment under independent European officers, who would be able to give their undivided time and attention to supervising the force. Superintendents of Police were appointed in every district. The arrangement was approved by the Court of Directors.

THE REVOLT OF 1857

The East India Company's charter for renewal was taken up for the last time in 1853. There was an elaborate enquiry by a select committee of Parliament. It was brought to light that police in Bengal was inefficient 'as evidenced by the prevalence of gang robberies and other crimes.'[59] As compared to that, police of the North-Western Provinces were found to be 'admirable'. In 1856, a prophetic memorandum was submitted to the Lieutenant Governor of Bengal by certain missionaries. They warned that 'the discontent of the rural population' was 'daily increasing' and that there was 'a bitter feeling of hatred towards their rulers.'[60] They suggested that a commission be appointed to enquire into the causes which had disaffected the

---

[58]Basudeb Chattopadhyay, *Crime and Control in Early Bengal 1770–1860*, KP Bagchi & Company, Calcutta, 2000, p. 161.
[59]Anandswarup Gupta, *Crime and Police in India (upto 1861)*, Sahitya Bhawan, Agra, 1974, p. 279
[60]Ibid. 345.

population, especially the working of the police and the judicial departments. The Governor did not agree with the views of the missionaries and recorded that measures for improvement were under consideration and that there was no need for any commission. The Governor General, Lord Canning, agreed with the Lieutenant Governor and stated that a commission may even lead to mischievous results.

The Court of Directors, in a despatch of 24 September 1856, diagnosed the problems of the police in the following words:

> That the police in India has lamentably failed in accomplishing the ends for which it was established is a notorious fact; that it is all but useless for the prevention, and sadly inefficient for the detection of crime, is generally admitted. Unable to check crime, it is with rare exceptions, unscrupulous as to its mode of wielding the authority with which it is armed for the functions which it fails to fulfil, and has a very general character for corruption and oppression.[61]

However, before any reforms could be initiated, the country was convulsed by the Revolt of 1857. Large areas of the country witnessed uprising against the British Rule. Hindu kings and Mughal rulers all fought against the tyrannical and, as they perceived, irreligious rule of the British. The rebellion was crushed, but it shook the foundations of the British Empire in India. It was felt that they must have a reorganized police all over the country which should be at their beck and call and carry out their orders, right or wrong, under all circumstances and put down any manifestations of dissent or signs of rebellion. As stated by the Secretary of State for India, Sir Charles Wood, in a despatch dated 6 July 1860 to

---

[61]Ibid.

the governor general, Lord Canning, they must have a police force 'capable of quelling all disturbances against the rulers' and its personnel may remain 'under the close and minute watch of the European Superintendents of Police in respect of their discipline and movements and of the European District Officers in respect of their functions and duties.'[62]

'It is difficult to escape the conclusion,' as stated by Basudeb Chattopadhyay, 'that the Revolt of 1857 radically altered the threat perception of the Raj. In the context of a civil rebellion looming large on the horizon, structural change in the police decisively emerged as a political imperative. It could no longer be postponed on grounds of either penury or expediency.'[63] According to Anandswarup Gupta also, a reorganization of the police system in India became 'a most urgent necessity in 1860 on account of political, military and financial reasons and not because of its inefficiency and impurity in the prevention and detection of crime.'[64]

POLICE ACT OF 1861

A Police Commission was, therefore, constituted in August 1860. It comprised the following:

MH Court, Esquire
S Wauchope, Esquire, C.M.
W Robinson, Esquire
R Temple, Esquire
Lieut-Colonel H. Bruce C.B.
Lieut-Colonel A.P. Phayre

---

[62]Ibid. 382.
[63]Basudeb Chattopadhyay, *Crime and Control in Early Bengal 1770–1860*, KP Bagchi & Company, Calcutta, 2000, p. 160.
[64]Anandswarup Gupta, *Crime and Police in India (upto 1861)*, Sahitya Bhawan, Agra, 1974, p. 377.

The commission was asked to:

i. propose a new system of police, applicable to India generally, whereby economy and efficiency might be secured.

ii. prepare for publication all available information regarding the best system of police organization.

iii. collate the most complete and comprehensive statistics obtainable regarding the cost and establishment of the police of all kinds throughout India.

It recommended that 'the present Police, Civil and Military be abolished, and an organized Constabulary substituted in all the Provinces of India where such a system does not already exist'.[65] It expressed its confidence that this arrangement would increase efficiency and diminish expense.

And so, the Police Act of 1861 was passed to reorganize the police and to make it a more efficient instrument for the prevention and detection of crime. Significantly, it was acknowledged that the new police should be 'politically more useful'.[66]

The Police Act of 1861 constituted a single homogenous force of civil constabulary for the performance of all duties which could not be assigned to the military arm. The management of the force in each province was entrusted to an Inspector General, who, apart from the functions assigned to him, was to act as 'Consultative Officer to the Government of India in matters of Police'. The importance the British government assigned to the office of the Inspector General is reflected in a letter dated 12 April 1862 which the secretary to the Government of India wrote to the secretaries to the governments of Bengal, North-West Provinces, Madras,

---

[65]*Compendium of Recommendations of the Police Commissions of India,* National Crime Records Bureau (MHA), 1997, p. 31.

[66]First Report of the National Police Commission, February 1979, p. 7.

Bombay, Oude, Central Provinces and the other provinces:

> His Excellency in Council has thought that it will be
> most satisfactory to the local Governments that the
> Inspector General should address to them direct, rather
> than to the Government of India, whatever report he
> may think it necessary to make on the Police of each
> Province, sending at the same time a copy of his report
> for the information of the Supreme Government. Under
> this arrangement, it will be optional with the local
> Government either to act on the suggestions of the
> Inspector General, or not to do so; and in the latter
> case, where points of importance, or involving financial
> considerations, are in question, the local Government
> will communicate to the Government of India the
> grounds of its dissent. With the report of the Inspector
> General and the objections of the local Government
> before it, the Government of India will be able to come
> to a satisfactory decision on the questions at issue.[67]

The Inspector General was assisted by superintendents of
police in each district. The superintendence of the police was
vested in the state government. The subordinate staff consisted
of inspectors, head constables, sergeants and constables. On
relations between the magistracy and the police, the commission
observed that no magistrate of grade lower than the district
magistrate should exercise any police functions.

THE AITCHISON COMMISSION, 1886

Lord Dufferin appointed a Public Service Commission under
Sir Charles Aitchison to investigate the problems of the civil

---

[67]*Compendium of Recommendations of the Police Commissions of India,*
National Crime Records Bureau (MHA), 1997, p. 36.

services in India. The commission suggested that the terms 'covenanted' and 'uncovenanted' be replaced by the terms 'imperial' and 'provincial', respectively, proposed the setting up of provincial civil service, members of which would be separately recruited in every province either by promotion from lower ranks or by direct recruitment, and suggested 19 and 23 as the minimum and maximum age limits for Indians at the open civil service examinations. The recommendations of Aitchison Commission were accepted and the covenanted civil service came to be known as Civil Service of India.[68]

The total strength of the organized civil police in the country in 1888 was 129,000 men, and it cost ₹242 lakh. In 1901, the strength went up to 145,000 men, and the cost increased to ₹328 lakh. The local village watchmen aggregated about 700,000 men.[69]

The functioning of the police unfortunately did not show any marked improvement. Sir John Woodburn, Lieutenant Governor of Bengal, recorded as follows on 12 December 1901:

> In no branch of the administration in Bengal is improvement so imperatively required as in the police. There is no part of our system of Government of which such universal and bitter complaint is made, and none in which, for the relief of the people and the reputation of Government, is reform in anything like the same degree so urgently called for...the improvement of the police must, in the interest of the people and of good government, take precedence of every other project in Bengal.[70]

---

[68]'The Aitchison Commission (1886); British Rule, Expansion and Administration, 30 November 2009, http://thebritishinindia.blogspot.com/2009/11/aitchison-commission-1886.html, accessed on 20 November 2021.

[69]The Imperial Gazetteer of India, Volume IV, p. 396.

[70]Anandswarup Gupta, The Police in British India, 1861–1947, Reprinted by Bureau of Police Research and Development, MHA, Government of India, 2007, pp. 183–84.

On 3 February 1902, Lord Curzon remarked that 'a government that gives good laws or good education, or the wherewithal to live, but that places the preservation of internal order and the detection, prevention and punishment of crime in soiled or incompetent hands cannot escape severe reproach,'[71] and decided to set up a strong commission to go into all aspects of the police administration.

THE FRASER COMMISSION (1902-03)

The Governor General in Council appointed, with the approval of the Secretary of State, a commission in 1902 to inquire into the administration of police in British India. The commission was headed by A.H.L. Fraser, Chief Commissioner of the Central Provinces. Four other members, all of them Europeans, included a High Court Judge of Bombay, a member of the Punjab Lieutenant Governor's Council, Inspector General of Police of Hyderabad State and a barrister of Allahabad. The two Indian members were the Maharaja of Darbhanga, Additional Member of Governor General's Council, and Srinivasa Raghava Iyengar, ex-Dewan of Baroda State and Additional Member of the Council of Governor of Madras.

The commission came to the conclusion that the system introduced in 1860 was, on the whole, a wise and efficient system. It had however failed due to the following reasons:

That the extent to which the village police must cooperate with the regular police has been lost sight of, and an attempt has almost everywhere been made to do all the police work through the officers of the department; that the importance of police work has been underestimated, and responsible duties have ordinarily been entrusted to untrained and ill-educated officers

---

[71]Ibid. 184.

recruited in the lower ranks from the lower strata of society; that supervision has been defective owing to the failure to appoint even the staff contemplated by the law and to increase that staff with the growing necessities of administration; that the superior officers of the department have been insufficiently trained and have been allowed from various causes to get out of acquaintance and sympathy with the people and out of touch even with their own subordinates; and that *their sense of responsibility has been weakened by a degree of interference never contemplated by the authors of the system.* (emphasis added)[72]

It is distressing that these comments are generally valid even today. The 'degree of interference' deplored by the commission in 1903 has, in fact, increased manifold.

The commission found that the 'police force is far from efficient; it is defective in training and organisation; it is inadequately supervised; it is generally regarded as corrupt and oppressive; and it has utterly failed to secure the confidence and cordial cooperation of the people.'[73] It came to the following conclusion:

The police force throughout the country is in a most unsatisfactory condition, that abuses are common everywhere, that this involves great injury to the people and discredit to the Government and that radical reforms are urgently necessary.[74]

This was the first time that a high-level body talked of police reforms. Ironically, the battle for reforms continues even after more than nearly 120 years.

---

[72]Ibid. 202.
[73]Ibid. 201.
[74]Ibid. 206.

The commission recommended *inter alia* that the police force should consist of (i) a European Service to be recruited entirely in England; (ii) a Provincial Service to be recruited entirely in India; (iii) an Upper Subordinate Service consisting of inspectors and sub-inspectors; and (iv) a Lower Subordinate Service consisting of head constables and constables. It also said that recruitment to the European Service should be through a competitive examination to be held in England, that large provinces should be divided into ranges and a Deputy Inspector General placed in-charge of each range, and that the authority of the District Magistrate over the criminal administration of the district should be of the nature of 'general control and direction and not a constant and detailed intervention.'[75]

The commission acknowledged that their proposal for reform was not of a 'revolutionary character' and that they consisted mainly of suggestions for the maintenance and development of indigenous local institutions so as to obviate the vexatious interference of the police in cases of little importance; for the conduct of investigation by the trained officers; for inspection of police by officers of capacity and integrity; for supervision and control by the best European and Native officers available; and for organized and systematic action against organized and professional crime.

The Maharaja of Darbhanga significantly recorded a Note of Dissent. He suggested *inter alia* a uniform method of recruitment by open competition both in India and England without any racial distinction. The commission, however, rejected the suggestion and took the stand that 'it is essential to have different methods of recruitment for Europeans and natives because it is essential for the Government to control

---

[75]*Compendium of Recommendations of the Police Commissions of India*, National Crime Records Bureau (MHA), 1997, p. 105.

the relative proportions of these two classes in the superior police service.'[76]

The Commission made very pertinent observations on the relations between the district magistrate and the Superintendent of Police:

> The administration of the police is vested in the Superintendent. He is the head of the police in the district. Though he must carry out all lawful orders of the District Magistrate, he is not his assistant in the sense in which an Assistant Collector is; and it destroys police work to put him in that position. No unnecessary interference with the Superintendent should be allowed. The police force... should be kept as far as possible departmentally distinct and subordinate to its own officers. And the District Magistrate should avoid acting so as to weaken the influence and authority of the Superintendent.[77]

It is relevant that the commission considered it advisable to have a single Police Act for the whole of India and felt that Act V of 1861, which was already in force in all provinces would, with a few amendments, be suitable for the whole country. 'The conditions of police service, machinery and work must be fairly uniform throughout India,' they said. It is also significant that the Commission was very critical of the statistical tests to judge the work of police officers and went so far as to recommend that 'no statistics of crime should be given in the reports of inspections of police stations'.[78]

The commission's recommendations were definitely not 'radical' as they themselves admitted. Nevertheless, as stated by Anandswarup Gupta, 'they amounted only to the

---

[76]Anandswarup Gupta, *The Police in British India, 1861–1947*, Bureau of Police Research and Development (MHA), 1979, p. 215.
[77]Ibid. 223.
[78]Ibid. 233.

minimum and most urgent and essential needs of the case, and their advocacy in this respect could not have been more powerful.'[79]

THE ISLINGTON COMMISSION (1912)

In 1912, a Royal Commission on Public Services in India was constituted with Lord Islington as its chairman. The commission invited recommendations for all departments including the police. The Imperial Police Service Association, which had been formed in 1911, submitted a memorandum deploring the condition of policemen thus:

> The policeman was nobody's child. He was the one department without which the Government could not carry on. He was charged with the most elementary and the most important of the functions of any civilized Government. Yet his importance had never been realized nor had he been assigned any official position befitting his station and his duties. He alone had been stamped with the brand of second class importance and everyone knew it. It was the same in the days of Kipling, when the mother of Strickland's refused to allow her daughter to marry into 'the worst paid department in the Empire.'[80]

Interestingly, a pamphlet titled *Police Reform* was published by Dinsha Edulji Wacha from Allahabad in 1911. Edulji called the police a 'rotten organization' and lamented that harsh and repressive laws had not only contributed to crime and perjury but also 'sown the seeds of wide discontentment and stimulated the corruption of the police.'

---

[79]Ibid. 251.
[80]Ibid. 310.

The Islington Commission made a number of recommendations regarding the civil services and suggested that these be reorganized into four categories: Imperial, Central, Provincial and Subordinate.[81] In the first group were services which were to be recruited exclusively in British India. In the second were the Indian Civil Service and Indian Police Service, whose members were to be recruited primarily in Britain, though some recruitment could be done in India. In the third group were services such as education and medical, which were to be filled up by recruitment partly in Britain and partly in India. The fourth group included scientific and technical services which were also to be recruited both in Britain and India. The commission rejected the demand for holding examinations simultaneously in India. The Islington Commission's recommendations were however overturned in 1918, when the Montagu-Chelmsford Report proposed the appointment of Indians to one-third of the posts, and action was taken to hold simultaneous examinations in London and New Delhi in 1922.

It is necessary to mention here that the first open competition for the selection of superior grade police officers was held in England in June 1893, and the successful candidates were appointed as probationary Assistant Superintendents of Police. In 1907, the officers were directed to wear 'I.P.' on their epaulettes to distinguish them from other officers. The age limit for the candidates was 19 to 21 years and candidates had to be unmarried. The compulsory subjects were English, Elementary Mathematics, French or German, English History and Geography. Two optional subjects had also to be taken. The candidates had to pass a riding test as well. The Islington Commission referred to these superior grade officers as

[81]'Islington Commission, 1912,' *Banglapedia*, http://en.banglapedia.org/index.php?title=Islington_Commission,_1912, accessed on 20 November 2021.

belonging to 'Indian Police Service'. In 1932, however, the word 'Service' was dropped and the simple designation of 'Indian Police' was officially adopted.[82]

STATE OF POLICING

The *Statement of the Moral and Material Progress of India during the period 1922-23*, prepared by L.F. Rushbrook Williams, who was formerly a professor of Modern Indian History in the University of Allahabad, contained the following significant observations:

> The policeman, it must regretfully be stated has a bad name in India: he is accused both of tyranny and of corruption. It would indeed be strange if these faults were entirely absent from a force which is still largely illiterate, none-too-well paid, and wholly unstimulated by healthy public opinion...
>
> Until the police of India, like the police of England, enjoy the whole-hearted support of the average citizen; until their efficiency becomes a matter of pride to their fellow countrymen; and until the supreme importance of their function is adequately appreciated, India can never possess the kind of force she needs.[83]

It is interesting to recall that some British police officers expressed their anguish very much like some police officers of our generation. P.M. Stewart, an IP Officer of Sindh, wrote a book titled *Policing India* in which he criticized the hegemony of the ICS over the police and also the political misuse of the Criminal Investigation Department. The malady is much worse today.

---

[82]Sir Percival Griffiths, *To Guard My People: The History of the Indian Police*, Ernest Benn Ltd, 1971, pp. 95-97.

[83]Anandswarup Gupta, *The Police in British India, 1861-1947*, Bureau of Police Research and Development (MHA), 1979, p. 401.

LEE COMMISSION, 1924

The Royal Commission on Superior Civil Services in India, 1924 (Lee Commission) was appointed by the British government to consider the ethnic composition of the superior Indian public services of the Government of India. It was of the view that 'more specialised training is now necessary to equip the present-day police officer for the efficient discharge of his duties' because their responsibilities had 'become more onerous and irksome'[84] The commission proposed that 40 per cent of the future entrants should be British, 40 per cent Indians directly recruited and 20 per cent Indians promoted from the provincial service.[85]

GOVERNMENT OF INDIA ACT, 1935

The Government of India passed an Act in 1935 granting a fair measure of autonomy to the provinces of British India. The Governor General remained the head of the central administration and enjoyed wide powers concerning administration, legislation and finance. Provinces were reorganized: Sindh was separated from Bombay; Bihar and Orissa were split into separate provinces of Bihar and Orissa; and Burma was separated from India. The Act contained a seventh schedule which had a Federal Legislative List, Provincial Legislative List and Concurrent Legislative List. The Provincial Legislative List had *inter alia* the following entries:

> Public order (but not including the use of His Majesty's naval, military or air forces in aid of the civil power); the

---

[84]Memorandum to the Seventh Central Pay Commission submitted by The IPS (Central) Association, p. 8.
[85]Lee Commission, *Britannica*, https://www.britannica.com/topic/Lee-Commission, accessed on 3 March 2022.

administration of justice; constitution and organisation of all courts, except the Federal Court, and fees taken therein; preventive detention for reasons connected with the maintenance of public order; persons subjected to such detention...[86]

It was a comprehensive legislation and, at the time of Partition, the two dominions of India and Pakistan accepted the Act of 1935 with minor amendments as their provisional constitution. The Indian Constitution endorsed the placing of public order and police in the state list. British intentions in placing these subjects in the provincial list were far from honourable. As commented by Oxford professor David Steinberg, 'by giving Indian politicians a great deal of power at the provincial level, while denying them responsibility at the Centre, it was hoped that Congress, the only national party, would disintegrate into a series of provincial fiefdoms.'[87] The Constituent Assembly, which started under British tutelage from 9 December 1946, according to Balachandran, was guided strictly by the Cabinet Mission's directive for a 'weak Centre' under a façade of 'instilling confidence among the minorities, but for a covert purpose of planting seeds of future disunity.'[88] It was unfortunate that the Constituent Assembly, which continued till 26 November 1949, did not think it necessary to modify this provision even after witnessing the Great Calcutta killings or the Noakhali massacres of 1946, which showed how the police had been rendered ineffective by the local politicians.

---

[86]Government of India Act, 1935 (As amended up to 15th August 1943), p. 169, https://bit.ly/3p2hJsO, accessed on 21 February 2022.

[87]Vappala Balachandran, 'Jinnah's Role in Weakening Indian Territorial Integrity,' *Outlook*, 24 September 2020, https://bit.ly/3LNl5tF, accessed on 22 November 2021.

[88]Vappala Balachandran, 'Link State Police System to Development,' *The Tribune*, 2 September 2019.

Today we are confronted with a situation where the states are not able to handle even minor law-and-order problems on their own and depend on the Central Armed Police Forces to deal with all kinds of situations: communal riots, mela arrangements, VIP security, terror incidents, separatist/secessionist movements, Maoist violence, etc. In most states, the police have been politicized and are misused by the party in power to further its political agenda. Every time the central government initiates any proposal which would give it some say in police matters, the state satraps raise a hue and cry and allege central encroachment over their turf. The Supreme Court of India gave directions to the state governments to carry out police reforms in 2006, but the states have been dragging their feet in the matter because they have developed a vested interest in maintaining the status quo. The remedy lies in bringing police and public order in the concurrent list, but no government at the Centre has so far shown the courage or the vision to initiate a constitutional amendment to achieve that.

Lord Linlithgow, who took over as Viceroy in 1936, issued a message to all the branches of the police in India. It was as follows:

> The services that you perform are essential to the welfare of the public, for your duty requires that you should be friends and protectors of all persons...
>
> I am confident that in your relations with the public, you will seek at all times to discharge your duties with firmness, tact and impartiality.
>
> You may rest assured that in the performance of your arduous duties, sometimes difficult, at moments dangerous, and always delicate, you may count upon my steady support.
>
> Your welfare will at all times be my anxious care.[89]

---

[89]Anandswarup Gupta, *The Police in British India, 1861–1947*, Bureau of

FREEDOM STRUGGLE

During the two world wars, the police remained loyal to the British. There was nevertheless an undercurrent of distrust and the military authorities insisted on police leadership remaining in European hands.

The police acted as the repressive arm of the British government in taking action against the freedom fighters. Lala Lajpat Rai suffered lathi blows in Lahore in 1928 which ultimately led to his death. Chandrashekhar Azad was surrounded by the police in Alfred Park of Allahabad in 1931; the revolutionary, after he ran out of ammunition, shot himself. Bhagat Singh, Rajguru and Sukhdev were charged with Saunders's murder in the Lahore conspiracy case by the police and later sentenced to death. An official report acknowledged that 'in no province was there at any time hesitation on the part of the police or other authorities in taking action against *satyagrahis*, either for fear of future victimisation or for any other reason.'[90]

On the eve of Independence, on 30 June 1947, the Indian Police had 516 officers. Their break-up was: Europeans 323, Hindus 130 and Muslims 63. The majority of European officers opted for retirement and compensation for loss of career. Almost all the Muslim officers opted for Pakistan. The Hindu officers opted for India.

THE LEGACY OF BRITISH RULE

When the British came, India was 'the leader of Asiatic civilization and the undisputed centre of light in the Asiatic world.'[91] The colonial rule of India however, as brilliantly

---

Police Research and Development (MHA), 1979, p. 495.
[90]Ibid. 523.
[91]Calcutta magazine, *Indian World*, quoted by US statesman William Jennings Bryan in 1906.

brought out by Shashi Tharoor, meant 'economic exploitation and ruin to millions, the destruction of thriving industries, the systematic denial of opportunities to compete, the elimination of indigenous institutions of governance, the transformation of lifestyles and patterns of living that had flourished since time immemorial, and the obliteration of the most precious possessions of the colonized, their identities and their self-respect.'[92] When the East India Company was established in 1600, Britain was producing just 1.8 per cent of the world's gross domestic product (GDP), while India was generating some 23 per cent. By 1940, after two centuries of British Raj, Britain accounted for nearly 10 per cent of the world's GDP, while India had been reduced to a poor 'third world' country, destitute and starving, a global poster child of poverty and famine.[93]

The assessment by Will Durant, the American historian who came to India in 1930, is even more damaging:

> The British conquest of India was the invasion and destruction of a high civilization by a trading company (the British East India Company) utterly without scruple or principle, careless of art and greedy of gain, overrunning with fire and sword a country temporarily disordered and helpless, bribing and murdering, annexing and stealing, and beginning that career of illegal and 'legal' plunder which has now (1930) gone on ruthlessly for one hundred and seventy-three years.[94]

The Indian Civil Service, the steel frame of British administration, as has been rightly said, was neither Indian nor civil nor a service. The Indian Police was structured, in

---

[92]Shashi Tharoor, *An Era of Darkness: The British Empire in India*, Aleph Book Company, 2016, pp. 252–53.
[93]Ibid. 254.
[94]Ibid. 2.

the words of the Second Administrative Reforms Commission, 'as an armed force, as an organisation oriented not to the service of the people of India but principally to maintain the authority of the Crown. It was an agency of oppression, of subjugation, used for protecting British interests and to sustain their empire.'[95]

The NPC made the following assessment of the pre-Independence police:

> Prior to Independence, police functioned *de jure* and *de facto* as an agency totally subordinate to the executive and ever ready to carry out its commands ruthlessly, even though they may not always have been in genuine 'public interest' as viewed by the public. Though the concept of 'rule of law' was introduced by the British regime, law enforcement was subject to the ultimate objective of protecting the British Crown and sustaining the British rule.[96]

Anandswarup Gupta described the police inherited from the British in the following words:

> Independent India received a Police Force with a very small Indian leadership and a subordinate body, which had been studiously trained in the use of brute force and in which extortion, corruption and malpractices had been tolerated with a callous indifference to the welfare and the dignity of the Indian citizen and had been allowed to acquire the sanctity of tradition; a system of supervision and control which prevented the development of professionalism in the force and was antagonistic to the establishment of the rule of law; a

---

[95]Fifth Report of Second Administrative Reforms Commission (Public Order), p. i.
[96]Second Report of the *National Police Commission*, August 1979, p. 21.

body of criminal laws which was hardly conducive to an effective control of crime and criminals; and a totally ineffective machinery for the security of the rural areas.[97]

The assessments are true. The regret however is that even today, more than 70 years after Independence, the subordination to the executive is still there like a millstone around the police neck and the environment is far from conducive to the development of professionalism and, what is worse, continues to be antagonistic to the establishment of the rule of law.

---

[97]Anandswarup Gupta, *The Police in British India, 1861–1947*, Bureau of Police Research and Development (MHA), 1979, p. xix.

2

WHY POLICE REFORMS?

Why do we need police reforms in the country? The answer is simple. The British had introduced a colonial system of policing based on the militaristic Irish constabulary. It was meant to exercise dominance over the indigenous population and maintain the imperial authority of the Crown. Unfortunately, after Independence, the politicians found it convenient to continue the system because it enabled them to misuse and abuse the police for their partisan ends. As beautifully summed up by the Commonwealth Human Rights Initiative (CHRI):

> Unfortunately, the post-independence histories of the countries of South Asia paint a grim picture of the state of policing. The British colonial government, with the sole intention to keep its subjects under control, introduced a formal, state-administered system of policing to the region. The foundation of policing in the region was imperialism. Alarmingly, neither the advent of independence nor democracy has changed policing models. Post-independence governments have retained archaic policing laws that perpetuate the ills of colonial policing towards their own ends and to maintain their own power. Illegitimate political interference in policing is endemic across the region and has shaped the subservient, partisan, and unaccountable nature of policing. By controlling powers to transfer, promote

or punish police officers, ruling regimes ensure that officers toe their line. Undeniably, police in the region are entirely dwarfed and most often controlled by executives that make little effort to check the huge constraints that the police work within, including lack of financial and human resources, immense working hours and extremely hostile conditions in conflict areas.[98]

It would be necessary at this stage to study as to how the police evolved after Independence.

INDEPENDENCE: STATUS QUO CONTINUES

The Constituent Assembly debates (1947 to 1949) show that several members had serious reservations about the role of the All India Services in independent India. Their attitude was coloured by their experience of these services during the Independence struggle, when the officers, at the behest of the imperial power, came down heavily on the freedom fighters. Sardar Vallabhbhai Patel stoutly defended the services and expressed his optimism that the services would, in the changed circumstances, be patriotic and motivated by the highest ideals of service to the country. Some of his observations are recorded below:

> They are as good as ourselves, and to speak of them in disparaging terms in this House, in public, and to criticise them in this manner, is doing disservice to yourselves and to the country.
>
> The Police which was broken has been brought to its proper level and is functioning fairly efficiently. The Heads of the Departments of the Police in every

[98]*Feudal Forces: Democratic Nations, Police Accountability in Commonwealth South Asia*, Commonwealth Human Rights Initiative, 2007, p. 6.

province are covered under this guarantee. Are you going to change that? Are you going to put your Congress volunteers as captains? What is it that you propose to do?

As a man of experience I tell you, do not quarrel with the instruments with which you want to work. It is a bad workman who quarrels with his instruments. Take work from them. Every man wants some sort of encouragement. Nobody wants to put in work when every day he is criticised and ridiculed in public. Nobody will give you work like that.

These people are the instruments. Remove them and I see nothing but a picture of chaos all over the country.

They are men who prefer honour, dignity, prestige and deserve the affection of the people.[99]

Patel's thinking ultimately prevailed. The Constitution of India, which was adopted on 26 November 1949, had a chapter devoted to the Services. Article 312(2) thereof stated: 'The services known at the commencement of this Constitution as the Indian Administrative Service and the Indian Police Service shall be deemed to be services created by Parliament under this article.'

The Partition in 1947 had thrown up problems of enormous magnitude. There was huge movement of populations across the borders and there were communal riots over large parts of the country. Subsequently, the country was witness to unrest over the reorganization of the states, Naga rebellion in the Northeast, language riots in the South and a host of other problems. The police, according to M.V. Narayana Rao, a celebrated police officer, came out, with rare exceptions, 'in flying colours'. Prime Minister Indira Gandhi, while addressing the Inspector Generals' (IGs) Conference on 23 February 1966

---

[99]Constituent Assembly of India Debates (Proceedings), Volume X, https://bit.ly/3LMNcJk, accessed on 22 November 2021.

paid tribute to the police for having handled the various problems very well.

In those turbulent years, what was lost sight of was that a new role, a new philosophy for the police needed to be defined, and that its accountability to the law of the land and the people of the country had to be emphasized in clear terms. As a result, 'the relationship that existed between the police and the foreign power before independence was allowed to continue with the only change that the foreign power was substituted by the political party in power'.[100]

For some years after Independence, however, there was no problem, thanks to the quality of political as well as administrative leadership. The politicians were men of great stature, endowed with vision and committed to pursuing national interests. The administrators were also thorough professionals, keen on playing their role in independent India. The politician drew from the professional experience and expertise of the civil servant who, in turn, benefited from the politicians' commitment to democracy and secularism. There was mutual respect, give and take in pursuit of the common objective of taking the nation forward on the road to progress and modernity.

POLICE ROLE DURING THE 1965 AND 1971 WARS

The police role during the Indo-Pak War of 1965 was recognized by the then prime minister, Lal Bahadur Shastri. In his broadcast to the nation on 23 September 1965, he said:

> At many places, they had to stand shoulder to shoulder with our armed forces to fight the invaders. In this task, many of them laid down their lives. But they have

---

[100] *Second Report, National Police Commission*, p. 35, https://bit.ly/3v4LLQS, accessed on 22 November 2021.

succeeded in adding a glorious chapter to the history of Indian police.[101]

In the 1971 Indo-Pak War, leading to the liberation of Bangladesh, Indian Police again played a stellar role. The BSF, which had been raised only five years back, was authorized by Prime Minister Indira Gandhi to take on Pakistani troops in erstwhile East Pakistan a few months before the war actually erupted. An important contribution of the BSF was to impart training to Mukti Bahini, waging war against the Pakistani Army.[102] Indira Gandhi, the then prime minister of India, in a letter dated 22 December 1971 addressed to K.F. Rustamji, director general of BSF, expressed the gratitude of the government and the people of India in the following words:

> As the first line of our defence, the Border Security Force had to bear the immediate brunt of the enemy onslaught. The manner in which they faced enemy fire and the support they gave the Army has played a crucial role in our ultimate success.[103]

As the years rolled by, however, there was unfortunately a qualitative change in the style of politics. The fire of idealism which had inspired the first generation of post-Independence politicians and civil servants, started becoming dim. Power became an end in itself, and gradually a symbiotic relationship developed between the politicians on the one hand and civil servants on the other. Vested interests grew on both sides and, as commented by the NPC, 'what started as a normal

[101]Lal Bahadur Shastri, *When Freedom Is Menaced*, Ministry of Information and Broadcasting Publications Division, 2018.

[102]South Asia Monitor, 'Role of BSF in Liberation of Bangladesh: Analysis,' *Eurasiareview*, 5 February 2015, https://bit.ly/3H63cCH, accessed on 22 November 2021.

[103]Navneet Anand, 'KF Rustamji: India's iconic police officer,' *The Pioneer*, 23 May 2016, https://bit.ly/3JJImuu, accessed on 22 November 2021.

interaction between the politicians and the services for the avowed objective of better administration with better awareness of public feelings and expectations, soon degenerated into different forms of intercession, intervention and interference with *mala fide* objectives unconnected with public interest'.[104]

THE EMERGENCY (1975–77)

In the late 1960s, the political leadership injected the concept of 'commitment' in administration. It caused havoc. Officers were selected and given key placements in consideration of their affinity and loyalty to the ruling party and its political philosophy. Their intrinsic merit and administrative qualifications were given secondary importance. The disastrous consequences of this were seen during the Emergency, when thousands of political opponents of Mrs Gandhi were imprisoned, press was censored, inconvenient officers were prematurely retired, slums were bulldozed and there was forced sterilization of men.

The Janata Party government, led by Morarji Desai, later constituted a commission headed by Justice J.C. Shah, a former Chief Justice of India, to inquire into the excesses committed during the Emergency.

As observed by the Shah Commission in its interim report:

The Commission views with anguish the evidence of patent collusion between the police and the magistracy in denying the citizens their basic freedoms by arrests and detentions on grounds which were now admitted to be non-existent or deliberately invented. Even when the slender legal remedies were attempted to be resorted to

---

[104] *Second Report of National Police Commission*, p. 82, https://police.py.gov. in/Police%20Commission%20reports/2nd%20Police%20commission%20 report.pdf, accessed on 22 November 2021.

by the aggrieved citizens, these were considered sufficient provocation for incarcerating them on fabricated or non-existent grounds...

The Commission invites the government's attention pointedly to the manner in which the police was used and allowed themselves to be used for purposes some of which were, to say the least, questionable. Some police officers behaved as though they are not accountable at all to any public authority. The decision to arrest and release certain persons were entirely on political considerations which were intended to be favorable to the ruling party. Employing the police to the advantage of any political party is a sure source of subverting the rule of law. The government must seriously consider the feasibility and the desirability of insulating the police from the politics of the country and employing it scrupulously on duties for which alone it is by law intended.[105]

In its third and final report (1978), the Shah Commission deplored the role of the civil services during the period:[106]

A large number of officers—District Magistrates and Commissioners of Police, who exercised the powers of District Magistrates ex-officio, obediently carried out the instructions emanating from politicians and administrative heads issued on personal or political considerations. Many of these officers who appeared before the Commission explained that in the circumstances that prevailed, they had no alternative. In light of the evidence concerning the conditions prevailing during the period of emergency,

---

[105]Ibid. 42.

[106]Shah Commission of Inquiry, Third and Final Report, Chapter XXIV, paras 24.3, 24.12 and 24.17. https://www.countercurrents.org/Shah-commission-of-Inquiry-3rd-Final-Report.pdf, accessed on 3 March 2022.

the Commission has generally accepted the plea of helplessness tempered by expressions of regret put forward by the detaining officers. This, however, does not minimize the basic fact that such conduct on the part of responsible officers is not in consonance with the best traditions of the services to which they belonged, and of the ethical considerations which must govern the exercise of powers involving deprivation of liberty, under an order based entirely on subjective satisfaction of the officers concerned without a trial and without affording an opportunity to the person detained or even his knowing what infraction he had, in the view of the official, been responsible for... Exhortations have in the past often been addressed by political leaders that public functionaries must be committed servants of the government. These have in no small measure been responsible for some of the serious consequences that had followed certain steps taken by the government servants during the emergency. The commitment of a public functionary is, however, to the duties of his office, their due performance with an accent on their ethical content, and not to the ideologies, political or otherwise, of the politicians who administer the affairs of the State. Commitment by the public servants, therefore, means only and entirely, commitment to the policy and programmes of the government insofar as the policy and programmes are in conformity with the fundamentals of the Constitution. Anything beyond these fundamentals should be construed to mean as falling outside the scope and the purview of the commitment.

The Commission went on to warn that:

If a recurrence of this type of subversion is to be prevented, the system must be overhauled with a view to strengthen it in a manner that the functionaries working in the system do so in an atmosphere free from the fear of consequences of their lawful action and in a spirit calculated to promote the integrity and welfare of the Nation and the rule of law.

The suggested overhaul was, unfortunately, never taken up. The Bureau of Police Research and Development (BPR&D), in a paper titled *Political and Administrative Manipulation of the Police*, published in 1979, warned that 'excessive control of the political executive and its principal adviser over the police has the inherent danger of making the police a tool for subverting the process of law, promoting the growth of authoritarianism, and shaking the very foundations of democracy'. The warning went unheeded.

ANTI-SIKH RIOTS (1984)

The anti-Sikh riots which convulsed the country following the assassination of Mrs Gandhi on 31 October 1984 was the darkest chapter in the history of India's criminal justice system post-Independence. Hooligans belonging to or supported by the Congress party organized pogrom against members of the Sikh community across India, particularly in Delhi. A total of about 3,000 Sikhs were killed in Delhi alone. No less than four commissions, nine committees[107] and two special investigating teams (SITs) were set up from time to time to investigate the incidents. However, as alleged by H.S. Phoolka, the lawyer who pursued relentlessly the criminal cases registered in

---

[107]Ved Marwah Commission, 1984; Ranganath Misra Commission, 1985; Dhillon Committee, 1985; Kapur-Mittal Committee, 1987; Jain-Banerjee Committee, 1987; Ahuja Committee, 1987; Poti-Rosha Committee, 1990; Jain-Aggarwal Committee, 1990; Narula Committee, 1993; Nanavati Commission, 2000; Mathur Committee, 2014; Central Government SIT, 2015; Supreme Court SIT, 2018.

respect of the riots, there was lack of political will, which led to the findings of the various committees not being properly followed up. On 10 January 2018, the Supreme Court ordered the setting up of an SIT to investigate the 186 cases that had been closed by the central government. The SIT headed by Justice S.N. Dhingra, in its report which was released in January 2020, slammed the then Union government and the Delhi Police for showing utter lack of interest in booking the rioters and for trying to hush up the criminal cases:

> Despite a large number of victims approaching various agencies (including Justice Ranganath Misra Commission) soon after the riots and for a few years thereafter, a large number of crimes of murders, rioting, looting, arson remained unpunished and untraced. The basic reason for these crimes remaining unpunished and culprits getting scot-free was lack of interest shown by the police and by the authorities in handling these cases as per law or to proceed with the intention of punishing the culprits... The whole effort of the police and the administration seem to have been to hush up the criminal cases concerning riots.[108]

The Government of India accepted the findings of the Dhingra Committee. What action is taken against the perpetrators of the riots and the delinquent officers who tried to shield the rioters, however, remains to be seen. The majority of police officers, barring a few honourable exceptions, had allowed the rioters a free run during the riots and, after the registration of cases, carried out such shoddy investigations that any court would find it difficult to punish the accused. Not that the judiciary played its role. The Commission headed by Justice Ranganath

---

[108]Dhananjay Mahapatra, 'Congress govt showed no interest in nailing 1984 rioters: Panel,' *The Times of India*, 16 January 2020.

Misra had received hundreds of affidavits with respect to the killings, lootings and incidents of arson in which the accused were named. But instead of directing the registration of FIRs on the basis of those affidavits, he recommended the appointment of other committees which delayed the process of law. The FIRs were actually registered in 1991 and 1992 on the basis of affidavits filed before the Misra Commission in 1985. The trial courts later rejected the testimony of witnesses on the grounds of delay in filing of FIRs, delay in recording statements of witnesses and other reasons related to unfair investigations.

There was thus all-round failure—lack of political will, administrative connivance, police collusion and judicial incompetence—which together contributed to justice being delayed and therefore denied to the hapless victims of the riots. The Justice Nanavati Commission of Inquiry, in its report on the Anti-Sikh Riots (submitted in 2005), significantly recommended that 'there should be an independent police force which is free from political influence and which is well equipped to take immediate and effective action.'[109]

I was Deputy Inspector General of Police, Agra Range those days. Suffice to say that Agra was the safest place for Sikhs on the Delhi-Kanpur axis during the riots. Hundreds of truckers had taken shelter at Guru ka Tal gurudwara on the outskirts of Agra under our protection. After the riots subsided, Agra police escorted them up to the Punjab border.

There were several other incidents also, where police, playing the tune of the political masters in power, abdicated its lawful functions with tragic consequences. These included the demolition of the disputed structure in Ayodhya on

---

[109]In the Supreme Court of India, (Civil original Jurisdiction), Writ Petition (Civil) NO. 310 of 1996, https://www.humanrightsinitiative.org/programs/aj/police/india/initiatives/prakash_singh_final_submissions.pdf, accessed on 22 November 2021.

6 December 1992,[110] assault on the Allahabad High Court on 13 September 1994[111] and excesses committed on the Uttarakhand agitators on 1 October 1994.

American political scientist David H. Bayley commented as follows on the distortions in police–politician relations in the country, which contributed in no small measure to the aforesaid unfortunate incidents:

> The police have been discredited by their colonial past and present defects in practice; politicians have been discredited by their unscrupulousness, partiality and parochialism. The problem for modern India is to establish a stable equilibrium between two imperfect forces so as to serve public interest.[112]

MY EXPERIENCE

During my nearly 35 years of career, I felt, more than once, that the police organization needed systemic reforms. External pressures, particularly from the political class, are quite often overwhelming. Only extraordinary officers are able to

---

[110]The Supreme Court, in its judgment on the Ayodhya case on 9 November 2019 observed that 'the destruction of the mosque took place in breach of the order of status quo and an assurance given to this Court' and that it was 'an egregious violation of the rule of law'. (https://www.thehinducentre. com/resources/article29929806.ece/binary/Ayodhya.pdf, accessed on 22 November 2021.)

[111]A procession of Samajwadi/Bahujan Samaj party workers, while enforcing Uttar Pradesh Bandh, moved into the High Court premises where they created lawlessness and beat up some advocates. The Chief Justice had to call the Army to secure the High Court. Police role during the incident was questionable.

[112]David H. Bayley, *Police and the Politicians*, published in Reading Material for Level-III Management Course by SVP National Police Academy, Hyderabad (1994).

withstand these, and even they have to pay the price. The majority of officers prefer to swim with the current. The overall result of this trend has been a gradual decline in professionalism and poor delivery of services to the people. A stage came when most of the serving officers of the state carried an invisible party stamp on their foreheads. As a consequence, every time there was change of government, there were wholesale transfers of officers. Those considered loyal to the party in power were given key assignments. Those whose loyalties were suspect usually found themselves on inconsequential assignments, irrespective of their merit and professional competence. This, I felt, was not a healthy state of affairs. I was convinced that the serving officers should be loyal to the laws of the land and the Constitution of the country and that they should, under all circumstances, uphold the rule of law.

However, it is easier said than done. Certain institutional arrangements are necessary to achieve political neutrality. These must be built in to protect the good officers if we want them to perform their duties and discharge their obligations in a manner consistent with the requirements of law.

But then, people would argue, this battle could have been fought departmentally by the serving officers. Why could the police chiefs or the IPS Associations not take up these matters and pursue them with the government? My experience was that our efforts in this direction over a period of decades had not led us anywhere. In UP, we have a unique system of observing Police Week every year. One of the highlights of the week is a conference of senior officers to which the chief minister of the state is invited. The occasion is utilized to make some recommendations, suggest systemic reforms and make specific requests to improve the working conditions of policemen. We found that the demands or suggestions which involved cosmetic changes had a fair chance of acceptance, but recommendations for any systemic changes would either be brushed aside or half-hearted assurances would be given, which would never be kept.

A classic example was the announcement by the Government of UP in 1978 that it would be introducing Commissionerate system of policing in Kanpur. Vasudev Panjani was handpicked to be the first commissioner of police of Kanpur. He, along with the then Home Secretary, K.K. Bakshi, were even sent to Mumbai, Pune and Chennai to study the Commissionerate system. The bureaucracy meanwhile got active and through their clandestine operations managed to scuttle the project. No reasons were given. The proposal was buried for well over 40 years until Yogi Adityanath, UP chief minister, resurrected it and Commissioners of Police were appointed in Lucknow and Noida in January 2020.

The executive stranglehold over police has a sinister side to it also. Officers trying to uphold the rule of law are harassed and humiliated by the establishment. I had my own share of traumatic experiences in this regard.

During my tenure as DIG Meerut (1977–78), I worked with crusading zeal and came down heavily on the corrupt elements. In the process, I never cared to look into the caste background of officers. Several Jat station officers suffered. Actually, a large number of Jat officers had managed their transfer to Meerut Range during the tenure of Chaudhary Charan Singh as home minister of India. It was not surprising therefore that many of the officers punished by me happened to belong to one community. These officers ganged up, carried on a tirade that I was anti-Jat and complaints to that effect were made to the home minister. Charan Singh was a man of great integrity, but he was vulnerable to any whispering campaign on the caste frequency. One morning, while I was holding a meeting of the station house officers in Muzaffarnagar, I got a call from the Special Assistant to Home Minister (Vijay Karan) that I should see the home minister immediately. I hurriedly concluded the deliberations and drove straight to Delhi. As I was ushered into the home minister's office, I found him visibly angry. He started shouting at me, accusing me of caste bias, and holding me responsible for victimizing police officers of the Jat community. I held my ground politely but firmly, tried to explain to him that these officers were corrupt and that my disciplinary action against them was not influenced by any extraneous considerations. Charan Singh was however in no mood to listen. I found that he was not prepared to hear any contrary arguments. At that stage, I saluted him and walked out of the room. By the time I reached Meerut, orders transferring me had already been issued.

If the story had ended there, I would have probably reconciled to the shift. However, the affected sub-inspectors/ inspectors had cooked up fictitious allegations against me and, on the basis of that, the home minister asked the chief minister of UP (Ram Naresh Yadav), who was his protégé, to suspend me. Fortunately, there was, I feel in retrospect, divine intervention and the suspension order could not be executed. The Chief Secretary (Dilip Bhattacharya) and Home Secretary (S.S. Bisen), both of whom knew me personally and were convinced that I was being victimized, insisted that a preliminary inquiry was necessary before I could be suspended. The chief minister reluctantly agreed to an anti-corruption inquiry, but insisted that the same should be completed within a week. The inquiry brought out that all the allegations were entirely fictitious and baseless. However, the threat of suspension did hang over my head like the Damocles sword for about a month and it caused me great mental trauma. Why should I have been humiliated when, in fact, I had embarked on a campaign against corruption? The question kept haunting me, and I never got a satisfactory answer.

Another terrible experience was when one fine morning I was disgraced and removed from the post of Director General of Police (DGP), UP without any provocation. On 30 September 1992, at about 11.30 a.m., I was asked by the chief minister to hand over charge by 1.30 p.m. It was a Bharatiya Janata Party (BJP) government and Kalyan Singh was the chief minister. I had no problem working with him for about a year. For the first time, a relentless campaign was carried out against the mafia. The terrorist movement in Terai area, an area geographically bigger than Punjab, was crushed. Large-scale recruitments were held without any taint. Police image was on the upswing and the DGP had acquired a larger-than-life image. The developments in and related to Ayodhya, however, led to sharp differences between me and the executive. The state government wanted the security arrangements around the disputed shrine to be diluted. These were resisted by me in light of the Supreme Court's directions to maintain the status quo. Personally, in my heart of hearts, I was all for Ram Mandir at the disputed site. However, as Police Chief of the State, I was quite clear that upholding the rule of law was the highest religion for me. There were two high-level meetings where I had the unpleasant duty of striking discordant notes. These meetings were attended by the chief minister, about half a dozen other ministers, the chief secretary, the principal secretary (Home), the principal secretary to the chief minister, the DGP of the State (myself), and DG Intelligence. Unfortunately, the chief secretary, principal secretary (Home) and the DG Intelligence kept quiet on the issue of scaling down the security arrangements. Every time a minister suggested lifting a barrier or removing concertina coils from a particular place, mine was the only dissenting voice. I was marked out as an officer who was unlikely to toe the official line. The bureaucracy was also not comfortable with my style of functioning. In quite a few cases, I had not complied with the Home Department's orders because I considered them against public interest or as undermining the performance of the police department. Of course, in all these cases, I took care to discuss the matter with the chief minister and get his approval on the orders being modified. The Home Department was miffed at some of its orders being firstly not complied with and then amended at the highest level. The bureaucrats kept on poisoning the ears of the chief minister. And finally one day, I was given marching orders even though nothing had gone wrong on the law-and-order front in the State. *The Times of India*, commenting on my ouster, said: 'This is not done' and observed that this would be 'a reprieve for mafia'.[113]

Why should I have been politically victimized? Why was I disgraced and humiliated at the peak of my career? During the months which followed, I was almost ostracized, socially and officially. I withdrew into a cocoon. It is another matter that after the demolition of the disputed shrine at Ayodhya, the state was engulfed in communal riots, President's rule was imposed and, to restore law and order, the government posted me again as DGP, UP on 23 December 1992. The basic question nevertheless remained unanswered. Should a police chief upholding the Rule of law and committed to ensuring compliance of judicial directions in a sensitive matter be unceremoniously thrown out? Does it not call for a systemic change, giving security of tenure to the police chief?

There were several other experiences also which left a bad taste behind. For reasons of brevity, I would not go into their details. One small interaction may be briefly mentioned. S.S. Bisen, an IAS officer of the UP cadre and a man of great integrity, once said, 'Prakash, who wants an honest police officer?' I have not been able to forget that observation and the question continues to haunt me to this day.

---

[113] 'This is not done,' *The Times of India*, 2 October 1992; 'UP DGP's ouster a reprieve for mafia,' *The Times of India*, 11 October 1992.

I knew that as long as I was in service, there was a limit beyond which I could not go. We are all bound by the All India Services (Conduct) Rules. I realized that there was one and only one option still left to be explored—and it was the Supreme Court of India. And so, after my retirement on 31 January 1994, my mind started working on the project. It was not easy to make up my mind. It would involve time, money and a lot of effort to challenge the establishment. I was not part of any non-governmental organization (NGO), had no financial backing and no infrastructure. However, I decided that the assault had to be made and the battle had to be fought.

Getting an advocate to pursue the PIL was a major problem, particularly because it would have been impossible for me to pay his fees. After contacting different advocates, I met Prashant Bhushan, advocate of the Supreme Court. He impressed me with his sincerity and dedication. When I broached the proposal to him, I encountered a Chinese wall of resistance. He had a very poor opinion of the police and criticized its working in unequivocal terms. We had several sessions. Ultimately, he agreed with my reasoning. The police system was corrupt and inefficient, but it was so essentially because it had been designed to serve the establishment. The police needed systemic reforms to become an instrument of service to the people. Once Prashant Bhushan was convinced, the rest was easy. I must place on record the fact that he never charged one paisa as fees, worked diligently for the next more than two decades and pursued the PIL in the Supreme Court at every stage. I had to pay only the court expenses and other miscellaneous charges. These were not much and I could afford them.

However, before we take up the long-drawn-out battle in the judiciary, it would be worthwhile mentioning certain other efforts to bring about reforms in the police at the state and national levels.

3

THE INITIAL EFFORTS

Several states appointed Police Commissions from time to time to review the working of police in their respective areas and suggest necessary improvements.
The following commissions were appointed:

1. Kerala Police Commission (1959) under Shri N.C. Chatterjee, senior advocate, Supreme Court
2. West Bengal Police Commission (1960-61) led by Shri K.C. Sen, ICS (Retd)
3. Bihar Police Commission (1960-61) headed by Shri B.P. Jamuar, Retd High Court judge
4. Punjab Police Commission (1961-62) led by Shri Mehr Chand Mahajan, Chief Justice of India (Retd)
5. Maharashtra Police Commission (1964) under Shri Y.V. Dixit, Retd High Court judge
6. Madhya Pradesh Police Commission (1966) headed by Shri C.M. Trivedi, ICS (Retd)
7. Delhi Police Commission (1968) led by Shri G.D. Khosla, Retd High Court judge
8. UP Police Commission (1970-71) led by Shri Ajit Prasad Jain, MP and Shri Gangeshwar Prasad, Retd High Court judge
9. Assam Police Commission (1971) headed by Shri Shanti Prasad, IP (Retd)
10. Tamil Nadu Police Commission (1971) led by Shri R.A. Gopalaswamy, ICS (Retd)

11. One-Man Police Commission of Andhra Pradesh (1984) under Shri K. Ramachandra Reddy, IPS (Retd)

The Kerala Police Reorganisation Committee (1959) observed that 'the greatest obstacle to efficient police administration flows from the domination of party politics under the state administration' and the result of partisan interference is often reflected in 'lawless enforcement of laws, inferior service and in general decline of police prestige followed by irresponsible criticism and consequent widening of the cleavage between the police and the public affecting the confidence of the public in the integrity and objectives of the police force'.[114] The West Bengal Police Commission (1960–61) found that there were frequent allegations that investigation of offences was sought to be interfered with by influential persons highly placed in society or office. The Bihar Police Commission (1960–61) made wide-ranging recommendations and emphasized the importance of public cooperation. The Punjab Police Commission (1961–62) deplored that 'members of political parties, particularly of the ruling party, whether in the legislature or outside, interfere considerably in the working of the police for unlawful ends...the result of this political interference is disastrous and it has considerably and very seriously affected the police work in the state. The police are demoralised'.[115] The Delhi Police Commission (1968) observed that political interference was a 'rich source of corruption'.[116] The Tamil Nadu Police Commission (1971) made recommendations for the reorganization of police establishments, modernization of the police and improvements in service conditions, and stated that the problem of political interference had

---

[114]Second Report of the National Police Commission, August 1979, p. 22.
[115]Ibid.
[116]Ibid.

grown over the years in spite of the most explicit public declarations made by the successive chief ministers. The Committee on Police Training set up by the Government of India in 1972 observed that 'there have been instances when the governments have been accused of using the police machinery for political ends.'[117]

The terms of reference of the State Police Commissions were generally restricted to improving the functioning of police within the framework of the Police Act of 1861 and the Commissions therefore, as stated by C.V. Narasimhan, who was member secretary of the NPC, did not examine 'the basic structure of the police and their statutory role as impartial and truthful agents of law.'[118] Consequently, while the police infrastructure was improved in terms of manpower, transport and communications, the overall quality of police service rendered to the public did not rise up to public expectations.

NATIONAL POLICE COMMISSION

The Government of India appointed, through a Resolution dated 15 November 1977, a National Police Commission (NPC) as it felt that far-reaching changes have taken place in the country after the enactment of the Indian Police Act, 1861 and the setting up of the Second Police Commission of 1902, particularly during the last 30 years of the Independence. However, despite radical changes in the political, social and economic situation in the country there has been no comprehensive review at the national level of the police system after Independence. It was felt that 'a fresh examination is necessary of the role and performance of the police—both as a law enforcement agency and as an

---

[117]Ibid.

[118]'Insulating the Police from Extraneous Pressure,' A paper by C.V. Narasimhan, IPS (Retd), p. 4.

institution to protect the rights of the citizens enshrined in the Constitution.'[119]

The Commission comprised the following:

1.	Shri Dharma Vira (Retired governor)	Chairman
2.	Shri N.K. Reddy (Retired Judge, Madras High Court)	Member
3.	Shri K.F. Rustamji (ex-Inspector General of Police (IGP), Madhya Pradesh and ex-Special Secretary, Home Ministry)	Member
4.	Shri N.S. Saksena (ex-IGP UP and ex-DG CRP and then, Member, UPSC)	Member
5.	Prof. M.S. Gore (Professor, Tata Institute of Social Sciences, Bombay)	Member
6.	Shri C.V. Narasimhan (The then director, CBI)	Full-time Member-Secretary

The terms of reference of the Commission were *inter alia* to:

- Redefine the role, duties, powers and responsibilities of the police,
- Examine the development of the principles underlying the present policing system,
- Examine if any changes are necessary in the existing method of administration, disciplinary control and accountability,
- Inquire into the system of investigation and prosecution,
- Examine the methods of maintaining crime records and statistics and suggest methods for making them uniform and systematic,
- Review policing in rural areas and recommend

---

[119]First Report of the National Police Commission, p. 1.

necessary changes,

- Examine the system of policing required in non-rural and urbanized areas including metropolitan areas and suggest the pattern that would be most suitable,
- Examine the steps taken for modernizing law enforcement,
- Examine the nature and extent of the special responsibilities of the police towards the weaker sections of the community and suggest steps to ensure prompt action on their complaints,
- Recommend measures and institutional arrangements to prevent misuse of powers by the police, misuse of the police by administrative instructions, political or other pressure or oral orders of any type, for quick and impartial inquiry of public complaints made against the police, redressal of grievances of police personnel and periodic evaluation of police performance,
- Examine the manner and extent to which police can enlist cooperation of the public in the discharge of their social defence and law-enforcement duties,
- Examine the methods of police training, development and career planning of officers, and recommend any changes that are required, as well as to make the leadership of the force effective and morally strong, and
- Examine the nature of the problems that the police will have to face in the future and suggest measures necessary for dealing with them.[120]

The NPC submitted eight detailed reports between 1979 and 1981 which contained comprehensive recommendations covering the entire gamut of police working.

---

[120]Ibid. 1–2.

First Report (February 1979)[121]

The Commission, while reviewing the developments since Independence, deplored that 'the relationship between the government and the people has not basically changed' and that 'the attitude of the elected representatives as well as the government servant towards the common man appears to the latter as the attitude of the ruler towards the ruled.'[122] The fundamental problem regarding the police, as analysed by the Commission, was how to make the police function as 'an efficient and impartial law enforcement agency fully motivated and guided by the objectives of service to the public at large, upholding the Constitutional rights and liberties of the people.'[123]

The Commission recognized that the constable of the present day had moved far from the predominantly mechanical role assigned to him by the 1902 Commission and had now to interact with the public in large numbers in a variety of situations 'where he has to apply his mind, exercise his judgment, use his powers of persuasion and appeal and enforce law with public understanding and cooperation.'[124] The constabulary constituted the bulk of the force and was the 'foundation and base for the entire police structure.'[125] It was necessary therefore that they should be so recruited and trained that they could be deployed on duties involving the exercise of discretion and judgment, and they should be able to assist the sub-inspectors in inquiries and investigation work in a positive and purposeful manner.

---

[121]Quotations are from the respective reports (there are eight such reports) of the National Police Commission. Sub-headings show the source.
[122]First Report of the National Police Commission, p. 9.
[123]Ibid. 7.
[124]Ibid. 11.
[125]Ibid.

The Commission also suggested a machinery for the redressal of grievances within the police organization. It was of the view that any arrangement for inquiry into complaints against the police should be acceptable both to the police and to the public as fair and just, not favouring one at the expense of the other and not damaging the morale of the police and their effectiveness in maintaining law and order. The large number of complaints against the police should be looked into and disposed of by the supervisory ranks in the police hierarchy. The Commission however recommended that a judicial inquiry should be mandatory and held in the following categories of complaints: (i) alleged rape of a woman in police custody; (ii) death or grievous hurt caused while in police custody; and (iii) death of two or more persons resulting from police firing in the dispersal of an unlawful assembly.[126]

Second Report (August 1979)

The second report of the Commission stressed that 'the basic role of the police is to function as a law enforcement agency and render impartial service to law, in complete independence of mere wishes, indications or desires expressed by the Government as a matter of policy which either come in conflict with or do not conform to the provisions in our Constitution or laws duly enacted thereunder'.[127] Elaborating on the law-enforcement function of the police, the Commission said that, having regard to the objectives mentioned in the preamble of our Constitution, it should cover the following two basic functions:

(i) Upholding the dignity of the individual by safeguarding his constitutional and legal rights. The police secure

---

[126]Ibid. 62.
[127]Second Report of the National Police Commission, p. 12.

this objective by enforcing laws relating to the protection of life, liberty and property of the people; and

(ii) Safeguarding the fabric of society and the unity and integrity of the nation. Police secure this objective by enforcing laws relatable to maintenance of public order.[128]

The Commission recommended that a new Police Act should be framed which should spell out the duties and responsibilities of the police to:

(i) promote and preserve public order;

(ii) investigate crimes and, where appropriate, to apprehend the offenders and participate in subsequent legal proceedings connected therewith;

(iii) identify problems and situations that are likely to result in commission of crimes;

(iv) reduce the opportunities for the commission of crimes through preventive patrol and other appropriate police measures;

(v) aid and co-operate with other relevant agencies in implementing other appropriate measures for prevention of crimes;

(vi) aid individuals who are in danger of physical harm;

(vii) create and maintain a feeling of security in the community;

(viii) facilitate orderly movement of people and vehicles;

(ix) counsel and resolve conflicts and promote amity;

(x) provide other appropriate services and afford relief to people in distress situations;

(xi) collect intelligence relating to matters affecting public peace and crimes in general including social and

---

[128]Ibid. 13.

economic offences, national integrity and security; and

(xii)   perform such other duties as may be enjoined on them by law for the time being in force.[129]

The Commission dealt at great length with interference in the working of police and its misuse by illegal or improper orders or through extraneous pressures from the political class or the executive, and deplored that 'the relationship that existed between the police and the foreign power before independence was allowed to continue with the only change that the foreign power was substituted by the political party in power.'[130] The Police Act of 1861 was retained and attempts were not made to redefine the relationship between the police and the politically oriented government. The observations made by the Commission are relevant to this day—with greater force, in fact. It would be worthwhile quoting these *in extenso*:

> Interference with the police system by extraneous sources, especially the politicians, encourages the police personnel to believe that their career advancement does not at all depend on the merits of the professional performance, but can be secured by currying favour with politicians who count. Deliberate and sustained cultivation of a few individuals on the political plane takes up all the time of a number of police personnel to the detriment of the performance of their normal professional jobs to the satisfaction of the general public at large. This process sets the system on the downward slope to decay and total ineffectiveness...
>
> Interference at the operational level in police stations, police circles, etc. results in the total bypassing

---

[129]Ibid. 18.
[130]Ibid. 21.

of the supervisory officers in the hierarchy. The frequent by-passing of the normal chain of command results in the atrophy of the supervisory structure. It, therefore, fails to operate effectively even in matters which do not attract any such extraneous interference...

A police force which does not remain outside politics but is constantly subjected to influences and pressures emanating within the system from the politicised police personnel themselves will in turn seriously disturb the stability of the duly elected political leadership in the State itself and thereby cause serious damage to the fabric of our democracy. This danger has to be realised with equal seriousness and concern by the politician as well as by the police.[131]

The Commission divided the police tasks into three categories: (i) investigative, (ii) preventive, and (iii) service-oriented. It stated categorically that 'the investigative tasks of the police are beyond any kind of intervention by the executive or non-executive.'[132] As regard the preventive tasks and service-oriented functions, the 'police should be subject to the overall guidance from the government which should lay down broad policies for adaption in different situations from time to time.'[133] There should however be 'no instructions in regard to actual operation in the field' and that 'the discretion of the police officers to deal with the situation, within the four corners of the overall guidance and broad policies should be unfettered.'[134]

The Commission expressed its view that the power of superintendence of the state government over the police

---

[131]Ibid. 24–27.
[132]Ibid. 30.
[133]Ibid.
[134]Ibid.

should be limited to ensuring that the police performance is in strict accordance with law. To achieve this, it recommended the setting up of a State Security Commission in each state, and said that the chief of police in a state should be assured of a statutory tenure of office 'without the Damocles sword of transfer hanging over his head all the time'.[135] The Commission also wanted the police officers to be effectively protected from whimsical and *mala fide* transfer/suspension orders.

Third Report (January 1980)

The third report dealt with the special role and responsibility of the police towards the weaker sections of society. It recommended that the state governments may set up special courts under the Protection of Civil Rights (PCR) Act to bring down the large pendency of cases under this head. The state police could also set up special cells to monitor the progress of investigation of cases under the PCR Act or other atrocities against scheduled castes/tribes registered in police stations. On rural police, the Commission was of the view that while the chowkidari system may be retained, it needed to be strengthened. On the subject of posting of officers-in-charge of police stations, the Commission was emphatic that there should be exclusive responsibility of the district Superintendent of Police. Likewise, the chief of police should have the exclusive responsibility of selecting and posting superintendents of police in charge of districts.

The Commission also laid down guidelines for making arrests and use of handcuffs. Arrest during the investigation of cognizable case would be justified only if it involved a grave offence, or the accused was likely to abscond or commit further offence unless his movements were restrained, or if

---

[135]Ibid. 30–31.

the accused was a habitual offender and likely to commit similar offence again.

The Commission recommended a separate economic offences wing in the state police to deal with offences of tax evasion, manipulation of stocks and shares, black marketing, hoarding, adulteration of drugs and essential commodities, etc. The report also dealt with modernization of law enforcement and laid emphasis on acquisition of scientific equipment.

Fourth Report (June 1980)

The fourth report emphasized the imperative need of co-ordinating the functioning of the investigating staff with the prosecuting agency and suggested reforms in procedural laws with a view to facilitating judicious conduct of investigations. It recommended an amendment to Section 154 CrPC, making it incumbent on a police station to register an FIR irrespective of whether the crime had taken place within its jurisdiction or not, and then transfer the FIR to the concerned police station, if necessary. This was done to avoid harassment to complainants whenever there was doubt about jurisdiction. It also said that the examination of witnesses should be conducted as far as possible near the scene of offence or at the residence of witnesses or at any other convenient place. The Commission further recommended that the police officers should be empowered to compound offences in simple cases during the investigation stage. This would reduce the workload of courts. There should however be safeguards to prevent any forced compromise.

To reduce the use of third-degree methods, the Commission recommended surprise visits of senior officers, including magistrates, to the police stations to question persons held in custody and ensure that they were not being subjected to any ill treatment. It also said that there should be a mandatory judicial inquiry in cases of death or grievous hurt caused while in police custody.

On the subject of social legislation, the Commission recognized that these could be of two kinds: the permissive type in which the law merely sought to enlarge the freedom of social action and interaction in certain fields and protect the person from any disability that might fall on him but for the law; and the prescriptive type which sought to restrict certain social practices and penalize any conduct that was specifically prohibited by law. Legislation concerning inter-caste marriages would come under the permissive type while laws relating to dowry, polygamy or untouchability would come under the prescriptive type. The Commission laid down the parameters of police involvement in such laws.

Fifth Report (November 1980)

The Commission recommended that future recruitments to the police should be at two levels only: (i) Constables and (ii) Indian Police Service, and that recruitment at other levels should be gradually phased out. Recruitment to the constabulary should be done at the district level to ensure adequate representation for every district in the police. The Commission laid great stress on psychological test and said that these should be introduced during the training to weed out those who are not likely to shape into good policemen. The Commission deplored the tardiness in the implementation of the recommendations of the Committee on Police Training, 1973 and suggested that the central government should undertake a leading role in the implementation process by providing the full capital costs for establishing the new training institutions and improving the existing ones. The posting in training institutions should carry attractive pay and other amenities.

On relations between the district police and the executive magistracy, the Commission made the following observations:

> The general control and direction of the District Magistrate cannot be construed as warranting any interference in the internal management of the police force. In fact, though the District Magistrate is referred to as the Head of the Criminal Administration by several State Police regulations and manuals, such a position is not conferred upon him by law either in the Police Act or the Code of Criminal Procedure. Legally, the District Magistrate's capability to control and direct the Superintendent of Police should only be restricted to selective and individual situations and should be exercised more as an exception than as a rule. We note that the present position in several states far exceeds this legal stipulation. This, in our view, is untenable and needs to be corrected.[136]

The Commission nevertheless recognized the role of the district officer as the Chief Coordinating Authority in the district, and said that it should be obligatory for the superintendent of police to give the utmost consideration and attention to a communication from the district officer and take prompt steps to look into and deal with any situation brought to his notice by the district officer.

A healthy police–public relationship on a continuing day-to-day basis, the Commission said, is vital 'to secure the desired measure of public involvement and cooperation in police work to make it meaningful and acceptable to society'.[137] It however took note of the fact that the police–public relations were in a very unsatisfactory state. While there were several

---

[136]Fifth Report of the National Police Commission, p. 35.
[137]Ibid. 47.

reasons for it, the Commission identified police partiality, corruption, brutality and failure to register cognizable offences as the most important factors which contributed to this sad state of affairs. The Commission felt that the remedies for the organizational constraints on police performance lie in proper living and working conditions for policemen and reform of the organization.

On the subject of women police, the Commission recommended that they should become an integral part of the police organization and handle investigation work in much greater measure than at present. They should be entrusted with investigation of cases especially relating to women and children, and employed in intelligence work connected with said crimes. The Commission recommended the same training to women police as for their male counterparts, both in terms of content as well as duration and suggested that they should be recruited in much large numbers than at present.

Sixth Report (March 1981)

The Commission, in a chapter devoted to police leadership, deplored the prevailing culture which were bureaucratic and structure oriented and not dynamic and performance oriented. It painted a lurid picture of the state of affairs:

> We have observed that for quite some time now police officers tend to abdicate their role, initiative and responsibility. Some of them have convinced themselves that they are helpless due to scarcity of resources, problems of staff and the overbearing control of and interference by the political leadership. Things would not have degenerated so much if the deficiencies of the politicians had been made up by the ability, courage, vision, competence and leadership of the senior civil servants and police officers. But it seems to us that the

very process of survival, and going up in the system, exhausts and dehydrates many of them. Those officers who do win and reach the top are too tired and worn out to be able to do much, or even want to do much.[138]

The Commission observed that 'the challenges of the future will require new skills in personnel management and a much higher level of professional knowledge, competence and leadership from the senior officers in the police'[139] and recommended that 'the terms and conditions of this service should be comparable with those of the best services.'[140]

The Commission also recommended that the management of the IPS cadre should be by police officers through the Central Police Establishment Board at the Centre and by the State Security Commissions in the states. It also recommended two Central IPS cadres—one for the paramilitary organizations such as the BSF, Central Reserve Police Force (CRPF), Indo-Tibetan Border Police (ITBP) and the other for organizations like the Intelligence Bureau (IB), Central Bureau of Investigation (CBI) and Research and Analysis Wing (RAW).

The Commission dealt at length with the problem of communal riots in the country. It analysed the reasons for the same and also the factors which contribute to failure in handling such riots. The Commission suggested that only 'specially selected experienced officers with an image of impartiality and fair play should be posted to the communally sensitive districts'[141] and that every district should have a riot scheme which must be rehearsed from time to time. It emphasized that 'only a strong political will, determined official commitment to duty, and impartial administration of the laws of the land, and

---

[138]Sixth Report of the National Police Commission, p. 3.
[139]Ibid. 1.
[140]Ibid. 4.
[141]Ibid. 31.

a widespread popular condemnation of all those who incite communal passions and instigate communal riots can in the long run contribute to solution of the problem.[142]

On the subject of urban policing, particularly in large cities, the Commission emphasized that the police should be organized in a unitary chain of command which embraces the two basic functions of decision-making and implementation. This was necessary because crime and law-and-order situations developed rapidly in large urban areas, requiring a speedy and effective operational response from the police. The Commission, therefore, recommended that in cities with a population of five lakh and above and even in places where there may be special reasons like speedy urbanization, industrialization, etc., the system of Police Commissionerate should be introduced. The Police Commissioner should have complete authority over his force and should be functionally autonomous.

Seventh Report (May 1981)

The report deplored that the police station is the most neglected unit of the police administration and emphasised that:

> The basic problems will have to be tackled at the level of Police Station itself. Therefore, the Police Stations have to be strengthened and made effective. The integrity, professional competence and impartiality of its members have to be improved. It is only then that the public expectation of a high quality of professional work and conduct from police will be fulfilled.[143]

On the question of separation of crime and law-and-order work,

---

[142]Ibid. 35.
[143]Seventh Report of the National Police Commission, p. 3.

the Commission made very pertinent observations. During the arguments in the Supreme Court over the implementation of its directions, I was dismayed to find that some of the most reputed lawyers of the country have quaint ideas on the subject. I had to take a firm stand in the Court against their recommendations on the subject. These will be discussed at the appropriate place later on. The NPC's views on the subject are being reproduced in full to clarify the position:

> We, however, feel that the nature of police duties is such that there are obvious disadvantages in placing the two branches *viz.* crime investigation and law and order in watertight compartments. If the lines of command and control for law and order and crime investigation are totally separate, the contact between the two wings will tend to be practically eliminated resulting in their isolation from each other. We are therefore of the view that the station house officer of police station should have an overall control and responsibility for all the police tasks within the police station limits. This should in no circumstances be diluted by making the crime investigation wings of the police station answerable to hierarchies other than the station house officer. It is essential that at the police station level the division of duties and functions is not carried out to the other extreme as would make the police station appear as a house divided into two separate compartments. Therefore, while maintaining the composite integrity of the police station under the station house officer, our main object of stressing the functional aspect in the bigger police stations is to ensure that adequate time and attention is given to crime investigation work which is often neglected at present.[144]

---

[144]Ibid. 5.

The Commission also emphasized that the role of the chief of police should be considerably enhanced and strengthened. It said, in unambiguous terms, that 'the internal management of the police force in the state should fall entirely within the purview of the Chief of the Police.'[145]

The report devoted a separate chapter to policing in the Northeast. It recognized that the problems of policing in the Northeast were complex and cautioned that the region should not blindingly imitate the police set-up of the rest of the country. The administration should not interfere with the traditional tribal customs, laws and institutions. 'The tribal sense of identity should not be threatened under the garb of introducing a modern system of policing.'[146] The Commission recommended that the best officers of the highest calibre should be posted to the region, and that a comprehensive police manual should be drafted for the Northeast, taking into consideration its special features.

Eighth Report (May 1981)

The Commission defined the three-fold accountability of the police—to the people, to the law and to the organization. In a democratic society, the police are accountable for its performance to the people. However, all activities of the police are governed by various provisions of law and each action of the police is to conform to the law of the land. The police are therefore accountable to the law. Besides, the police functionaries are accountable for their performance to the organization. The Commission however clarified that: '[The] police on their part should also clearly understand that the ultimate accountability is to the people and to the people

---

[145]Ibid. 14.
[146]Ibid. 83.

alone. Their accountability to law and to their organisation are only complementary to the ultimate objective of accountability to the people.'[147]

While concluding, the Commission reiterated that the present police organization based on the Police Act of 1861 was not suited for the present time because 'an authoritarian police working under an imperialist regime cannot function well in an independent democratic country'.[148] The police subculture should take into account 'the fundamental rights of the people, the supremacy of laws and not of executive fiat and our constitutional goal towards a developed and egalitarian society'.[149] The Commission therefore drafted a new Police Act incorporating its recommendations.

The NPC's recommendations, however, received no more than a cosmetic treatment at the hands of the Government of India. The political leadership was just not prepared to give functional autonomy to the police because it found this wing of the administration a convenient tool to further its partisan objectives. As for the bureaucracy, control over the police was—and continues to be—an intoxicant they have become addicted to and are just not willing to give up. And so, the Act of 1861 continues to be on the statute book even after more than 160 years—a millstone around the police neck. It is true that, after the Supreme Court's directions of 2006, several states have passed new Police Acts. However, as we shall see later, these Acts have generally legitimized the status quo and merely given legal cover to the prevailing equations.

The NPC's recommendations remain broadly relevant to this day. It is a very comprehensive document, covering all the important aspects of police functioning. Its recommendations formed the core of the PIL filed in 2006.

---

[147]Eighth Report of the National Police Commission, p. 11.
[148]Ibid. 14.
[149]Ibid.

OTHER COMMITTEES

Several other committees were also constituted from time to time to go into the question of specific issues related to police reforms. These were:

1. Gore Committee on Police Training (1971–73)
2. Ribeiro Committee on Police Reforms (1998)
3. Padmanabhaiah Committee on Police Reforms (2000)
4. Group of Ministers on National Security (2000–01)
5. Malimath Committee on Reforms of Criminal Justice System (2001–03)

Gore Committee

A Committee headed by Prof. M.S. Gore was appointed by the Government of India on 10 November 1971 'to undertake a review of the existing police training programmes in the country and to suggest ways in which they should be modified so that the country may have a police force which is professionally well-equipped and capable of responding effectively to the changing social situation.' Its members included M.M.L. Hooja, formerly director, IB; K.F. Rustamji, director general, BSF; N.S. Saksena, former IGP, UP and A. Gupta, director, BPR&D.

The Committee felt that the police have 'a difficult role, and a role that they are often called upon to perform in the most provocative and trying circumstances.'[150] There are agitations which pose a threat to law and order and yet have a claim to social legitimacy. The police, under the circumstances, run the risk of being cast in an anti-people role. It should, while maintaining law and order and supporting the constitutional

---

[150] *The Gore Committee Report on Police Training*, Chapter IV, para 17, https://bit.ly/3v4usPC, accessed on 21 February 2022.

processes in society, also show an understanding of the 'cause' but distinguish that from the 'means' which are adopted if those threaten peace or law and order. The Committee, therefore, recommended the following considerations to be given special emphasis in the training of police:

i) Loyalty to the Constitution, commitment to the goals of the nation and the concepts of an egalitarian society, and the need for national integration.

ii) Awareness of the problems that arise in the wake of the developmental process including conflicts, social disorganization, scarcity and controls, regional imbalances, etc.

iii) A deep social awareness for comprehending and reacting to complex situations.

iv) Development of analytical and innovative skills since situations will continue to change and no ready-made solutions can be prescribed.

v) A new orientation in dealing with the masses, which come from various strata of society, divided among many contours such as religion, caste, region and income as may lead to the correct response in individual cases.

vi) The need for the application of scientific techniques, management concepts and skills, and constructive attitudes and values in police work.[151]

The Committee, while examining improved training methods for the police, also commented on certain areas of police functioning which needed systemic reforms. It made a total of 186 actionable recommendations. Forty-five of these are related to police reforms. While the training-related recommendations

---

[151] *The Gore Committee Report on Police Training*, Ministry of Home Affairs, Government of India, https://bit.ly/3H7xhlg, accessed on 24 November 2021.

were by and large implemented, those relating to structural reforms did not get the required degree of traction.

Ribeiro Committee

The Ribeiro Committee was set up by the Supreme Court on 25 May 1998 while it was deliberating over the PIL filed for police reforms. The Court wanted the Committee to examine if the NPC's recommendations were still relevant.

The Committee found that 'the passage of time has in no way affected the usefulness of most of the recommendations (of the National Police Commission) and they can and must be implemented by the governments concerned.'[152]

Padmanabhaiah Committee

The Padmanabhaiah Committee was set up in January 2000 to examine the challenges the police would face in the next millennium, suggest ways to transform the police into a professional and competent force, identify mechanisms to insulate police from political interference, and examine the need for 'federal crimes' and creation of a Federal Law Enforcement Agency. The Committee submitted its report in August 2000.

The important recommendations of the Committee were as follows:

i) New legislation is needed to replace the Police Act of 1861.

ii) Recruitment should aim at bringing the tooth-to-tail ratio to 1:4, that is one senior officer (sub-inspector and above) against four constables.

---

[152]Recommendations of the Committee have been dealt in detail in the next chapter.

iii) Police Training Advisory Council should be set up at the Union level and in each state to advise the relevant home minister on police training.

iv) Promotions should be subject to completing mandatory pre-promotion training and passing pre-promotion examinations.

v) A tenure policy should be put in place to prevent illegitimate political interference in police functioning. The minimum tenure of all officers should be two years.

vi) The Director General of Police should be appointed by the government from two names put forward by a selection committee comprising chief justice of the State High Court, state chief secretary and an eminent public person.

vii) The Police Establishment Board comprising the DGP and three other members of the police force selected by the DGP should be constituted to approve transfers of all officers of the rank of deputy superintendent of police and above.

viii) Confessions made to identified officers (superintendent of police and above) should be admissible in evidence.

ix) Specific offences that have inter-state, national and international ramifications should be declared federal offences and investigated by the Special Crimes Division of the CBI, which should function under the administrative control of the Ministry of Home Affairs.

x) A comprehensive law to address terrorist offences should be enacted. The standard of proof and legal procedures in terrorism-related crimes should be reviewed.

xi) Police personnel should be given one day off each week and required to go on earned leave every year.

xii) Community policing philosophies should be embraced.

Group of Ministers on National Security

The Group of Ministers (GoM) examined the reports of various task forces which were set up in the wake of Pakistan's aggression in Kargil to review internal security, intelligence, border management and defence. The Committee felt that the apparatus and systems which we had inherited from the British were no longer suitable in this day and age and it therefore made comprehensive recommendation under each head. Regarding the state police, it made the following observations:

> The state police is the most visible symbol of administrative authority and its failure to effectively maintain law and order has not only eroded the credibility of the Government but has also emboldened criminal elements to persist with their unlawful activities with impunity. Hence, there is a need to restore the fitness, capacity and morale of the State police forces through a transparent recruitment and promotion process, a well thought-out training regimen and improved living and working conditions. The police forces have also to be adequately sensitised to the demands of their profession and the expectations of the people. Thus, an exercise to modernise the police apparatus and simultaneously improve its image has to be undertaken on a priority basis.[153]

The GoM also emphasized the need to strengthen and modernize the state police forces, and recommended that the states should be encouraged to set up first-class forensic

---

[153]*Reforming the National Security System: Recommendations of the Group of Ministers*, February 2001, p. 42.

science laboratories, establish state-of-the-art training institutions, raise specialized forces and maintain updated data/information base with regard to the activities of the organized crime/mafia networks, smugglers and racketeers. It also suggested that the states be requested to introduce a shift system in order to ensure that the police constables do not have to work more than eight hours a day and, on an average, six days a week.

Borrowing from the NPC's recommendations, the GoM suggested the setting up of a state-level Police Establishment Board headed by the state chief secretary/home secretary to decide transfer, posting, rewards, promotions, suspension, etc. of gazetted police officers. Another board, under the state DGP should decide these matters in respect of non-gazetted police officers.

Regarding the central paramilitary forces, the GoM expressed the following views:

> The Central Paramilitary Forces (CPMFs), while playing a commendable role have often been diverted for prolonged deployment on a variety of duties other than those for which they were raised. This has adversely affected their training and recuperation schedules. It is strongly felt that each paramilitary force should revert to its original role, for which it was raised, equipped and trained. These forces should also be suitably modernised and trained to cope with the tasks expected of them in the prevailing internal security scenario.[154]

The GoM recommended the principle of 'One Border One Force' to optimize the utilization of border guarding forces. It also stated that the border guarding forces, which were deployed on counter-insurgency and other allied duties,

---

[154]Ibid. 42.

should revert to their role of border management and 'the counter-insurgency role be progressively taken over by the CRPF'.[155]

The GoM also suggested that a Special Duty Group (SDG) should be created in the Central Industrial Security Force (CISF) for VIP security. Regarding the National Security Guard (NSG), the Group stated unambiguously that the force should not be deployed for duties which stretch far beyond its original mandate.

The Criminal Justice System, according to the Group, needed an urgent revamp. In this context, it endorsed the Law Commission's recommendation to separate the staff engaged in investigation from those to be deployed on law-and-order duties. The Group suggested enactment of a Prevention of Terrorism Bill as early as possible to deal effectively with terrorism.

Malimath Committee

The Committee on Reforms of Criminal Justice System headed by Justice V.S. Malimath, formerly chief justice of Karnataka and Kerala high courts, was constituted by the Government of India in November 2000. It submitted its recommendations in March 2003.

The Malimath Committee made a total of 158 recommendations. The important ones are summarized below:

1. Quest for Truth: The Committee felt that the present adversarial system could be improved by adapting some useful features of the inquisitorial system, such as the duty of the courts to search for truth. All the functionaries should have an inspiring ideal to pursue, a sense of purpose and direction. The ultimate

---

[155]Ibid. 50.

objective of the system is to render justice, and justice should ideally be founded on truth. The Committee therefore recommended that 'Quest for Truth' shall be the guiding star of the entire criminal justice system. For this purpose, the Court shall be empowered to summon and examine any person as a witness as it considers necessary, and to issue any directions to the investigating officers as may be necessary to assist the Court in its search for truth. The courts, the police and the prosecution have to play a dynamic and proactive role in the process.

2. Standard of Proof: A fundamental principle of criminal jurisprudence is that the accused is presumed to be innocent unless there is 'proof beyond reasonable doubt'. The Committee felt that this places a very unreasonable burden on the prosecution. In continental countries, the standard of proof is much lower, namely, 'preponderance of probabilities'. The Committee therefore recommended that we should have a standard higher than 'preponderance of probabilities' and lower than 'proof beyond reasonable doubt'; it should be 'clear and convincing' standard of proof.

3. National Police Commission: The Committee endorsed the recommendations of the NPC that there should be state security commissions in the states, National Security Commission at the Union level, Police Establishment Boards to decide the posting, transfers and promotions of police officers, and that Police Commissionerate system should be introduced in the urban cities and towns.

4. Cognizable/Non-Cognizable Offences: The distinction between cognizable and non-cognizable offences should be done away with and all offences should be investigated. In the schedule to the Code, in place

of cognizable and non-cognizable, we should have offences 'arrestable without warrant' and 'arrestable with warrant or order.'

5. Federal Crime: The Committee made recommendation to deal with organized crime, terrorism and economic crimes, and recommended the enactment of a central law to deal with federal crimes.

6. Amendments: Some significant amendments suggested were as follows:

    i) Section 25 of the Evidence Act should be amended so that confession recorded by the superintendent of police or an officer above him is admissible in evidence.

    ii) Audio/video recording of statement of witnesses, dying declarations and confessions should be authorized by law.

    iii) Section 162 of CrPC should be amended to require that the statement is read over and got signed by the person making the statement, to whom a copy of the same should be furnished.

    iv) Section 167 (2) of CrPC should be amended to increase the maximum period of police custody to 30 days in respect of offences punishable with sentence of more than seven years.

    v) Identification of Prisoners Act should be amended to empower the magistrate to take fingerprints, footprints, photographs, blood sample, etc. of the accused.

7. Disposal of Cases: To expedite the disposal of cases the Committee recommended that:

    i) All cases in which punishment is three years or less should be tried summarily.

    ii) Vacations for high courts and the Supreme Court should be reduced.

iii) An 'Arrears Eradication Scheme' was proposed for all cases pending for more than two years.

iv) All compoundable cases should be sent to Legal Service Authority for settling those through Lok Adalats.

v) Adjournments should not be allowed.

vi) Cases may be settled without trial where the interest of society is not involved.

8. New Punishments: The Committee recommended new forms of punishments such as community service, disqualification from holding public offices, confiscation orders, imprisonment for life without commutation or remission, etc.

9. Director of Prosecution: Every state should have a Director of Prosecution in the rank of DGP. He should work in consultation with the advocate general.

10. Justice to Victims of Crime: The Committee made several recommendations including the right of the victim to participate in cases involving serious crimes and to adequate compensation.

The recommendations of the Malimath Committee were unfortunately not followed up mainly because of the chorus of protest from the human rights lobbies. The Amnesty International, in particular, launched a vehement attack on the Committee's recommendations.

MINISTERIAL EFFORTS

Pilot's Letter

At the ministerial level, efforts made by three distinguished politicians of the country deserve special mention.

Rajesh Pilot, minister for internal security, in a letter which he addressed to all the state governments on 27 July 1994, drew their attention to the recommendations of the NPC and stated that while a view might have been taken in the past on some of the recommendations, it was necessary 'to have a relook at the whole issue as the situation has undergone substantial change since then, warranting acceptance of the recommendations'.[156] He expressed hope that the state governments will give their serious consideration and take necessary steps to implement the recommendations of the NPC. Pilot, in his letter, made specific mention of giving a fixed tenure to the chief of police so that he could withstand extraneous influences and guide and supervise the men under his command. He also stressed the need to set up State Security Commissions which would aid the state government in discharging the superintending responsibility in an open manner within the framework of law with due regard to healthy norms and conventions.

Indrajit Gupta's Letter

Indrajit Gupta, as home minister of India, sent a letter to all the state governments and Union Territories on 3 April 1997, saying that 'a time has come when all of us may have to rise above our limited perceptions to bring about some drastic changes in the shape of reforms and restructuring of the police before we are overtaken by the unhealthy developments which appear to have been taking place all over the country'.[157] He urged the state governments to 'break out of our colonial system of policing and bring about certain reforms and structural changes in consonance with the developments which have taken place during the last 50 years or so in the administration of criminal justice in general and police

---

[156]Vide Appendix A.
[157]Full text of Indrajit Gupta's letter may be seen in Appendix B.

functioning and practices in particular'. Gupta analysed the malaise within the police in the following words:

> The popular perception all over the country appears to be that many of the deficiencies in the functioning of the police in our country have arisen largely due to an overdose of unhealthy and petty political interference at various levels starting from transfer and posting of policemen of different ranks, misuse of police for partisan purposes and political patronage quite often extended to corrupt police personnel. This is the general perception of the people and we all should share our quota of blame in this regard irrespective of our party affiliations. Added to this malady is the prevailing system of inadequate public accountability of police performance, extremely poor level of police-public relationship, increasing levels of police misconduct, poor state of police leadership and discipline and virtual absence of an effective public grievances redressal mechanism. In fact, within the police forces also there is strong resentment against political and other extraneous interference or pressure in the discharge of their lawful professional duties.

His exhortation to the state governments had a ring of sincerity not generally seen among politicians:

> It is, therefore, of great national importance that we rise above any narrow and partisan considerations to insulate the police from the growing tendency of partisan or political interference in the discharge of its lawful functions of prevention and control of crime including investigation of cases and maintenance of public order. Unless this task is taken up by us all, we at the Centre or in the States may soon find ourselves to be incapable of maintaining our democratic institutions to which we are all committed.

Paying a handsome tribute to the police and the paramilitary forces, he said that 'it should also be recognised by us that quite often it is the police, including the paramilitary forces, which have stood between lawlessness verging on anarchy and functioning of our democracy'.

Unfortunately, none of the state governments responded to Union home minister's exhortations. They did not extend him the courtesy of even a formal acknowledgement.

Antony's Initiative

A.K. Antony, the chief minister of Kerala, also deserves special mention in this context. He made a bold attempt to introduce police reforms in the state during the period 2001–04. He issued strict instructions that no ruling party member would go to the police station with any recommendation. There was tremendous appreciation of this bold step by the general public. The people's representatives, particularly of the ruling party, were however quite unhappy. The police were allowed to function without any political interference for over three years. N.R. Madhava Menon, the then vice chancellor, West Bengal National University of Juridical Sciences, Kolkata, praised Antony for not 'using the police as a stooge of the party in power'.[158] The Police Performance and Accountability Commission, which was set up by the state government in 2003, noted that although many officers were 'for the first time, emboldened to act according to the dictates of their conscience', there were others 'who felt that autonomy was a licence to misuse vast political powers'. The Commission pointed out that the common people lost the political conduit to reach the police without the fear of

---

[158]N.R. Madhava Menon, 'Police, People and Politicians', *The Hindu*, 12 November 2002.

ill treatment or intimidation, a function which the politicians were discharging rather effectively by accompanying complainants to the police station and interceding with the police, and protecting the citizens from police ill treatment. The Commission noted that 'autonomy to the police is the ideal, but it should be tempered with measures to prevent its misuse.'

Antony stepped down towards the end of 2004. His successor, Oommen Chandy, was not committed to police reforms and was keen on having full support of the MLAs. The police reforms experiment in Kerala ended with that.

4

JUDICIAL INTERVENTION

Having exhausted all other options and once I was free from the constraints of All India Services (Conduct) Rules, I decided to knock at the doors of the Supreme Court for police reforms in the country.

In early 1996, I drafted a writ petition in public interest under Article 32 of the Constitution, to be filed before the Supreme Court. I requested for the issuance of a writ of mandamus or any other writ, order or direction to the Union of India and the state governments to initiate positive steps to reform and overhaul the police organizations at the central and state levels. This is to make them accountable primarily to the law of the land and to the people.

Advocate Prashant Bhushan, who had agreed to take up the petition, suggested that I should get some other co-petitioners to sign the petition so that it did not appear to be the handiwork of just one individual. I approached N.K. Singh, who had worked under me as the additional director general, BSF and asked him whether he would like to join hands with me in the petition. He readily agreed. He, however, felt that we should get the petition endorsed by a well-known activist also. He suggested the name of H.D. Shourie, director, Common Cause. Shourie had an impeccable reputation. Bhushan talked to him about the petition and thereafter I personally called on Shourie, who was happy to sign the petition. We had a pleasant interaction.

The petition was thus jointly signed by me, Singh and

Common Cause through its director, Shourie. Singh took interest in the petition in the initial stages. An officer of great integrity and with vast experience of police work, he made valuable contribution during our interactions with Bhushan. Singh however entered politics in October 1996 and thereafter withdrew from active involvement in the petition. Common Cause's participation was notional. None of their representatives ever came to any hearings in the Court or discussions with the lawyer. For about a year, I used to apprise Shourie telephonically about the progress in the petition after every hearing. It was always a pleasure talking to him. However, as there was no active interest from Common Cause, the telephonic contacts also tapered off. The involvement of Common Cause with the petition remained on paper only.

The PIL had a long gestation period in the Supreme Court. It dragged on for more than 10 years. Most of the time, I found myself waging a lone battle before the highest court of the land. Bhushan was, of course, there. He was sincere, committed and painstaking. Any words of appreciation for his contribution would be inadequate. He was ably assisted by his junior, Rohit Kumar Singh, also a very hard-working and dedicated professional.

The one organization which supported me throughout was the CHRI. Maja Daruwala, its director, took great interest in police reforms. The CHRI, under her leadership, organized a series of workshops and round table conferences in Delhi and other parts of the country to mobilize public opinion in favour of police reforms.

THE PETITION (1996)

The petition stated that there was 'alienation of people from the police due to the increasing incidents of aggression on their fundamental and even human rights by the latter, and the steadily mounting criticism of this wing of the government by different sections of people, including the media and the judiciary, and being convinced that the executive authorities, at the political and bureaucratic levels, are not taking—and are not likely to take—any initiative to restructure the police department and introduce such reforms as would make it truly an instrument of service to the law and to the people.' It therefore urged the Supreme Court to 'direct the executive authorities of the Central and state government to introduce such reforms as are essential to make the police, in letter and in spirit, accountable to the law of the land and the people of the country.'

It was argued that the executive has been 'using, misusing and abusing the law enforcement agency to further its own selfish, partisan and political objectives' and the following glaring examples were given to illustrate the point:

i) Anti-Sikh riots of 1984
ii) Demolition of the disputed structure at Ayodhya on 6 December1992.
iii) Assault on the Allahabad High Court on 13 September 1994.
iv) Excesses committed on the Uttarakhand agitators on 1 October 1994.
v) The inaction in pursuing the various criminal cases against Chandraswami.
vi) The inaction in pursuing the St. Kitts forgery.
vii) The initial inaction in pursuing the Hawala case.

The petition contended that 'we would have been saved the trauma of several riots and massacres, scandals and scams which have rocked the country if the police had not become a pliable instrument in the hands of the executive, as it has unfortunately become.'

The thrust of the petition was that:

The present distortions and aberrations in the functioning of the police have their roots in the colonial past, the structure and organisation of the police which have remained basically unchanged during the last nearly 135 years, and the complete subordination of the police to the executive—an arrangement which was designed originally to protect the interests of the British Raj but which unfortunately continues to this day.

The petition was divided into four parts: (i) historical background; (ii) recommendations of various commissions at the state and central levels on the subject of police reforms; (iii) misuse and abuse of the police; and (iv) the need to redefine the scope and functions of the police, frame a new Act for the purpose and implement the core recommendations of the NPC.

The Police Act of 1861, the petition stated, was designed 'essentially to subserve the colonial interests of the British Raj.' The Frazer Commission had, as far back as in 1902-03, commented that certain rules and regulations framed by the provincial governments were contrary to the spirit of the Police Act and that there had been 'a degree of interference which the law did not contemplate and which have been prejudicial to the interest of the (police) department.'[159] The NPC, which was constituted to comprehensively review the working of the police system in India, had mentioned in its concluding report that the police have a three-fold accountability only: to the people, the law and the organization. There was no mention of accountability to the political executive or the bureaucracy, which between them were exercising total control over the police today.

---

[159]Anandswarup Gupta, *The Police in British India, 1861-1947*, Bureau of Police Research and Development (MHA), 1979, p. 222.

The petition quoted extensively from the reports of the Kerala Police Reorganisation Committee (1959), the West Bengal Police Commission (1960-61), the Punjab Police Commission (1961-62), the Delhi Police Commission (1968) and the Tamil Nadu Police Commission (1971), all of which had deplored members of political parties, particularly of the ruling party, whether in the legislature or outside, interfering considerably in the working of the police for unlawful ends. The petition also drew attention to the recommendations of the NPC to set up State Security Commission in every state, make investigative functions of the police completely independent of any extraneous influences and have a procedure for the appointment of Police Chief, giving him a minimum statutory tenure.

The executive misuse and abuse of the police, according to the petition, had manifested generally in the following forms:

- frequent postings and transfers
- recruitment procedures vitiated by political recommendations
- promotions influenced
- investigations tampered with
- unlawful directions to the police
- intelligence apparatus utilized for political purposes.

As a result, police standards had declined and there was growing alienation from the people. The petition acknowledged the sorry state of police affairs:

> Professionalism is at a discount. Officers spend a lot of time hobnobbing with politicians in an effort to be on their right side. The chain of command has been weakened. The control mechanisms have become dysfunctional. People in general have little confidence in the police. There is criticism from all the quarters including the media and the judiciary. What is particularly disturbing is that a

large segment of police officers are getting politicized. They are identified with one political grouping or the other. This is another reason which leads to widespread displacement of officers whenever there is a change of regime. It is indeed a vicious chain. Yet another—and this is the most devastating by-product—development is the growing nexus between the politicians, criminals and the bureaucrats/police which, as mentioned in Vohra Report, is 'virtually running a parallel government, pushing the state apparatus into irrelevance.' The existing criminal justice system, as a result, is proving inadequate to control the activities of this unholy alliance.

The petition expressed its view that the role and functions of the police need to be redefined and, in this context drew attention of the Court to the draft of a new Police Act prepared by the NPC, though it was felt that even this would perhaps need a fresh look and have to be updated. The petition emphasized that police accountability to law needs to be recognized statutorily.

Strange though it may seem, neither the Police Act of 1861 nor the Constitution or any Act of Parliament have stressed this obvious point. The police functions as a law enforcement agency under powers vested to it under the Criminal Procedure Code and several other enactments. In actual practice, under the Act of 1861, the police is answerable essentially to the executive—and we have seen the damage this arrangement has caused to the social fabric and the political structure of the country.

The petition quoted David Bayley's observations that 'the rule of law in modern India, the frame upon which justice hangs, has been undermined by the rule of politics.'[160] It also

---

[160]'Politics should not undermine justice,' *Deccan Chronicle*, 28 May 2017.

referred to the National Human Rights Commission of India's (NHRC) recommendation that 'serious action be taken on the Second Report of the Police Reforms Commission which, in 1979, made a series of proposals that remain highly pertinent today—including those suggesting the insulation of the investigative function of the police from political pressure.'

The following prayers were made in the petition to 'protect and safeguard the fundamental rights of the citizens of this country which are being rampantly violated on account of the political and bureaucratic control over the police':

i)   The role and functions of the police be redefined and a new Police Act framed on the lines of the Model Act drafted by NPC in order to ensure that the police is accountable essentially and primarily to the law of the land and the people.

ii)   The Government of India and the state governments be directed to constitute (a) State Security Commissions in each state to ensure that the police functions strictly in accordance with the laws of the land, (b) National Security Commission/Council at the central level which would take a macro view of the country's security-related matters and inter alia lay down the policies to be followed in dealing with various terrorist, insurgent and other anti-national groups threatening to destabilize or even disintegrate the country.

iii) The Union and state governments be directed to ensure that the investigative work at the state level is separated from the law-and-order functions, as has been recommended by several police commissions, and that all investigating agencies in states as well as at the Centre function uninfluenced by any extraneous pressure or consideration.

iv)   The Union and the state governments be directed to prescribe a procedure for appointing chiefs of state police and the Central Police Organizations which would inspire confidence and ensure that only the finest officers reach the top and also give them a minimum statutory tenure so that there is stability and long-term planning in the functioning of the organizations.

PROGRESS OF PIL IN THE SUPREME COURT

The Writ Petition (Civil) No. 310 of 1996, *Prakash Singh and Others vs. Union of India and Others,* was heard in the Supreme Court of India for 10 years. It turned out to be a long battle.

The Writ Petition was admitted on 30 July 1996. The first hearing took place on 30 September 1996, when the Court issued notices to the Respondents to state what action, if any, had been taken on the recommendations made by the NPC.

The NHRC had already expressed itself in favour of police reforms. It had repeatedly emphasized, in its annual reports, that the police needed to be shorn of the image of the hand-maid of the party in power and that, in a pluralistic society such as ours, it had to function, and be seen to function, with impartiality and integrity by all elements of society. The Court, on being apprised of the NHRC's views, directed on 4 November 1996 that it may be impleaded as a respondent and notice issued to the Commission. The secretary general of the NHRC thereupon filed an affidavit on 22 January 1997, emphasizing 'the need for systemic reforms in the police and endorsed the reforms suggested by the National Police Commission which are of crucial importance for improving the quality of policing'.[161] The affidavit drew attention to the English common law which had developed the doctrine

---

[161]Counter Affidavit filed by NHRC on 22 January 1997, para 18, p. 38.

of 'constabulary independence'. It quoted a former chief constable, who had said:

> 'In operational matters, a Chief Constable is answerable [to] God, his Queen, his conscience and to none else.'

It also quoted the following observations of the British Royal Commission of Police (1962):

> The case of Fisher vs. Oldham Corporation established that, whatever else he might be, the constable was not a servant of any organ of local government... The constable's position was described as that of an officer whose authority is original, not delegated, and is exercised at his own discretion by virtue of his office: he is a ministerial officer exercising statutory rights independently of contract.[162]

STATES' RESPONSE

Several states filed their affidavits.[163] A synopsis of some of these is given below:

Andhra Pradesh: The state in its affidavit dated 30 October 1996 apprised the Court that a comprehensive draft bill titled 'Andhra Pradesh Police Bill, 1996' has been prepared on the recommendations of the NPC and that the same was under scrutiny of the government. It nevertheless went on to say that the recommendation regarding setting up of State Security Commission is not acceptable to the state government.

---

[162]Ibid. para 20. pp. 39–40.
[163]'Police Reforms hit a Snag,' *Sunday Times of India*, 31 December 2006; 'States disagree with SC on Police Reforms,' *Sunday Hindustan Times*, 31 December 2006.

Arunachal Pradesh: In the first affidavit filed on 10 February 1997, the state drew attention of the Supreme Court to the fact that 'the criminal justice system in the State of Arunachal Pradesh is at variance with the rest of the country as it is [a] combination of customary and formal laws,' and pleaded that the 'Special Acts governing the criminal administration in the state should not be replaced to disturb the traditional system of criminal administration existing for centuries.'

Goa: In its affidavit filed in September 1996, the state government said that it had considered the recommendations of the NPC and accepted most of those.

Gujarat: In its affidavit filed on 21 January 1997, the state government struck a note of defiance. It argued that there is a need to wait for the Model Police Act and that till then 'we may not be able to take up genuinely radical reforms as suggested by the NPC or as pleaded in the petition.' It expressed its opposition to the setting up of the State Security Commission because either the institution will be relegated to mere advisory role or it will become another power centre to influence decision of the police machinery. The state did not agree even with the suggestion to separate investigative functions from law-and-order duties, and argued that this 'needs to be viewed from the constitutional obligation of the executive wing of the state.' The state was also against giving a fixed tenure to the DGP. It further informed the Court that the state government had undertaken an exercise to revise the Bombay Police Act.

Himachal Pradesh: The state government, in its first affidavit filed on 28 December 1996, said that it was 'not in favour in any type of change' and argued that 'drastic measures' like setting up a State Security Commission would 'erode the basic powers of the state government and are not acceptable.'

Madhya Pradesh: The state government in its affidavit of 30 November 1996 took the stand that it was for the Government of India to amend the Police Act, 1861, and that, under the existing arrangement, the state was not competent to set up a State Security Commission or make other changes.

Maharashtra: The state government in its affidavit filed on 2 November 1996 categorically stated that none of the recommendations highlighted in the petition were feasible or acceptable. The constitution of State Security Commission, it said, would be 'inconsistent with the spirit of the Constitution of India.' It did not agree with the suggestion to give minimum statutory tenure to the Police Chief either. The state also expressed its opposition to the separation of the investigative function from the regular police machinery.

Manipur: The state took the stand that the recommendations of the NPC were directly related to the enactment of a new legislation and till that was done the state government has 'nothing to comment.' It submitted a detailed response to the recommendations of the NPC.

Orissa: The affidavit filed by the state government on 4 December 1996, made a refreshing reading. It agreed that 'it is high time to introduce progressive reforms keeping in view the ground realities' and conveyed its willingness to consider restructuring of the police and introducing reforms on the basis of a 'national consensus.' The state government agreed with the 'desirability of insulating police from various unwholesome interests' and assured that it will do everything once the necessary arrangements are put in place. The affidavit clearly stated that 'it is necessary in the larger interest of justice that the recommendations of the National Police Commission may be implemented.'

Rajasthan: The state's affidavit of 13 July 1997 was surprisingly filed by a police officer of the rank of Additional Superintendent of Police, Crime Investigation Department (CID). The affidavit conceded that reforms are necessary in the existing system and that the recommendations of the National Police Commission should be implemented with such modifications as may be necessary.

Sikkim: The government in its affidavit dated 24 October 1996 claimed to have implemented the recommendations of the NPC 'in all sincerity'.

West Bengal: The state government in its affidavit dated 18 October 1996 stated that most of the recommendations of the National Police Commission were in the nature of major policy decisions and that, therefore the implementation would depend on the 'finalization of such major policy decisions'.

Government of India: The Government of India, in its affidavit filed in September 1996, took the stand that 'most of the issues raised by the petitioners are general in nature having wider overtones embracing some of the policies of the government'. It disagreed with the averments made in the petition and asserted that the first report of the NPC was considered at a Conference of the Chief Ministers held at New Delhi in June 1979 and it was agreed to implement its recommendations. The remaining seven reports were sent to the state governments in March 1983 with the remarks that 'the recommendations made therein should be considered thoroughly and appropriate action taken'.

A number of states did not file their responses. These included Tamil Nadu, Karnataka, Kerala, Bihar, Haryana and UP. On 24 January 1997, the Court recorded its presumption that the defaulting states did not propose to file affidavits.

A rejoinder affidavit filed by the petitioners on 12 February 1997 deplored that 'the respondents have gone off at a tangent and tried to obfuscate the main points highlighted in the petition' insofar as they have commented at length on such recommendations of the National Police Commission which were not even mentioned in the petition. The affidavit drew attention to the Indian Society of Criminology's *Bangalore Declaration on Police Autonomy and Accountability* adopted at the XXIV Criminological Congress, 1996, seeking immediate implementation of the NPC Report and giving police of the country the autonomy and professionalism which it needs to discharge its functions under the law. The affidavit also quoted from Prime Minister, Deve Gowda's speech at the Conference of DGPs/IGPs on 23 July 1996, where he had admitted that 'in each state, the political bosses try to mishandle the police machinery.'

A supplementary affidavit by the petitioners was submitted on 14 July 1997; it gave details of institutional mechanisms in other countries to ensure the independence of the investigative machinery.

On 6 January 1998, some counsels appearing for the states submitted that they were required to re-examine the position in light of the decision of the Court in *Vineet Narain and Ors. Vs. Union of India, 1997* and the observations made therein relating to the state police forces. They wanted more time to file their responses.

The Supreme Court was gradually getting convinced that the salient recommendations of the NPC, as summarised in the petition, needed to be implemented. A question was, however, raised that the NPC had submitted its reports between 1979 and 1981—nearly two decades back—and, therefore, it was necessary to check if those recommendations were still relevant or required any modifications in light of changes and developments which had taken place since then. It was suggested by us that a committee could be appointed to go into the relevance of the NPC's recommendations in the present context. This was the background to the setting up of Ribeiro Committee.

RIBEIRO COMMITTEE

The Ribeiro Committee, which was set up on 25 May 1998, was specifically tasked to examine if the NPC's recommendations, which formed the core of the PIL, were still relevant or that any modifications were called for. The Committee was asked to:

i) Review action taken by the central government and the state governments/UT Administrations for implementation of the recommendations of the NPC, Law Commission, NHRC and Vohra Committee;

ii) Suggest ways and means for implementation of the pending recommendations of the above commissions/ Committee; and

iii) Consider and make recommendations regarding any other matter which the Government may refer to the Committee or which the Committee considers necessary in this behalf.

The Committee submitted two reports, one in October 1998 and the other in March 1999. The salient features of these reports are summarized below:

1. A Security Commission called the 'Police Performance and Accountability Commission' should be set up in each state comprising the minister in charge of police as the chairman, leader of the Opposition, chief secretary of the state, a sitting or retired judge nominated by the Chief Justice of the state's High Court, and three other non-political citizens of proven merit and integrity as members. These three citizens should be chosen by a committee to be set up by the chairman of the NHRC.

2. The Commission will have advisory and recommendatory powers for the present. The DGP of the State will be its Secretary and Convenor.

3. The Commission will oversee the performance of the Police and ensure that it is accountable to the law of the land.

4. A District Police Complaints Authority be set up in each Police District as a non-statutory body to examine complaints from the public of police excesses, arbitrary arrests and detention, false implications in criminal cases, custodial violence, etc. and to make appropriate recommendations to the Police Performance and Accountability Commission as well as to the government and to the State or National Human Rights Commission. The Principal District and Sessions Judge, the Collector of the district and the Senior Superintendent of Police (SSP) should constitute this authority.

5. A Police Establishment Board should be constituted in every state with the DGP and his four senior-most officers, borne on the IPS cadre of the state but who are immediately junior to the DGP, as members to monitor all transfers, promotions, rewards and punishments as well as other service-related issues.

6. The DG of Police will be selected by the chief minister of the state from a panel of three names prepared by a committee headed by the chairman of the UPSC and consisting of the Union home secretary, the director of the IB, the state's chief secretary and the state's incumbent DGP. This selection committee may consult the Chief Vigilance Commission (CVC) before drawing up the panel. The DGP will have a fixed tenure of three years. He can be removed within the period of tenure only on the recommendations of the

Police Performance and Accountability Commission (PPAC) and for specified reasons, made in writing to the government.

7. All investigating officers should be specially trained in scientific methods of investigation and not utilized for law-and-order duties except in small rural police stations where it may not be possible to strictly demarcate the two important police functions. The investigating officers should not be shifted to law and order or other duties for five years at least.

The Ribeiro Committee emphasized that 'the passage of time has in no way affected the usefulness of most of the recommendations (of the NPC) and they can and must be implemented by the governments concerned'.[164]

The Committee ran into rough weather only on the setting up of Police Performance and Accountability Commission. It was of the view that a statutory institution would be the most satisfactory and efficient way of solving this problem. However, during its visit to the state capital and discussions with the chief ministers/home ministers, the Committee encountered stiff opposition to the idea of any monitoring body supervising the political executive. 'Every CM/HM denied vehemently the suggestion of interference in the performance of the legitimate duties of the police or the use of pressures like transfers or suspension on unobliging police officers.'[165] In light of such strongly held views, the Committee veered round the view that the Commission should be a non-statutory, advisory and recommendatory body for the present. But for this dilution, the Ribeiro Committee endorsed all the other prayers relating to the selection of the DGP, setting up of Police Establishment Board, Police Complaints Authority,

---

[164]Second and Final Report of the Ribeiro Committee (1999), para 14, p. 10
[165]Ribeiro Committee Report (1998), para 22, p. 9.

and separation of investigation from law-and-order duties. The recommendations of the Ribeiro Committee were brought to the notice of the Apex Court on 1 February 1999.

FINAL SUBMISSIONS

On 28 January 1999, in light of recommendations made by the Ribeiro Committee, the petitioners filed their *Final Submissions*, urging the Apex Court, in the interest of upholding the fundamental rights of citizens and ensuring the rule of law, to pass appropriate writ, order or orders directing the Government of India and the state governments to:

- Constitute State Security Commission/Police Performance and Accountability Commission in each state;
- Set up National Security Commission at the central level;
- Ensure, through a system of empanelment, that only good and honest officers get promoted, and especially prescribe a procedure for the appointment of police chief, both in the states as well as at the Centre, giving him a minimum tenure;
- Set up District Police Complaints Authority in each district to look into complaints against the local police;
- Constitute a Police Establishment Board in each state to monitor and supervise the service-related matters of the subordinate staff and make recommendations to the state government regarding senior appointments;
- Take measures to insulate the investigative wing of the police by separating it from the law-and-order functions, ensuring at the same time that there is complete coordination between the two wings.

A note on police in the UK and Japan was also submitted to the Supreme Court around this time to buttress our arguments.

PIL IN A DARK TUNNEL (1999–2005)

The PIL moved in slow motion. Dates were fixed on 22 March 1999, 11 May 1999, 28 July 1999, 8 September 1999, 23 January 2000, 23 January 2001, 10 April 2001, 18 July 2001, but there was hardly any progress. The Hon'ble Court directed the case to be listed in the week commencing 4 September 2001 for hearing, but it was not listed. On 6 August 2002, an application for early hearing was given, which was registered as Interlocutory Application (I.A.) no. 4 of 2002. An additional affidavit was filed on behalf of the petitioners on 19 August 2002 in the context of the developments in Gujarat and the observations made by the NHRC which drew attention to the 'deeper question of police reform.'

The one silver lining during the period was a positive contribution by Chief Justice Sam Piroj Bharucha (January 2001–May 2002). During one of the hearings, while we were emphasizing the need to give at least a two-year tenure to the DGP, Justice Bharucha's terse comment was: 'Why not security of tenure to the Station House Officer (SHO) also?' We seized this observation to modify our prayer subsequently to demand security of tenure not only for the DGP but to all the officers holding operational posts in the field.

The matter thereafter came up for hearing on 21 February 2003, when the Hon'ble Court was pleased to issue *rule nisi* in the petition and directed it to be listed on a non-miscellaneous day. The service of *rule nisi* was completed by the petitioners on all the respondents and a letter to that effect was given to the Registry on 3 September 2003. The petitioners submitted another application for early hearing on 9 October 2003.

GUJARAT RIOTS

Gujarat was convulsed with riots in 2002 after 59 karsevaks travelling in a train were burnt alive on 27 February by a crowd of fanatic Muslims of Godhra town. The NHRC, of which Justice J.S. Verma was the chairperson, made the following observations on the riots:

> The tragic events in Gujarat, starting with the Godhra incident and continuing with the violence that rocked the State for over two months, have greatly saddened the nation. There is no doubt, in the opinion of this Commission, that there was a comprehensive failure on the part of the state government to control the persistent violation of the rights to life, liberty, equality and dignity of the people of the State. It is, of course, essential to heal the wounds and to look to a future of peace and harmony. But the pursuit of these high objectives must be based on justice and the upholding of the values of the Constitution of the Republic and the laws of the land. That is why it remains of fundamental importance that the measures that require to be taken to bring the violators of human rights to book are indeed taken.[166]

The Commission also drew attention to the 'deeper question of Police Reform' and expressed its view that 'recent events in Gujarat and, indeed, in other states of the country, underline the need to proceed without delay to implement the reforms that have already been recommended to preserve the integrity of the investigative process and to insulate it from extraneous influences.'[167]

---

[166]*National Human Rights Commission Proceedings*, 31 May 2002, para 64, p. 78

[167]*National Human Rights Commission Proceedings*, 6 March 2002, p. 26.

On 2 December 2003, the Court gave an order that the Writ Petition be tagged with W.P. (Crl.) No. 109 of 2003, *National Human Rights Commission vs. State of Gujarat and Ors.* (Best Bakery case). The matter came up before the Court on 27 February 2004. The Counsel for the Petitioner contended that cases like the Best Bakery would not have happened if police reforms had been addressed, as prayed for in the petition. The matter came up on 2 April and again on 6 August 2004, but the Court remained preoccupied with the Gujarat case. Police reforms could not be taken up. It was, therefore, felt that the case should be delinked. Orders to that effect were eventually passed by the Court on 17 August 2004.

There was thus hardly any progress in the PIL for a period of about six years from March 1999 to January 2005. It was as though the PIL had gone into a dark tunnel during this period.

THE FINALE

The case was eventually listed for final hearing on 1, 2 and 10 February 2005. The judges, after hearing our submissions, decided that notices be issued to the central government and the state governments for their response on (i) action taken on the Apex Court's directions in the *Vineet Narain* case that 'credible mechanisms' be put in place in the states to give security of tenure to the police chief and officers of the rank of superintendent of police and above; and (ii) action taken on the Ribeiro Committee's recommendations, and that the case be listed again after eight weeks.

On 19 April 2005, the PIL was taken up by a Bench presided over by the Chief Justice of India (R.C. Lahoti) himself. He fixed 6 May for directions. On that date, as the majority of states had not filed their responses, another date, 18 July, was fixed for directions. Actually however the case was listed on

22 August 2005. The Chief Justice wanted to know how much time the case would take. Prashant Bhushan, Counsel for the Petitioner, said that he would take at least five hours and, considering that Counsels for the Union and the states would also take time, the PIL would take at least three days to be disposed of. The CJI thereupon said that he would take up the petition after the Constitution Bench had completed its work.

JUSTICE SABHARWAL DELIVERS THE PUNCH

Y.K. Sabharwal took over charge as the CJI on 1 November 2005. His tenure proved to be decisive. The case was taken up by the Supreme Court on 25 November 2005. The Solicitor General took the plea that the Government of India had already constituted Sorabjee Committee to examine the Model Police Act prepared by the NPC and suggest modifications as per the changing role/responsibility of police in view of the new challenges before it, and that therefore the Court may await the recommendations of the Committee.

The matter came up next on 3 February 2006. The Court was told that the Sorabjee Committee had not finalized its recommendations yet. On 13 April 2006, the case was again taken up. The Court recognized the importance of the matter but wanted to await the recommendations of the Sorabjee Committee. It directed that the case be listed for directions in the third week of July 2006.

On 17 July 2006, Prashant Bhushan argued that the Court may not wait any longer for the Sorabjee Committee Report. The CJI agreed and directed that 1 August 2006 be fixed for the final hearing of the case.

The case was listed on 1, 2 and 3 August 2006 but could not be taken up because the items which preceded it could not be concluded. The case was thereafter listed on 8 and 10 August. It met the same fate on those dates also.

The petition was finally heard on 17 August 2006 at 1513 hours (3.13 p.m.). We got about 45 minutes only. It was stated at the outset that the Sorabjee Committee had produced a draft and the same had been put on the website. Prashant Bhushan drew the attention of the Court to the fact that, apart from the NPC, several other bodies had gone into the question of Police Reforms such as the NHRC, the Law Commission, the Ribeiro Committee, the Padmanabhaiah Committee and the Malimath Committee. The recommended reforms had, however, not been introduced. Under the circumstances, there was no guarantee that the Sorabjee Committee's recommendations would be accepted and, if accepted by the Centre, the same would be endorsed by the states. The CJI indicated that he would like to conclude the final hearing next week.

The PIL was thereafter taken up on 22 August 2006. Prashant Bhushan, advocate for petitioners, presented at length the *Summary of Submissions*. He elaborated the concepts of:

- State Security Commission
- Police Chief, procedure for his appointment and tenure
- Separation of Investigation from Law and Order
- Police Establishment Board and
- Police Complaints Authority

He also shed light on the constitutional/administrative arrangements for the functioning of police in progressive countries like the UK and Japan. Summing up, he said that police reforms are essential for good governance, to uphold the rule of law, ensure protection of human rights, survival of the democratic structure and the economic progress of the country.

The Solicitor General, appearing on behalf of the government, said they were in broad agreement with the points raised in the petition. However, he was still awaiting the Ministry of Home Affairs's (MHA) response on the various points made by the petitioners. Besides, the Soli Sorabjee Committee was yet to finalize its report. He therefore wanted time till the end of September. We protested, arguing that the term of the Sorabjee Committee was expiring at the end of August and therefore, the government may be given another opportunity till the first week of September only. The Chief Justice agreed with our contention and fixed 8 September as the last date for the government to make its representation.

I was concerned over the prospect of the Soli Sorabjee Committee coming up with recommendations which may be contrary to our prayers for Police Reforms, and therefore got in touch with members of the Police Act Drafting Committee (PADC), and was able to see the draft report which they had prepared. I was relieved that there was no substantive difference. Nevertheless, in consultation with the lawyer, I made minor changes in the final submissions so that there was no divergence whatsoever in what we were praying for and in the recommendations of the Sorabjee Committee. (The Supreme Court judgment came on 22 September 2006 while the PADC's Model Police Act was released on 30 October 2006.)

The states had been asked to come up with their responses. The Meghalaya representative stood up to say something, but it was found that the lawyer was talking about recruitment and training which were not relevant to the petition. Kerala supported the points made in the petition and drew the attention of the Court to certain progressive measures they had initiated. The Hon'ble Judges wanted to know if the bigger states like UP, Bihar and Maharashtra had anything to say. No advocate stood up. The hearing thereafter concluded, much earlier than what we had anticipated.

The concluding hearing of the PIL was on 11 September 2006 before a Bench headed by Sabharwal, CJI, and including Justice C.K. Thakker and Justice P.K. Balasubramanyan.

Prashant Bhushan read out the draft order (which I had prepared for the benefit of the Court). The Court generally agreed with the draft submitted, though they suggested minor changes here and there.

It was a very satisfying finale. The proceedings ended with some flattering comments for the petitioner. The Solicitor General (G.E. Vahanvati), addressing the judges, said: 'Every officer I have talked to said that Mr Prakash Singh is one of the finest police officers of the country...' The CJI also said, 'We have to thank Mr Prakash Singh for this (petition).'

HISTORIC JUDGMENT

The Supreme Court gave a historic judgment on 22 September 2006. It felt that it was 'absolutely necessary' to issue directions for the following reasons:

> Having regard to (i) the gravity of the problem; (ii) the urgent need for preservation and strengthening of rule of law; (iii) pendency of even this petition for last over ten years; (iv) the fact that various Commissions and Committees have made recommendations on similar lines for introducing reforms in the police set-up in the country; and (v) total uncertainty as to when police reforms would be introduced, we think that there cannot be any further wait, and the stage has come for issue of appropriate directions for immediate compliance so as to be operative till such time a new model Police Act is prepared by the Central Government and/or the state governments pass the requisite legislations.[168]

The Court emphasized that 'the commitment, devotion and accountability of the police has to be only to the rule of law'

---

[168]Vide Appendix C.

and that 'the supervision and control has to be such that it ensures that the police serves the people without any regard whatsoever to the status and position of any person while investigating a crime or taking preventive measures.'[169]

With a view to achieving these objectives, the Court gave seven directions, six of which were for the state governments and one for the central government.

The Court ordered the setting up of three institutions at the state level with a view to insulating the police from extraneous influences, giving it functional autonomy and ensuring its accountability. These institutions were:[170]

1. **State Security Commission:** 'The state governments are directed to constitute a State Security Commission in every State to ensure that the state government does not exercise unwarranted influence or pressure on the State police and for laying down the broad policy guidelines so that the State police always acts according to the laws of the land and the Constitution of the country. This watchdog body shall be headed by the Chief Minister or Home Minister as Chairman and have the DGP of the State as its ex-officio Secretary. The other members of the Commission shall be chosen in such a manner that it is able to function independent of Government control. For this purpose, the State may choose any of the models recommended by the National Human Rights Commission, the Ribeiro Committee or the Sorabjee Committee. The recommendations of this Commission shall be binding on the state government. The functions of the State Security Commission would include laying down the broad policies and giving directions for the

---

[169]Ibid.

[170]The portions in quotes are all from the judgment which is given in Appendix C of the book.

performance of the preventive tasks and service oriented functions of the police, evaluation of the performance of the State police and preparing a report thereon for being placed before the State legislature.'

2. **Police Establishment Board**: 'There shall be a Police Establishment Board in each State which shall decide all transfers, postings, promotions and other service related matters of officers of and below the rank of Deputy Superintendent of Police. The Establishment Board shall be a departmental body comprising the Director General of Police and four other senior officers of the Department. The state government may interfere with decision of the Board in exceptional cases only after recording its reasons for doing so. The Board shall also be authorized to make appropriate recommendations to the state government regarding the posting and transfers of officers of and above the rank of Superintendent of Police, and the Government is expected to give due weight to these recommendations and shall normally accept it. It shall also function as a forum of appeal for disposing of representations from officers of the rank of Superintendent of Police and above regarding their promotion/transfer/disciplinary proceedings or their being subjected to illegal or irregular orders and generally reviewing the functioning of the police in the State.'

3. **Police Complaints Authority**: 'There shall be a Police Complaints Authority at the district level to look into complaints against police officers of and up to the rank of Deputy Superintendent of Police. Similarly, there should be another Police Complaints Authority at the State level to look into complaints against officers of the rank of Superintendent of Police and above. The district level Authority may be headed by a retired District Judge while the State level Authority may be headed by a retired Judge of the High Court/Supreme Court. The

State level Complaints Authority would take cognizance of only allegations of serious misconduct by the police personnel, which would include incidents involving death, grievous hurt or rape in police custody. The district level Complaints Authority would, apart from above cases, also inquire into allegations of extortion, land/house grabbing or any incident involving serious abuse of authority. The recommendations of the Complaints Authority, both at the district and State levels, for any action, departmental or criminal, against a delinquent police officer shall be binding on the concerned authority.'

Besides, the Apex Court gave the following other directions:

4. **Appointment and Tenure of Director General of Police:** 'The Director General of Police of the State shall be selected by the state government from amongst the three senior-most officers of the Department who have been empanelled for promotion to that rank by the Union Public Service Commission on the basis of their length of service, very good record and range of experience for heading the police force. And, once he has been selected for the job, he should have a minimum tenure of at least two years irrespective of his date of superannuation. The DGP may, however, be relieved of his responsibilities by the state government acting in consultation with the State Security Commission consequent upon any action taken against him under the All India Services (Discipline and Appeal) Rules or following his conviction in a court of law in a criminal offence or in a case of corruption, or if he is otherwise incapacitated from discharging his duties.'

5. **Tenure of Officers on Operational Duties:** 'Police Officers on operational duties in the field like the Inspector General of Police in-charge Zone, Deputy Inspector General of Police in-charge Range, Superintendent of Police in-charge district and Station House Officer in-charge of

a Police Station shall also have a prescribed minimum tenure of two years unless it is found necessary to remove them prematurely following disciplinary proceedings against them or their conviction in a criminal offence or in a case of corruption or if the incumbent is otherwise incapacitated from discharging his responsibilities. This would be subject to promotion and retirement of the officer.'

6. **Separation of Investigation from Law and Order**: 'The investigating police shall be separated from the law and order police to ensure speedier investigation, better expertise and improved rapport with the people. It must, however, be ensured that there is full coordination between the two wings. The separation, to start with, may be effected in towns/urban areas which have a population of ten lakhs or more, and gradually extended to smaller towns/urban areas also.'

7. **National Security Commission**: 'The Central Government shall also set up a National Security Commission at the Union level to prepare a panel for being placed before the appropriate Appointing Authority, for selection and placement of Chiefs of the Central Police Organizations (CPO), who should also be given a minimum tenure of two years. The Commission would also review from time to time measures to upgrade the effectiveness of these forces, improve the service conditions of its personnel, ensure that there is proper coordination between them and that the forces are generally utilized for the purposes they were raised and make recommendations in that behalf. The National Security Commission could be headed by the Union Home Minister and comprise heads of the CPOs and a couple of security experts as members with the Union Home Secretary as its Secretary.'

The aforesaid orders were to be implemented by the end of

2006. The time limit was, at the next hearing, extended till 31 March 2007.

On 11 January 2007, the Supreme Court actually reviewed the affidavits of compliance. The defaulting states had engaged the top lawyers of the country like Arun Jaitley, Rajeev Dhavan, Gopal Subramanium, etc. The Chief Justice was not impressed by their arguments. He took the stand that the Court could not permit review of its judgment of 22 September 2006 because there was a proper procedure for seeking review on permissible grounds. The matter had been heard for several days and 'practically no state government /Union Territory objected to the suggestions contained in various reports'. Prashant Bhushan also punctured holes in their arguments.

The Supreme Court, after heated arguments for more than three hours, directed that the self-executing directions, that is those which did not involve any administrative arrangement or financial implications—those regarding selection and minimum tenure of the DGP, fixed tenure of officers in the field and setting up of Police Establishment Board—should be implemented without any delay, in any case within four weeks. The other directions—those regarding setting up of State Security Commission, Police Complaints Authority and separation of investigation work from law-and-order functions—should also be complied with by 31 March 2007. The Government of India was told that the National Security Commission constituted by it was not in accordance with the directions given by the Court. All the states/UTs and the Centre were asked to submit fresh affidavits of compliance by 10 April 2007.

SIGNIFICANCE OF JUDGMENT

It was a landmark judgment by the Supreme Court with a view to transforming what had so far been a ruler's police into a people's police, answerable to the Constitution of the country and the laws of the land and upholding the rule of law. The judgment was hailed by all the right-thinking people.

A.K. Doval, who later became the national security advisor, wrote as follows in a leading national daily:

> It is an irony that India, a vanguard of crusade against colonialism suffered colonial style of policing for six decades, the only change being that the white man was replaced by the brown. But the bigger irony was that in the world's biggest democracy, the change came, not through the legislature, but by judicial intervention. The temptations of the post-independence elite to use this potent instrument to subserve its power interests were too strong to allow any change. Lacking political sincerity and will, scores of political commissions and committees failed to prevent use, misuse and abuse of the police machinery for the advantage of a select few at the cost of those who needed their help and protection most.
>
> The judgment is also a tribute to a single man's determination and resoluteness, Prakash Singh, one of the most brilliant professionals that Indian police has ever produced, who held high positions not because of, but in spite of, politicians, single-handedly challenged the system and fought the battle for a decade with his meagre resources. He filed a Public Interest Litigation in March 1996 and pursued it against heavy odds to give a policing system to a billion people which they deserved and which their elected representatives would not care to give.[171]

---

[171]'Don't cop out,' *The Times of India*, 26 September 2006, https://timesofindia.indiatimes.com/edit-page/dont-cop-out/articleshow/2027012.cms, accessed on 25 November 2021.

The Times of India, in its editorial on 26 September 2006, commented as follows on the Supreme Court judgment:

> The Supreme Court's call for substantial reforms in the police force has not come a day too late. The deadline set by the apex court may appear ambitious, but the directive should push central and state governments to set in motion changes that had been suggested by the first National Police Commission in the 1970s and various committees subsequently. The Police Act of 1861 is in letter and spirit a legal instrument meant to facilitate and legitimise oppression by a colonial power. It needs drastic revision. That the Act has remained unchanged even decades after India became independent points to the limitations of Indian democracy. Legislators have refused to revamp the Act because it enables them to use the police as an oppressive instrument to control and contain legitimate forms of dissent. A pliant police force is a useful ally for corrupt lawmakers and politicians.

Minhaz Merchant beautifully summed up the significance of the judgment in the following words:

> Taken together, the seven directives of the Supreme Court provide the architecture of an independent, well-paid, accountable police force equipped to deal firmly and fairly with local law enforcement, intelligence gathering from communities, counter-terrorism operations and day-to-day policing. It will sever the umbilical cord that today binds the police with politicians and the underworld.[172]

---

[172]Minhaz Merchant, 'After Lokpal Bill, next reform is police autonomy,' *The Economic Times*, 29 August 2011.

Leading English dailies of the country lauded my role as that of a 'crusader'.[173] I could however, foresee that there would be fierce resistance to the implementation of judicial directions. In an article titled 'Police of the People' published in *The Indian Express* on 26 September 2006, while welcoming the landmark judgment which had 'demolished in one stroke the colonial police structure', I said that 'the transition is, however, not going to be smooth' and that the 'vested interests whose power to manipulate and abuse the police has been taken away, will try to scuttle such reform through every means possible'. My concluding observations in the article were:

> The present generation of police officers will have to rise to the occasion and fulfil the expectations of the people. They will have to demonstrate that the Force is now a service and that what was the ruler's police is now a people's police.

---

[173]'SC Verdict just beginning: Police reform crusader,' *The Indian Express,* 25 September 2006.

According to one commentator, 'what could not be achieved by several Commissions (the NPC, the State Police Commissions, the Ribeiro Committee, the Padmanabhaiah Committee and the Malimath Committee on Criminal Justice System) was single-handedly achieved by Prakash Singh.' (However, I consider this an exaggeration.)

5

STRUGGLE FOR IMPLEMENTATION OF COURT'S ORDER

It took 10 years for the Supreme Court to give its historic verdict on police reforms. It is difficult to say how many years the battle for the implementation of those directions will take. The struggle goes on.

It has already taken nearly 15 years and the end is not in sight. The most formidable opposition that one could think of in the country is against police reforms. The political class and the bureaucracy are both opposed, for the simple reason that it would disturb the status quo which enables them to have a stranglehold over the police and use and misuse it for all kinds of purposes. The political class particularly has developed a zamindari mindset and they look upon the police as an instrument to further their political agenda and, whenever necessary, harass and prosecute elements opposed to it. The bureaucracy has become addicted to lording over the police. It gives them a sense of power they cannot do without. It must also be admitted that several top cops are not keen on police reforms either. Having climbed up the ladder and struck certain equations with the political bosses, they would like to work in the same environment. We are thus against some kind of a Berlin Wall. The wall has to crumble one day, but for the time being, it has slowed down, if not stalled, the process of reforms.

Soon after the Supreme Court judgment, I sent a letter on 26 September 2006 to the Chief Secretaries of all the state governments and Union Territories, with copies to all the DGPs, apprising them of the Court's directions and enclosing with my letter a copy of the judgment. I said that 'it would be my privilege to extend you any professional help in setting up the new institutions (mandated by the Supreme Court) and ensuring a smooth change over.' Needless to say, there was no response from any state.

THE NATIONAL INVESTIGATION AGENCY

A brief mention may be made here of a significant achievement. The Court took note of our request to issue directions for:

> Dealing with the cases arising out of threats emanating from international terrorism or organized crimes like drug trafficking, money laundering, smuggling of weapons from across the borders, counterfeiting of currency or the activities of mafia groups with trans-national links to be treated as measures taken for the defence of India as mentioned in Entry I of the Union List in the Seventh Schedule of the Constitution of India and as internal security measures as contemplated under Article 355 as these threats and activities aim at destabilizing the country and subverting the economy and thereby weakening its defence.[174]

The Court conceded that the suggestion, on the face of it, seemed quite useful. However, it sought the views of the NHRC, Sorabjee Committee and the BPR&D on the subject. The Government of India was also asked to submit its views.

The NHRC responded as follows:

> The challenges posed by the multifaceted forms of growing terrorism and other connected activities, narcotics menace, human trafficking especially that of

---

[174]Vide Appendix C, para 15.

women and children, organized crimes, the phenomena of crimes syndicates and cybercrimes are indeed too grave to be ignored or steps not taken to provide adequate response. The state police forces who have been traditionally recording and investigating such offences are finding themselves increasingly handicapped to deal with such offences... There is thus an acute need to identify certain offences as federal crimes, the need arising from the stark reality of the national and international ramifications and implications of these crimes. It is also desirable that the task of their investigation should be entrusted to one central agency.[175]

The Soli Sorabjee Committee also expressed itself 'in favour of creation of a specialised agency to deal with crimes affecting national security or having international linkages and ramifications.'[176]

The BPR&D stated that 'we do have a pressing need to declare certain offences having inter-state and international ramifications as "federal offences" to be investigated by a designated Federal Agency having the required level of expertise.'[177]

In an affidavit filed on 10 November 2008, while drawing the attention of the Court to the views of the NHRC, the Sorabjee Committee and BPR&D, it was further stated that the Second Administrative Reforms Commission had also

---

[175]Affidavit on behalf of the National Human Rights Commission on the suggestions of Mr Prashant Bhushan regarding Federal Crime on 16 January 2007.

[176]Views of Sorabjee Committee regarding Investigation of cases of terrorism and organized crimes, 31 January 2007, para 26.

May also see 'Most Wanted: A Federal Investigative Agency,' *Sunday Hindustan Times*, 18 February 2007.

[177]*Federal Crimes: A Study by the Bureau of Police Research & Development*, para IV(1).

recommended that there is the need to re-examine certain offences which have inter-state or national ramification and include them in a new law, which should prescribe the procedure for investigation and trial of such offences.

While the matter was still under examination, the country witnessed the traumatic events of 26/11 in Mumbai. It was felt that a central agency was absolutely necessary to deal with terror-related cases. The National Investigation Agency Act was accordingly passed on 31 December 2008. The preamble to the Act defined its objective in the following words:

> An Act to constitute an investigation agency at the national level to investigate and prosecute offences affecting the sovereignty, security and integrity of India, security of State, friendly relations with foreign States and offences under Acts enacted to implement international treaties, agreements, conventions and resolutions of the United Nations, its agencies and other international organisations and for matters connected therewith or incidental thereto.

The National Investigation Agency (NIA) has since given a good account of itself. The seeds of the agency could be traced to the petition on police reforms, though its founding was no doubt precipitated by the terrorist attack on Mumbai.

THE CENTRE AND STATES DRAG THEIR FEET

The Supreme Court, on 9 April 2007, heard an application by the Union of India and the Union Territories, seeking modification in the Supreme Court order of 22 September 2006 and 11 January 2007. It was contended by them that a committee rather than a (National Security) Commission would serve the purpose, that the heads of the Central Police Organizations (CPOs) need not be its members, that a two-year tenure may not be given to the heads of the CPOs, that one single State Security Commission could cater to all the UTs, etc. Some other states' advocates also jumped into the fray, seeking more time, saying they wanted to file review applications. Prashant Bhushan firmly said that the states could not seek review in the garb of interim applications. He also said that the judgment had been given as far back as 22 September last year and questioned the propriety of states seeking review after more than six months. The CJI (K.G. Balakrishnan) said that if the states had not complied with the Court's directions, the petitioner could move for appropriate action. A softening in the Court's attitude to police reforms was discernible.

The Supreme Court, to our great relief, nevertheless dismissed the review petitions filed by the states of Andhra Pradesh, Gujarat, Karnataka, Maharashtra, Punjab, Tamil Nadu and UP on 23 August 2007.

The case was listed for 11 March 2008 but could not be taken up on that date because one of the judges was on leave and the matter had to be heard by a three-judge Bench. It was again listed for 12 March and was item no. 1. However, the day began with a part-heard Gujarat case which went on and on till the end of the day. It was a frustrating wait the whole day. The case was again listed on 13 March and fortunately taken up at about 1155 hrs. Prashant Bhushan presented the case at length. He drew attention of the Court to the fact that orders had been given as far back as 22 September 2006, reiterated on 11 January 2007 and that the extended date for compliance was 31 March 2007. About a year had passed and yet the level of compliance was far from satisfactory. Only 10 states had shown some compliance, while nine were very partially compliant. Eleven states had passed bills/acts essentially to circumvent the implementation of the Supreme Court's directions. The two defiant states were UP and Tamil

Nadu. It was argued that we had wanted six states to be issued contempt notices but would now want such notices to be issued only to UP and Tamil Nadu. The partially compliant states could be given another chance to implement the directions. It was felt that even if two states were hauled up by the Supreme Court, which would have a sobering effect on the other states which were dragging their feet. The CJI was however disinclined to issue any contempt notice and the judges wanted that the states be persuaded to implement the Court's directions.

CONTEMPT PETITIONS

Contempt petitions were filed against the states at different stages. In May 2007, the Court was apprised that the following states had not complied with its directions:

(a) Gujarat: The state government had taken the stand that the directions are in direct contravention of the constitutional scheme of allocation of powers as enshrined in the Constitution, which has specifically allocated 'public order' and 'police' to states, and that the directions, therefore, impinge on the federal character of the Constitution and undermine its basic structure.

(b) Jammu and Kashmir: The state had set up a committee comprising additional director general (ADG, CID), IGP (Modernization), Special Secretary (Home) and Director Prosecution to prepare a revised Police Act. Meanwhile, it had not taken any steps to implement the Court's directions and had vaguely asked for some more time.

(c) Maharashtra: The state government argued that the directions of the Hon'ble Court were 'inconsistent with statutory provisions in existence'. It had not complied with any of the directions except the direction regarding separation of investigative work from law-and-order work, which was already in place at the state level and at the level of Commissionerate and district police.

(d) Rajasthan: The state had asked for time to draft the Rajasthan Police Act. However, the 'Preliminary Observations' submitted by the state, which had actually been drafted by the Bar Council of Rajasthan, made a disturbing reading. They said that the structure of the Model Police Act drafted by the Soli Sorabjee Committee was 'faulty', that the Model Act suffered from 'bad draftsmanship', that the police force had to be kept under a 'tight leash' and so on. These were unacceptable observations. It appeared that the Rajasthan Police Act would follow neither the guidelines of the Supreme Court nor the model prescribed by the Sorabjee Committee.

(e) Tamil Nadu: The state took the stand that 'courts have no power to pass directions by way of judicial order to affect the legislative autonomy of the State', and stated that it was drafting a comprehensive legislation on the subject. The state was of the view that a statutory tenure for the DGP may lead to practical difficulties and prejudice the autonomy of the state. It also said that fixed tenure for field officers could not be rigidly enforced. Besides, the Police Complaints Authority would act as a parallel authority to the existing constitutional remedies.

(f) UP: The state had expressed its reservations on all the directions given by the Supreme Court. It said that the establishment of State Security Commission would be a direct infringement of the rights of the state government and a dilution of its authority. It also expressed its opposition to giving a minimum tenure of two years to the DGP and the field officers on the ground of 'practical and operational difficulties'. Setting up of a Police Establishment Board, it argued, would be 'against the established canons of the administrative system of the state'. Police Complaints Authorities, it was further said, would be 'superfluous', considering the number of institutions already in existence to look into complaints against the police.

The aforesaid six states, namely, Gujarat, Jammu and Kashmir, Maharashtra, Rajasthan, Tamil Nadu and UP, it was contended by us, had committed contempt of the Supreme Court's directions. It was, therefore, necessary that the Court should initiate contempt proceedings against these states.

In August 2007, in light of subsequent developments, we submitted to the Court that now there were only four states which had not complied with any of the directions of the Supreme Court and had adopted an attitude of defiance. These states were Gujarat, Maharashtra, Rajasthan and UP. Contempt proceedings were suggested against the above states only.

In December 2007, in the context of the level of compliance by that time, it was submitted to the Court that the following states came in the category of Notionally Compliant/Almost Non-Compliant States:

i) Maharashtra: The state had taken the stand that the directions of the Hon'ble Court were 'inconsistent with statutory provisions in existence'. It had not complied with any of the directions except the direction regarding separation of investigative work from law-and-order work.

ii) Tamil Nadu: The state had argued that 'courts have no power to pass directions by way of judicial order to affect the legislative autonomy of the State.' It further said that a statutory tenure for the DGP may lead to practical difficulties and that fixed tenure for field officers could not be rigidly enforced. Police Complaints Authority, according to the state, would act as a parallel authority to the existing constitutional remedies.

iii) Uttar Pradesh: The state pleaded that it had already a Civil Services Board comprising Principal Secretary (Home), Principal Secretary to Chief Minister and the DGP. The body was, however, completely dominated by the government. The state had also not taken any steps to comply with the directions regarding the selection and minimum tenure of the DGP and the tenure of officers posted in the field. It was brought to the notice of the Court that 526 IPS officers had been transferred in the state during the period 1 January to 31 August 2007. The Police Establishment Board had not been constituted, nor had the Complaints Authority been set up. The state had set up a Police Reforms Commission to make recommendations in light of the Supreme Court's directions and draft a bill which could be passed by the legislature. The exercise had been undertaken with the sole object of gaining time.

The Court was urged to initiate contempt proceedings against the aforesaid states which had, even after the passage of one year and two months, very partially complied with its directions.

Meanwhile, the Supreme Court had, on 17 May 2008, constituted a Monitoring Committee headed by Justice K.T. Thomas to look into the implementation of its directions by the central and state governments and the Union Territories. In light of findings of the Thomas Committee, another contempt petition was filed in September 2010 against the states of Bihar, Maharashtra, Tamil Nadu and UP.

The position in these states at the time was as follows:

Bihar: It provided for a Rajya Police Board (State Security Commission) comprising the Chief Secretary, Home Secretary and the DGP. The Board was thus completely government dominated and did not have any independent members. The DGP would be selected by the state government (there was no reference to any panel to be prepared by the UPSC) and his tenure would generally be two years; he may however be removed, among other reasons, on administrative grounds, which gave a long handle to the state government. There was no provision for the creation of a Police Establishment Board nor was there any mention of separating investigation work from law-and-order work. The Accountability Authority had been set up at the district level only and here also it was headed by the district magistrate, the other members being the additional district magistrate and the superintendent of police. The arrangement made a mockery of the Complaints Authority stipulated by the Hon'ble Court. Some provisions of the Bill, Section 30 for example, strengthened bureaucratic control over the police which was not visualized even in the Act of 1861. The Bihar Police Bill was thus a highly regressive piece of legislation. Significantly the Bihar Police Association, which represented the non-gazetted officers of the state, also moved a contempt petition against the state government for having passed the Bihar Police Bill, 2007, whose provisions were in complete violation of the directions given by the Hon'ble Supreme Court of India.

Maharashtra: The state had taken the stand that the directions of the Hon'ble Court were 'inconsistent with statutory provisions in existence'. It had set up a State Security Commission but given it advisory powers only. The state was not agreeable to giving fixed tenure to the DGP and argued that flexibility was needed in the transfer of police officers. The composition of the Complaints Authority had been diluted, apart from the fact that it had no binding powers.

Tamil Nadu: The state argued that 'Courts have no power to pass directions by way of judicial order to affect the legislative autonomy of the State.' It took the stand that a statutory tenure for the DGP may lead to practical difficulties and that fixed tenure for field officers could not be rigidly enforced. Police Complaints Authority, according to the state, would act as a parallel authority to the existing constitutional remedies.

UP: The state pleaded that it had already a Civil Services Board comprising Principal Secretary (Home), Principal Secretary to Chief Minister and the DGP. The body was, however, completely dominated by the government. The state had not taken any steps to comply with the directions regarding the selection and minimum tenure of the DGP and the tenure of officers posted in the field. The mandate of the Police Establishment Board had been diluted, and the state had refused to set up any Complaints Authority.

The Court was requested to initiate contempt proceedings against the states which had, even after the passage of nearly four years, not complied with or very partially complied with the directions of the Court dated 22 September 2006 and 11 January 2007. The Court, however, took no action on our contempt petitions.

JUSTICE THOMAS COMMITTEE (2008–10)

At this stage, we suggested that a Monitoring Committee presided over by a retired CJI be appointed to assist the Supreme Court in the matter. The suggestion was made because we felt that our assessment on compliance—in fact, the lack of it—by the states was not being taken seriously by the Court. The assessment of a committee headed by a retired Justice would have greater credibility.

The Court was told that we had already taken the liberty of sounding a retired CJI (Justice R.C. Lahoti) and that he had given his consent to undertake the responsibility, if so desired by the Apex Court. The Bench was impressed by the suggestion. They were almost going to issue an order on those lines. At this stage, the advocate representing the Government of India came up with serious reservations on certain aspects, like fixed tenure being given to DGPs, etc. He was pulled up by Justice Raveendran, who said: 'You have no such problem in giving fixed tenures to Secretaries.' The advocate however insisted that the Solicitor General, who was not present in the Court, may be heard before the Supreme Court issued any fresh directions.

The PIL came up before the Supreme Court on 16 May 2008. The issue was constitution of a Monitoring Committee. The government wanted the Committee to be under the MHA. This was opposed by us. The Court upheld our view and ordered the Committee to be set up under Justice K.T. Thomas. CJI K.G. Balakrishnan had his own reasons for selecting Justice Thomas based in Kerala rather than Justice Lahoti based in the NCR region, suggested by us. Justice Thomas was to be assisted by two members, one to be nominated by the MHA and the other to be chosen by the Justice himself.

The terms of reference of the Committee were as follows:

(i)   To examine the affidavits filed by the different states and Union Territories in compliance to the Court's directions with reference to the ground realities.

(ii)   Advise the respondents wherever the implementation is falling short of the Court's orders, after considering the respondents' stated difficulties in implementation.

(iii)   Bring to the notice of the Court any genuine problems the respondents may be having in view of the specific conditions prevailing in a state or Union Territory.

(iv) Examine the new legislations enacted by different states regarding the police to see whether these are in compliance with the letter and spirit of this Court's directions.

(v) Apprise the Court about unnecessary objections or delays on the part of any respondent so that appropriate follow-up action could be taken against that respondent.

(vi) Submit a status report in compliance to this Court every six months.

Dharmendra Sharma (IAS), Joint Secretary (MHA) and Kamal Kumar IPS (Retd), former Director of the National Police Academy, were chosen to assist the Committee. The matter came up before the Supreme Court on 18 December 2008. Prashant Bhushan argued that the progress of Monitoring Committee was very slow and insisted that the Court issue contempt notices against the states which were particularly defiant. The CJI took the stand that in the context of appointment of a Monitoring Committee, it would be proper to await its recommendations. The Court nevertheless agreed to direct the Monitoring Committee to expedite its work. The exchanges between Prashant Bhushan and the Chief Justice (K.G. Balakrishnan) were quite heated. Bhushan pressed his point quite forcefully. The CJI was however unmoved.

The case was thereafter listed before the Supreme Court on 28 April 2009. However, it could not be taken up that day. The whole day was wasted. It was listed the next day also, but again the CJI was preoccupied with the Constitution Bench. The matter was thereafter taken up on 30 April. It turned out to be a damp squib. I mentioned (in the absence of Prashant Bhushan, who was held up in another Court) that the Justice Thomas Committee had submitted an interim report and another report dated 15 April. Copies of these reports had however not been made available to us. I requested the Hon'ble Court that copies of reports furnished by the Justice Thomas Committee be furnished to the petitioner. The CJI agreed. However, what surprised me was that the impugned reports of the Thomas Committee were not in the files before the Bench also. The CJI ordered that the reports be obtained. The case was deferred to be taken up after the vacations in the month of July 2009.

Meanwhile, the Thomas Committee continued to function in slow motion. There was no sense of urgency. They had, by that time, held seven sittings including two in Kochi. Fourteen states were supposed to have been discussed, but only seven could be analysed in depth. Kamal Kumar, the retired IPS officer, was doing his best but his efforts were thwarted by Dharmendra Sharma IAS, the other member of the Committee. Actually, more often than not, the deliberations degenerated into some kind of a slugfest with Kamal Kumar and Dharmendra Sharma taking diametrically opposite stands. Justice Thomas, instead of throwing his weight on the side of reason and logic, always tried to balance the opposite points of view. In the process, no concrete decisions were taken. More than once, I said that all the correspondence that the Committee was entering into would not lead us anywhere. The Committee should recommend to the Supreme Court to make an example of at least one or two states which were defiantly non-compliant. Justice Thomas was however averse to taking any hard decision. And so, the charade continued.

The matter was next taken up by the Court on 21 July 2009 to discuss the report submitted by the Thomas Committee. Prashant Bhushan argued that 14 months had passed, but the Committee had not made any specific recommendation in respect of any state. He insisted that the Committee be asked to submit its recommendations on a priority basis in respect of the states which were recommended for issuance of contempt notices. He emphasized that 26/11 in Mumbai had underscored the urgency of police reforms. Police all over the country were completely demoralized under the existing arrangement. Soli Sorabjee, former attorney general, also appeared on our behalf. He contended that this state of affairs could not be countenanced. The states had been given a time frame. Their review petitions had been dismissed. There was no excuse or justification for not complying with the Supreme Court's directions. He urged the Supreme Court to take a strict view. The Chief Justice said that the states were not cooperating with the Monitoring Committee. It was disappointing to see the CJI (K.G. Balakrishnan) pleading helplessness. Prashant Bhushan suggested that the Monitoring Committee should be asked to give specific recommendations about some states within the next one month. He was supported by Soli Sorabjee.

The Monitoring Committee met in Delhi on 20 and 21 April 2010. They invited me and the CHRI also to attend the deliberations on 21 April. The CHRI representative suggested that the Monitoring Committee should continue its work even after the expiry of two-year period. Justice Thomas wanted my views on states which had passed laws contrary to the letter and spirit of the Court's directions. I took the stand that these could be struck down under Article 21 of the Constitution.

On 23 April 2010, the PIL came up before the Supreme Court. Prashant Bhushan was out of station. So, I presented the case. I argued that on the basis of the fourth report of the Monitoring Committee, the Supreme Court should consider taking action against six states (UP, Tamil Nadu, Madhya Pradesh, Jammu and Kashmir, Orissa and West Bengal) which had neither complied nor responded to communications from the Monitoring Committee. The CJI wanted to know as to when would the final report of the Monitoring Committee be available. The amicus said that the same might take another month or so whereupon the CJI said that the PIL may be listed after the vacation in July.

The Thomas Committee submitted its report to the Supreme Court in August 2010. The Committee recorded its findings in the following words:

> Insofar as the implementation of the six specific Directives of the Supreme Court is concerned, the Committee has no hesitation in concluding that practically no State has fully complied with those Directives so far, in letter and spirit, despite the lapse of almost four years since the date of the original judgment. In the States, where new police legislations have not been enacted, the directions are purported to have been complied with by issuing executive orders but the contents of such executive orders clearly reflect dilution, in varying degrees, of the spirit, if not the letter, of the Court directives.[178]

About states which had enacted legislation, the Committee observed that the Acts passed by them reflects the same story. The Committee expressed its dismay over the total indifference to the issue of reforms in the functioning of Police being exhibited by the states.

The Committee verified the ground realities in four states only: UP, Maharashtra, Karnataka and West Bengal. One state was chosen from each geographical zone. Here also, the Committee found that the level of compliance of the Supreme Court directives in these states range from total non-compliance to partial/marginal compliance to mere paper implementation.

The Thomas Committee Report was a disappointing document. The Committee could have verified the ground realities in all the states of the country and made specific

---

[178]Vide Appendix E.

recommendations on action to be taken by the Apex Court. The Committee was however content to say that the Supreme Court may, to start with, 'initiate action as deemed appropriate' against the four states and, as for the remaining states, it left the matter to the Supreme Court 'to decide on the course and modalities of such verification, to assess the exact level of compliance of the directives by them, before deciding on the action to be taken in respect of them.'[179]

It was obvious that the Committee had not done its best. The main reason for that was that the two members—Dharmendra Sharma, IAS and Kamal Kumar, IPS (Retd)—generally disagreed on all the vital points. I was told that the bureaucracy had deliberately planted Dharmendra Sharma in the Committee to ensure that it did not disturb the status quo in any significant manner. Sharma, I could see, was a brilliant officer, but unfortunately he used the sharpness of his intellect to scuttle the progress of police reforms. Having seen him from close quarters, I distressingly felt that we have a class of officers for whom the primacy of their service is more important than what is good for the country or its people. Justice K.T. Thomas was an honest judge, but more than once I got the feeling that he was under some compulsion to play it cool. The report could be given a presentable shape in the last few months only, thanks to the hard work put in by Kamal Kumar.

JUSTICE KAPADIA: STARTS WITH A BANG

The PIL was listed for hearing on 27 September 2010. The amicus (Raju Ramachandran) stated that the Monitoring Committee would be submitting its final report to the Court by the end of the month. Prashant Bhushan, advocate, utilized the occasion to brief Justice Kapadia about the slow progress

---

[179]Ibid.

in the implementation of police reforms. He stated that it was now four years since the Supreme Court had delivered its historic judgment, but the states had not cared to implement its directions. The Monitoring Committee had also taken more than two years to submit a report which should not have taken more than three or four months. Bhushan also mentioned that the Court had been urged twice in 2007 to issue contempt notices to the defaulting states and the request was reiterated at subsequent hearings.

Justice S.H. Kapadia, showing a sense of urgency, promised that the matter would soon be heard at length by his Bench or a special Bench. He also ordered the PIL to be listed again for directions on Monday next.

The PIL was taken up by Chief Justice Kapadia on 4 October 2010. The other judges on the Bench were Justice Aftab Alam and Justice K.S. Radhakrishnan. It was mentioned that the Thomas Committee had submitted its report to the Supreme Court in a sealed cover. Prashant Bhushan thereupon requested that copy of the report be made available to the petitioners and the other parties. This was acceded to by the CJI. The Court Registry was directed to furnish copies of the report to the petitioner, Union of India and the states/Union Territories. The parties were asked to give their response to the Court at the earliest. The Court desired that the petitioner, amicus curiae and learned Solicitor General should work in tandem and give them a chart on the basis of which orders could be passed from time to time. The general impression was that the CJI was quite serious and that he would give the required push to police reforms.

On 8 November 2010, the PIL was heard by the Chief Justice of India. The amicus presented a brief history of the entire case, concluding with the Thomas Committee Report and drawing attention of the Court to its finding that there was 'total indifference to the issue of reforms in the functioning of police exhibited by the states'.[180] He also pointed out that the Thomas Committee had suggested 'action as deemed appropriate' against the states of UP, West Bengal, Maharashtra and Karnataka, and recommended that notices be issued to these states. This was endorsed by the Solicitor General (Gopal Subramanium). Justice Alam, who was on the Bench, expressed his happiness that the Government of India was supportive of police reforms. The Court, after some discussions, finally agreed to issue notices to the states of UP, West Bengal, Maharashtra and Karnataka 'to start with' to explain their non-compliance. The Chief Secretaries of these states were asked to personally appear before the Supreme Court on the next date of hearing, which was on 6 December 2010.

The best part of the day's proceedings was that the amicus, Solicitor General and Prashant Bhushan all talked on the same wavelength. This could be possible because during the preceding one week I had separate sessions with each one of them. I was able to convince them on a 'common minimum programme'. Under the circumstances, the Supreme Court had no difficulty in agreeing to the suggestion to hold at least some states, one each from north, south, east and west, accountable.

On 6 December 2010, the PIL was again taken up by the CJI. Compliance in the four states of Karnataka, Maharashtra, West Bengal and UP was reviewed. At the very outset, the CJI made it clear that the Court was going to ensure implementation of its orders, that 'the orders would not remain in a limbo' and that this message should go to all the states. West Bengal was taken up first. The Court took exception to the fact that the constituted State Security Commission (SSC) did not follow any of the three models prescribed by the Court, and also expressed surprise that the SSC was headed by the health minister and not by the chief/home minister. Karnataka was pulled up for

---

[180]Ibid.

giving fixed tenure to the DGP 'subject to superannuation'. The CJI was emphatic that it will have to be a full two years. The state was also cornered for not giving fixed tenure to SP I/C district/DIG Range/IG Zone. Maharashtra was asked to explain the absence of a serving/retired judge in the SSC. The advocate for the petitioner made adverse observations about the non-official members chosen to be members of the SSC. UP had filed an affidavit on 6 December only, and therefore its compliance could not be examined in detail. I nevertheless mentioned that the state was one of the worst defaulters.

Several states had expressed objection/difficulty in getting a panel prepared by UPSC for the selection of DGP. UPSC had expressed its own reservations about the arrangement. The matter was referred to the Solicitor General to get the final views of the UPSC/government in the matter.

For the first time, after the judgment on 22 September 2006, the Supreme Court had taken up the implementation of its directions in a serious, business-like manner. States were asked to respond on the various points and asked to explain their non-compliance.

The matter was listed next on 10 January 2011. Compliance in the state of UP was taken up. The Court expressed satisfaction with the setting up of SSC by the state government. Regarding the credentials of the independent members, the Court said it would examine that at a later stage. It then moved on to the selection and tenure of the DGP. The Solicitor General representing the Government of India tried to give the matter a twist. He argued that the UPSC should be kept out of the selection process and that the two-year tenure should be subject to superannuation. The CJI snubbed him by saying, 'Do you want the judgment to be reopened?' The amicus added that the review petition by the state had already been dismissed. The Solicitor General said that the propriety of UPSC involvement was perhaps not considered at that stage. The CJI wanted to know if this aspect was raised and considered when the review petition was taken up. There was no satisfactory response to the query. The CJI said that the matter should be looked into, and posted the case to next Monday (17 January).

On 17 January 2011, the amicus put up an analysis of all the review petitions and proved to the satisfaction of the Court that the points being raised now had been raised earlier by some states and rejected by the Court. He argued that these matters had acquired finality and there could be no question of going back. Amendment in Fundamental Rule 56 was brought to the notice of the Court, though Prashant Bhushan clarified that the amendment only talked of extension in service on 'case-to-case basis' subject to the condition that 'the total term of the incumbents of the above posts (Cabinet Secretary, Defence Secretary, Home Secretary, DIB, Secretary RAW, and Director CBI) who are given such extension in service does not exceed two years'.

Harish Salve thereafter spoke for almost an hour on reforms needed in the criminal justice system. The points highlighted by him were (a) separation of investigation wing from the law-and-order wing, (b) creation of a Directorate General of Public Prosecution to ensure fair and independent prosecution of criminal cases, and (c) training of investigating police and prosecutors in forensic skills and nuances of criminal law.

The most encouraging part of the day's proceedings was the keenness of the CJI to give a constitutional basis to the mandated reforms under Article 21 of the Constitution.

On 11 April 2011, the Solicitor General sought time to take instructions from the government on the question of functional segregation of the investigative wing from the law-and-order wing of the police. Similarly, with regard to the selection and minimum tenure of the DGP, IGP and other officers also, the Solicitor General sought one week's time to take instructions.

On 12 December 2011, when the matter was next taken up, the Supreme Court wondered whether in view of the 'legislative activity' which was taking place, it would be proper for the Court to issue any further directions. The Lokpal Bill was under consideration of Government of India. Prashant Bhushan clarified that the Lokpal Bill did not impinge on the Supreme Court's directions on police reforms. Bhushan was one of the leading members of the Anna Hazare Team campaigning for the Lokpal Bill and whatever he said on the subject had the imprint of authority. The Hon'ble Judges were however not convinced. They asked the Additional Solicitor General for his views; he was evasive and said that he would need to check on this point. The Supreme Court thereupon asked the amicus and the Additional Solicitor General to examine this aspect in depth and come before the Court with their views/recommendations at the next hearing on 9 January 2012. I was disappointed with the attitude of the Hon'ble Judges. It appeared that they had developed cold feet and were now looking for alibis to shelve the case. The PIL was never listed during the next nine months and Justice Kapadia retired on 28 September 2012. A tenure which had started with a bang ended, unfortunately, with a whimper as far as police reforms matter was concerned. Justice Kapadia, while hearing another case, had reportedly remarked that it had become difficult to proceed with the police reforms matter in view of the resistance of the states. He was aware of this resistance when he took up the case. What led him to jettison the petition halfway remained a mystery to me.

JUSTICE ALTAMAS KABIR: STALEMATE

The PIL was next listed before the Supreme Court on 16 October 2012. The Bench comprised Chief Justice Altamas Kabir, Justice Surinder Singh Nijjar and Justice

J. Chelameswar. It was a completely new Bench. None of the judges had dealt with the PIL earlier. Our first anxiety therefore was to educate them about the case. I had prior discussions with the amicus, Raju Ramachandran, and Prashant Bhushan to work out a strategy. Accordingly, the amicus gave a brief background of the entire case and concluded with the findings of the Thomas Committee. We had gone with three prayers: (i) the state governments of West Bengal, Maharashtra, Karnataka and UP be asked to file fresh affidavits to show the follow-up action taken by them subsequent to the assurances given by their Chief Secretaries; (ii) the Chief Justices of the High Courts of states which had not passed any legislation be asked to constitute a Committee headed by a retired judge to monitor the implementation of the Court's directions in the respective states and submit a report to the Apex Court; and (iii) the Supreme Court to examine the constitutional validity of the Acts passed by the (12) state governments.

The CJI however wanted to go step by step. He gave directions to all the state governments/UTs to file fresh affidavits, showing the latest position in compliance to the Court's directions. I wanted to interject and insist on the Court taking the process forward beyond the Thomas Committee Report. The amicus and Prashant Bhushan however both restrained me. Looking at the brighter side, the matter had been revived and the states would be compelled to do fresh stock taking. There was in a way need for that also because the Thomas Committee Report had been submitted two years back and maybe there had been changes since then in some of the states.

The actual context was an IA filed by the State of Tamil Nadu, seeking the intervention of the Court to direct the UPSC to prepare a fresh panel for selection to the post of DGP. The IA was allowed. We took advantage of the occasion to resurrect the PIL. However, the case was not taken up by the Bench again. In retrospect, the petition was taken up incidentally. Justice Kabir had no interest in police reforms.

JUSTICE SINGHVI: A CRUSADE

Meanwhile, something strange happened which gave fresh impetus and momentum to the police reforms case. There were reports in the media of alleged police brutalities in Tarn Taran district of Punjab and Patna in Bihar. The Bench headed by Justice G.S. Singhvi and including Justice Kurian Joseph took *suo moto* cognizance of these reports on 11 March 2013. The Court expressed concern over 'the gross violation of human rights as well as the constitutional rights of the people', and issued notices to Directors General of Punjab and Bihar to file affidavits indicating the action taken against the delinquent policemen. Notices were also sent to all the state governments through their Chief Secretaries, Home Secretaries and Directors General of Police and to the Union Territories through their Administrators and Police Commissioners to file affidavits on the issue of 'implementation of the directions contained in the judgment of this Court in *Prakash Singh and Ors. Vs. Union of India and Ors.*'

It amounted to almost hijacking the police reforms case, which was actually pending before the Chief Justice. I was worried that the Attorney General may object to it on technical grounds. He might say that the Bench should limit itself to the merits of the Tarn Taran and Patna incidents and not go into the implementation of the Supreme Court judgment of 2006 on police reforms, which were pending before Court No. 1. I talked to the Attorney General (Goolam Vahanvati). He was half inclined to raise the point but was diffident. In my presence, he talked to the Solicitor General (Mohan Parasaran) on the subject. I pleaded with them not to raise any objection and let the matter take its natural course. They very graciously accepted my suggestion and did not throw a spanner in the proceedings.

The Supreme Court's order also contained a direction to the following effect: 'Notice be issued to Shri Prakash Singh, former Director General of Uttar Pradesh to remain present on the next date of hearing and assist the Court.'

I was given the status of Amicus Curiae in the case. Perhaps this was the first instance of a police officer being appointed amicus in a case. (I did not know Justice Singhvi and had never met him before.)

On 1 April 2013, I filed my submissions before the Court, giving a synopsis of the Court's directions and the tardy compliance by the state governments. Reference was made by me to the findings of the Justice Thomas Committee and also the recommendations of Justice Verma Committee. Recommendations—short term and long term—were made. On 4 April, another submission was filed, giving an overall picture of compliance by the state governments and the Government of India.

On 11 April, I was given time to make my presentation. I explained the significance of the six directions to the state governments. Justice Singhvi said that monitoring the implementation was going to be a complicated affair and that they shall take up each of the six directions one by one. He announced that at the next hearing, the Court shall take up Direction No.1 relating to SSC. The states were asked to file their fresh affidavits on what they had done to constitute the Commission and to indicate whether these were functioning and meetings were being held.

On 25 April, the reconstituted Bench of the Court took up the compliance of Direction No.1. Harish Salve explained that the states had done half-hearted compliance in the sense that the Commissions did not conform to any of the prescribed models and their powers had been diluted. I brought to the notice of the Court that the SSC had not been constituted in the states of Andhra Pradesh, Odisha and Jammu and Kashmir. Twenty-five states had constituted these Commissions but 23 of these had recommendatory powers only whereas the Supreme Court had clearly laid down that its recommendations shall be binding on the state governments. Karnataka was the only state which had accepted that the recommendations of the SSC shall be binding; Kerala had made the recommendations binding on the state police but not on the government. It was also brought to the notice of the Court that the SSCs were meeting very infrequently and even at these meetings, they were discussing routine and not policy matters.

The Court expressed its unhappiness and made it clear that there will have to be full compliance of the Supreme Court's directions and the states will not have the discretion to mix features of different models as some of them had done. The Court said that it will specifically examine compliance in the six states of Andhra Pradesh, Goa, Haryana, Maharashtra, Rajasthan and UP at the next hearing.

May 6, 2013 was a landmark day in the efforts to get police reforms implemented in the country. The proceedings started on a sedate note. State Security Commissions, as set up in the states of Andhra Pradesh, Goa, Haryana, Maharashtra, Rajasthan and UP were reviewed one by one. Andhra was pulled up for setting up SSC on 4 May 2013 only and even that did not conform to the Supreme Court's guidelines. Goa was reprimanded for filing its affidavit on 3 May only. Haryana was chided for setting up an SSC which would only 'aid and advise'. Maharashtra cut a sorry figure insofar its SSC had not met even once during the last one year. Rajasthan was ridiculed for not having set up the SSC even though an Act had been passed. UP was hauled up as the SSC constituted by it had never met.

The Bench was quite exasperated. They asked Attorney General (Vahanvati), Harish Salve and me to give specific suggestions to the Court after the vacation so that effective implementation of its directions could be ensured.

MAHARASHTRA DGP MATTER

Meanwhile, something strange was happening in the state of Maharashtra. According to Julio Ribeiro, the home minister was virtually the de facto police chief of the state.[181] As he wrote:

> Maharashtra Home Minister R.R. Patil now runs the Maharashtra police force with the help of his four personal assistants. Police officers of all ranks approach him for postings and transfers knowing that it is the minister who decides where personnel is transferred. The director general of police has no say on such crucial instruments of discipline. By administrative fiat, Patil has appropriated all powers, including the power to promote or punish. The DGP has been reduced to a non-entity and figurehead...[182]

I talked to Julio Ribeiro on the subject and, on the basis of what he told me and the material he furnished, I prepared a petition and submitted that to the Court through Harish Salve.

On 6 May 2013 there were interesting exchanges in the Supreme Court. On the erosion of authority of DGP Maharashtra, I said that even the most imperious Governor General of British India, Lord Curzon, never thought of usurping police powers in the manner the Home Minister of Maharashtra had done. Such a thing had never happened before in the history of Indian Police. On Police Acts passed by different states, I said that the Bihar Police Act was particularly

---

[181]'Why does RR Patil meddle so much in police affairs?' *DNA Analysis*, Mumbai, 8 August 2012.
[182]'A police force of his own,' *The Indian Express*, 4 May 2013.

atrocious. The Act takes you back not to British India, but to the East India Company days.

On non-compliance by the majority of states, I said that two factors had contributed to that. One was that the Government of India itself had not shown commitment to police reforms. Soli Sorabjee had drafted a Model Police Act, but the same had not been legislated so far. Secondly, the Supreme Court itself had not wielded the whip against the defiant states.

At one stage, Justice Singhvi appeared despondent. He was thoroughly disgusted with the farcical compliance by the state governments. He said:

> Let us ask all the state governments if they are serious at all about police reforms. If all of them say 'No', we might as well say the game is over. After all, what is the point in giving directions if they are not complied with. See what happened to Justice Verma's directions in Vineet Narain case. There is no point in imposing fines or giving contempt notices.

There was complete silence in the Court. It appeared as if Justice Singhvi may also give up. I could not restrain myself. I got up and said, 'If you would permit me, I want to say something.' Justice Singhvi nodded his head in approval whereupon I said:

> My Lord, the future of this country is linked with police reforms. If we do not reform the police, rejuvenate it, restructure it, there will be no democracy in the country. You can also forget about economic progress. Besides, there would be lawlessness and anarchy in large areas of the country. We cannot allow that to happen. The highest Court of the land cannot give up. The people of the country look up to the Supreme Court, and I am saying this as a citizen of this country. The political

executive has established some kind of a zamindari over the police. This zamindari has to be abolished. The battle has to go on.

The Bench listened to me without showing any sign of disapproval.

STATE ACTS CHALLENGED

I had a session with Harish Salve at his residence on 30 April 2013. One of the decisions taken during the discussions was to challenge the constitutionality of the Acts passed by the 15 state governments. I had already prepared an analysis of all the Acts, showing their deviations from the Court's directions. Salve asked his juniors (four of them were sitting at the meeting) to prepare a petition under Article 32 of the Constitution and send the draft to me for whatever changes I may like to make. This exercise was completed by 2 May and the amended draft was sent to Salve, who finalized the petition on 6 May. This petition was given to the Court directly. It was a long jump forward.

On 9 May 2013, Harish Salve's writ against the Police Acts passed by the state governments was admitted by the Supreme Court. Fifteen states had (by that time) passed Police Acts. These were: Assam, Bihar, Chhattisgarh, Gujarat, Haryana, Himachal Pradesh, Kerala, Meghalaya, Mizoram, Punjab, Rajasthan, Sikkim, Tripura, Uttarakhand and Karnataka.

It was contended that the directions of 22 September 2006 flowed directly from interpretation of the Constitutional guarantees under Part III generally and Articles 14 and 21 of the Constitution, and the underlying principle of Rule of law. These directions therefore constituted the bare minimum action to be taken by the executive as a constitutional imperative to ensure that the functioning of the police was consistent with the Constitution. Conversely, any executive or legislative action that deviated in its substantive content from the constitutional mandate as specified in the said decision was *ex hypothesi* null, void, illegal and *ultra vires* the Constitution of India for failure to comply with the requirements of Part III and was therefore liable to be set aside.

The following prayers were made:

(a) Issue an appropriate Writ, direction or declaration, declaring that the directions contained in the decision of this Hon'ble Court in *Prakash Singh v. Union of India (2006) 8 SCC 1* set out the basic minimum requirements consistent with Art. 14 and Art. 21 and any law or executive action that seeks to dilute these directions would be violative of Part III and of the basic structure of the Constitution of India.

(b) Issue an appropriate Writ, direction or declaration, declaring that the Police Acts legislated by the 15 states aforesaid are violative of Art. 14 and 21 and *ultra vires* the Constitution.

(c) That the 15 states being Respondent 2 to Respondent 16 be directed to issue executive orders in conformity with this Court's directions of 22 September 2006 within the next one month and submit fresh affidavits of compliance by the end of June 2013.

(d) Grant any other or further relief that the Hon'ble Court may deem fit in the circumstances of the case.

Notices were issued to respective state governments, and it was said that the matter would be taken up after the vacations in the second week of July.

The police reforms case came up before Justice Singhvi's Bench on 16 July 2013. The Bench expressed annoyance over several states not filing affidavits and some states not marking them to the Attorney General or the Amicus. Justice Singhvi said that he was left with no option but to summon the Chief Secretaries to explain the status of compliance in their respective states.

To start with, on my suggestion, the Bench decided to summon the Chief Secretaries of Andhra Pradesh, Karnataka, Maharashtra and UP. Justice Singhvi further directed me to submit by 27 July a chart showing the exact status of compliance in different states.

On 31 July 2013, Chief Secretaries of Andhra Pradesh, Maharashtra, Tamil Nadu and UP appeared before the Court. They were given a dressing down by Justice Singhvi, not so much for non-compliance as for not filing affidavits on time in response to the Court's directions. All of them had to apologize. It was interesting to see the paper tigers grovelling before the Apex Court. The Court thereafter examined compliance in the four states. The Attorney General's office had prepared a chart with my help showing the latest position of compliance. Entries against every state were under two heads: (1) Factual position of compliance and (2) Prakash Singh's comments. The Attorney General took up the states one by one and explained the position. That the Attorney General and I were on the same page was significant. The Court kept on making critical observations in between.

The battery of advocates representing different states were perturbed at Justice Singhvi's crusade for police reforms. They knew that unless they came with a clever strategy, it would be difficult to stop Justice Singhvi. Shekhar Naphade, senior counsel appearing for Maharashtra, led the charge. He argued that there was difficulty in implementing some directions of the Apex Court because those were in conflict with the existing laws. Thus, giving a two-year tenure to the DGP irrespective of superannuation, it was said, would require amendment in All India Services Rules. Another advocate said that the Court's directions had not taken State Police Rules into account. I controverted their arguments, but could see that the lawyers had thrown a spanner.

Copies of Attorney General's note with my comments thereon were given to the advocates of all the four states. Justice Singhvi added that the states and Union Territories should point out in writing the difficulty, if any, faced by them in implementing any particular direction of the Court. It was however made clear that 'any so-called conflict between the directions given by this Court and the rules framed under proviso to Article 309 of the Constitution or any other legislation shall not be considered as a ground for non-compliance of the directions contained in the judgment.'

STATES FRUSTRATE REFORMS

The states of Maharashtra, Andhra Pradesh, UP and Madhya Pradesh, among others, filed affidavits mentioning the difficulties faced by them in implementing the Supreme Court's judgment. The Attorney General prepared a rebuttal of all the objections raised by them. Unfortunately, however, the matter could never be taken up. The specious pleas of the states and the Attorney General's response thereto are nevertheless summarized below.

It was argued by the state of Maharashtra that under Article 154 of the Constitution, the executive power of the State is vested with the Hon'ble Governor and, under Article 163, the Governor acts on the aid and advice of the Council of Ministers. All the directives contained in *Prakash Singh's case* related to the executive powers and functions of the state government and they could only be exercised by the Governor on the aid and advice of the Council of Ministers. This, it was argued, was the basic constitutional scheme and, therefore, recommendations of any authority could never be binding on the state government. If such recommendations were made binding, the same would be inconsistent with and contrary to the procedure laid down by the Constitution. The state government was nevertheless, the affidavit added, attempting to 'harmonise the basic constitutional scheme and the directives contained in *Prakash Singh's case*.' The Attorney General's response to it was as follows:

> Article 141 of the Constitution provides that the law declared by the Supreme Court shall be binding on all courts; Article 142 enables the Supreme Court, in the exercise of its jurisdiction, to pass such decree or make such order as is necessary for doing complete justice in any cause or matter pending before it.
>
> Article 144 of the Constitution lays down that *all* authorities in the territory of India shall act in aid of the Supreme Court.
>
> Therefore, the question of a threat to the constitutional scheme does not arise. The state government has to act upon the recommendations made by various authorities constituted under the judgment. The directions as laid down now have the force of law under Articles 141 and 142, and must be enforced by the state governments, as laid down under Article 144.

The state of Andhra Pradesh, while referring to the directions of the Court regarding the constitution of the SSC and Police Complaints Authority, also stated that under the provisions of Article 154 read with Article 163 of the Constitution, the executive power of the State vested with the Governor who acts on the aid and advice of the Council of Ministers, and that, therefore, if the recommendations of the SSC or Police Complaints Authority were binding, the same would conflict with the powers vested with the concerned authorities under the law. The Attorney General's response in this case was similar to the stand taken on the affidavit of Maharashtra.

The state of UP in its affidavit, argued that if the

recommendations of the SSC were to be binding, that could only be done through a legislative enactment passed by the State Legislature. The Attorney General's response was that the powers and the functions of the SSC have been laid down in office memorandum (O.M.) dated 2 December 2010 and repeated in the O.M. dated 26 July 2013 issued by the state government. It was not clear why any change in the powers and functions could not be given effect by a similar notification of the state government. Besides, the affidavit did not identify any statutory provision contradicting the grant of such powers to the SSC. The state government had only to issue a notification to give effect to the directions of the Supreme Court in *Prakash Singh's case.*

The state of Madhya Pradesh took the stand that the state government was not competent to provide a minimum tenure of two years to the DGP irrespective of the date of superannuation. That would require an amendment in the All India Rules by the Union Government. The Attorney General's response was that the amendment could be carried out by the competent authority.

It was obvious that the state governments were raising untenable technical difficulties in the implementation of the Court's directions. The case was listed on 13 August, 22 October, 12 November and again on 19 November 2013, but unfortunately, it could not be taken up on any of those dates. Justice Singhvi's tenure was coming to an end and he was to retire on 11 December 2013. He probably felt that he would not be able to conclude the police reforms petition. Besides, he was also exasperated with the objections of the state governments. Justice Singhvi decided to devote the remaining few months of his tenure to cases which he thought he would be able to conclude with a touch of finality. And thus ended what was, in retrospect, the most determined effort to push through the police reforms agenda.

JUSTICE DATTU: CONVENIENT DISPOSAL

The matter came up before another Bench headed by Justice H.L. Dattu on 4 March 2014. While hearing the matter, Justice Dattu wanted to know if the allegations regarding police brutalities in Tarn Taran and Patna had been suitably addressed. The Attorney General replied in the affirmative and also clarified that police reforms were actually part of another petition and that the Court's directions in that petition were only being monitored in the present case. Justice Dattu promptly passed a cryptic order that 'the *suo moto* proceedings are discharged' and the writ petition disposed of. While what Justice Dattu did was legally unexceptionable, it was unfortunate that all the good work done by Justice Singhvi was conveniently buried. Justice Dattu was keen to dispose of the petition, which he did. It would however have been better if Justice Dattu had taken forward the good work done by Justice Singhvi and pursued the matter to its logical conclusion.

JUSTICE J.S. VERMA COMMITTEE REPORT (2012–13)

The Government of India appointed a committee comprising Justice J.S. Verma (Chairman), Justice Leila Seth and Gopal Subramanium on 23 December 2013 to look into possible amendment of the Criminal Law to provide for quicker trial and enhanced punishment for criminals committing sexual assaults of extreme nature against women. The Committee was set up in the wake of the infamous Nirbhaya case in Delhi on 16 December 2012.

NGOs working on police reforms—CHRI, Common Cause, Foundation for Restoration of National Values and Manushi—submitted a joint memorandum to Justice J.S.

Verma on 5 January 2013, emphasizing that 'any proposals and efforts to change laws around sexual assaults will yield no results until police organizations that are the first port of call for every victim of sexual abuse are reformed' and that 'fundamental and core changes in policing are the need of the hour'.[183] In an indictment of the Government of India, the NGOs categorically stated that 'had the government passed and earnestly implemented the proposed (Delhi Police) Act, we would have a much safer Delhi and may be Nirbhaya and many others would not have suffered loss of life and dignity which is their right in a free, democratic India'.[184]

The Justice Verma Committee submitted its report within a month on 23 January 2013. Significantly, the report devoted one full chapter running into 28 pages to police reforms.

The Committee expressed the following views on police reforms:

> The need for police reform was strongly stated by the Supreme Court, six years back, in *Prakash Singh & Ors. Vs. Union of India & Ors.* and in the Committee's perspective ensuring full compliance with this judgment across all of India is of utmost priority to national welfare; including the welfare of women and children and towards the weaker sections of the community. Proper policing can ensure a safer community which is accessible to all for enjoyment; especially women and children without fear of sexual harassment or violence.[185]

---

[183]Submissions from NGOs working on Police Reform – Commonwealth Human Rights Initiative, Common Cause, Foundation for Restoration of National Values and Manushi, p.1.
[184]Ibid.
[185]Report of the Committee on Amendments to Criminal Law, 2013, p. 313, https://spuwac.in/pdf/jsvermacommitteereport.pdf, accessed on 21 February 2022.

The Committee deplored that the Supreme Court's judgment had not been substantially implemented across India. It urged all states to fully comply with all six Supreme Court directives in order to tackle systemic problems in policing which exist today.

The Committee went on to observe:

> We believe that if the Supreme Court's directions in *Prakash Singh* are implemented, there will be a crucial modernisation of the police to be service oriented for the citizenry in a manner which is efficient, scientific, and consistent with human dignity.[186]

Unfortunately, the Committee's emphasis on police reforms and, in that context, the need to implement Supreme Court's directions did not get due attention from the governments at the Centre and in the states.

JUSTICE THAKUR: MAIN PETITION REVIVED

The main Police Reforms PIL, Writ Petition (Civil) No. 310 of 1996 was taken up on 15 July 2014 after a gap of almost three years.

The Writ Petition was last heard on 11 April 2011, 12 December 2011, 9 January 2012 and 11 March 2014. On 11 April 2011, the Court had made some observations on the separation of investigation and law and order and tenure of the DGP. On 12 December 2011, there was no progress. On 9 January, the matter could not be taken up. On 11 March 2014, the matter was only 'mentioned'.

On 15 July 2014, the Bench, headed by Justice T.S. Thakur and comprising Justice C. Nagappan and Justice Adarsh

---

[186]Report of the Committee on Amendments to Criminal Law, 2013, p. 321, https://spuwac.in/pdf/jsvermacommitteereport.pdf, accessed on 21 February 2022.

Kumar Goel, took up the original petition. The Bench listened to Prashant Bhushan. It allowed me also to speak, which I did for about eight to 10 minutes. I gave a brief synopsis of the case, summarized the present position, stating that 15 states had passed laws which were against the letter and spirit of the Court's orders and that the remaining states had passed executive orders which diluted the Court's directions. I drew the attention of the Court to the findings of Justice Thomas, who had expressed his 'dismay' over the indifference of the states to the subject of police reforms. Later, though in a different context, the Justice Verma Committee had also highlighted the need to implement the Court's directions on police reforms. The central government, I added, had been lukewarm. They had a ready-made Model Police Act drafted by Soli Sorabjee but had yet to enact the Delhi Police Bill. I concluded with four recommendations:

1. The constitutionality of the laws enacted by the state governments would need to be examined by the Court. A separate petition had been filed by Harish Salve in this regard.

2. The IPS Amendment Rules, 2014 passed by the Ministry of Personnel, Public Grievances and Pensions in violation of the Supreme Court's judgment of 2006 deserved to be quashed. The Court had already stayed the operation of the order.

3. Monitoring the implementation of the Court's directions should be decentralized. The State High Courts should constitute committees headed by a judge, serving or retired, of the Supreme/High Court, and including a retired DGP of the state and another member drawn from the civil society. This body should study the ground situation and prepare a report on actual implementation of the Court's directions. The Committee's report should be sent,

through the Chief Justice of the State High Court, to the Supreme Court. The Apex Court should then, on the basis of recommendations received, issue appropriate directions. I suffixed my remarks on this point by saying that every time the case moved forward, the battery of lawyers representing the states (pointing my hands at about 10/15 advocates representing the state governments) managed to confuse the Bench or derail the proceedings by raising irrelevant issues. (There was suppressed laughter at my remarks.)

4. The Government of India should be directed to pass the Delhi Police Bill at the earliest.

The Court appreciated my presentation. Justice Thakur, in fact, said: 'Mr. Singh, we find you are very clear-headed and you have all the facts. In fact, we wonder why you need Prashant Bhushan.' The Court wanted a brief history of the case to be prepared with the suggestions to take the process forward.

The matter was next taken up on 29 August 2014 by a three-judge Bench comprising Justice T.S. Thakur, Justice Adarsh Kumar Goel and Justice Banumathi. Several connected petitions were also listed—the contempt petition filed by me in 2007 against the defiant states, the petition filed by Harish Salve challenging the constitutional validity of the State Acts, the petition filed by me against the Government of Maharashtra and another contempt petition filed by the Bihar Police Association against the Government of Bihar for having enacted a law contrary to the directions of the Supreme Court.

The irrepressible Harish Salve was the first to get up and started arguing on his Writ Petition No. 286/2013. Earlier, while briefing him, my advice was that if one had to sink a ship all he needed to do was to make a small hole at the bottom. In other words, he should pick up the most outrageous Act— the Bihar Police Act—and completely demolish it. That would send the right message to the other states. The Supreme Court could, in fact, give an opportunity to the other states to amend and revise their laws and make them conform to the Court's directions else their deviations could also be taken cognizance of. Salve stuck to this line. The Bihar Police Act was targeted. The Court agreed that while it would take up the Bihar Act in detail at the next hearing, the other states could also intervene if their deviations were on similar lines. The next date was fixed as 3 November 2014.

Discussions on the main petition, Writ Petition No. 310/1996 were, however, inconclusive. Justice Thakur kept on saying that instead of concentrating on all the six directions, they would like to take them up one by one, starting with separation of investigation from law and order. I protested but was not allowed to develop my arguments. Prashant Bhushan and Raju Ramachandran, based on the affidavit filed by me, argued for monitoring work to be delegated to the states. The Court was however not responsive to the idea.

In the course of discussions, which were tangential, a suggestion was made by Justice Adarsh Kumar that investigating officers should constitute a separate cadre and that they could be centrally recruited. It was mentioned by Bhushan that the Criminal Procedure Code was under the Concurrent List and that therefore such a cadre could be created.

The petition was taken up by the Supreme Court next on 3 November 2014. It turned out to be a very tough day for me—tough because I discovered to my horror that Harish Salve and Prashant Bhushan, who had both supported me throughout, were going to take a different stand on the separation of investigation from law and order. My contention was that, as recommended by the NPC, the separation should be at the police station level only and that the SHO should coordinate the two wings. Harish Salve and Prashant Bhushan were however of the view, independently though, that there should be total separation right up to the DG level. The Second

Administrative Reforms Commission, headed by Veerappa
Moily had, for inexplicable reasons, recommended one DGP
for investigation and another DGP for law and order. This
idea was perhaps planted by a bureaucrat member of the
Commission. Salve, when I met him two days before the
hearing to brief him about the case, was of the view that in
the US also there was complete separation. I did not agree with
him. However, he held his ground. I met Prashant Bhushan
on the evening of 2 November and tried to convince him, but
he too had reservations. I had prepared a detailed note on
the subject, bringing out that the Law Commission, Ribeiro
Committee, Malimath Committee and Sorabjee Committee
had all endorsed the NPC's recommendations on the point
and that ARC[187] was the only body which had struck a different
note. Prashant Bhushan said that he would read my note and
convey his views the next day.

On 3 November 2014, the case was to be taken up at 1400
hrs (2.00 p.m.). There was a lot of drama before that which
caused me considerable tension. Prashant Bhushan rang up at
11.00 a.m. to say that he did not agree with the contents of my
note. I pleaded with him that we had been on the same page
for the last 18 years and that it would be very unfortunate if
we take different views on the separation of investigation from
law and order now. Prashant Bhushan was not prepared to
change his views. Thereupon, I said, 'Could you just be quiet
on the subject?' He said, 'Yes, I will be quiet, but if they ask
for my opinion, I would have to express that.' I felt terrible
and, in sheer desperation, said: 'In that case, please do me
a favour. Could you abstain from the proceedings?' Bhushan
reluctantly agreed. His junior later told me that Bhushan was
very upset at my suggestion. At about 1330 hrs (1.30 p.m.),
I met Raju Ramachandran, Amicus, in the Supreme Court.

---

[187](Second) Administrative Reforms Commission which was headed by
Veerappa Moily.

Earlier, I had sent him my note on separation of investigation from law and order. To my great relief, he expressed broad agreement with my views.

At 1400 hrs (2.00 p.m.), we were in the Court. So was Harish Salve. We learnt that the case would be taken up at 1415 hrs (2.15 p.m.). That gave me about 10 minutes to talk to Salve, who was amicus in Writ Petition (Civil) No. 286/2013, challenging the constitutional validity of the Police Acts passed by the state governments. I again tried to convince him that he should argue on the lines of NPC recommendations, but he insisted that complete separation would be desirable. Finding no other alternative, I suggested that he should leave the main petition to me and concentrate only on Writ Petition No. 286. He said that as amicus he had to express his views on police matters. His contention was, strictly speaking, wrong. The Court had sought his help only on determining the constitutional validity of the Police Acts passed by the state governments. However, I felt that it would hurt his ego if I pressed this point. As an alternative, I requested him if he could just keep quiet on the subject. I said it would be tragic if from police reforms we moved on to police destruction. A vertical split of the department would have devastating consequences. Salve's response was: 'Alright, I will keep quiet provided you do not give your note on the subject to the Court.' I agreed. It was some kind of a *quid pro quo*. I agreed not to press my point. He agreed not to speak on the subject. It was a very torrid experience for me, asking Bhushan to stay out of the Court and Salve not to open his mouth on the subject.

When the hearing actually began, Salve took up the Bihar Police Act. Actually, the Act had been challenged at the state level also. There were procedural problems in taking up the matter in Supreme Court. These were discussed at length.

The petition was next taken up on 13 January 2015. Salve challenged the constitutional validity of the Police Acts passed by the state governments. The Bihar Police Act was picked up as an example. Salve examined its provisions with reference to the Supreme Court's directions and proved to the satisfaction of the Court that the provisions regarding the SSC, the appointment of the DGP, the tenure of field officers and the Police Establishment Board had been violated. The Police Complaints Authority issue could not be taken up even though the case took the entire day. A lot of time was taken up on separation of investigation from law and order. Unfortunately, Salve argued for complete separation in investigation and law-and-order wings— from DGP downwards. The Bench also had some ideas about separation of investigation. In the evening, I got the opportunity to speak. I controverted Salve and argued that the kind of vertical split he was suggesting would fracture the department. To prove my point, I read out from the National Police Commission Report. I also said that we had (thanks to Arvind Varma and Rama Sastry) collected information about practices in the other countries and that what was being suggested was not practised in any progressive country of the world. The Bench was apparently not happy with whatever I said because it went against their thinking on the subject. They therefore decided to call the DG (BPR&D) on 15 January to get his views on having a separate cadre of investigating officers within the department.

On 15 January 2015, Rajan Gupta, DG (BPR&D) addressed the Court and made the following points:

(i) If investigations and law and order are to be separated, more manpower will have to be provided at police stations for carrying on investigations.

(ii) A complete vertical separation of investigation and law and order is neither possible nor desirable. The BPR&D does not support the Administrative Reforms Commission's recommendation on the subject.

(iii)   Investigation and law and order can be separate wings, not separate cadres.

The BPR&D had prepared a Draft Model Police Act and forwarded the same to the Ministry of Home Affairs. The provisions of this Draft Act relating to separation of law and order and crime investigation were read out in the Court. The Supreme Court asked the BPR&D to suggest ways to insulate investigation and investigating officers from extraneous influences. Salve asked for time to submit a detailed note to the Court on the subject, throwing light on practices in foreign countries. He was obviously not happy with the DG, BPR&D endorsing my views on separation of investigation from law and order. The proceedings of the Guwahati Police Science Congress were also placed before the Court; paragraphs 5, 6 and 7 thereof on separation were read out. The Court showed special interest in Para 7, which talked of separation of investigation of heinous crimes in the first instance (I was not present on that day because I had to go to Bangalore on some other work.)

The PIL was to be taken up next on 8 April 2015. However, it was actually not listed on that date because it was a three-judge Bench matter and the Court could not constitute such a Bench. The petition was again listed on 28 April 2015. Salve suggested that the matter be taken up after the vacations. I protested that it was being delayed and suggested that it could be listed within the next couple of days. Salve was however adamant that the matter be taken up after the summer vacations only. The Bench was also in no mood to take up what was essentially a complicated matter, and they rose for lunch. I felt frustrated over delay in the matter, but there was little that I could do beyond expressing my anguish.

The PIL was taken up after the vacations on 14 July 2015. Justice Thakur, at the very beginning, wanted to know as to where was Salve. He was told that Salve was out of the country.

Bhushan argued that monitoring the implementation of the judgment was proving to be a long-drawn-out affair, and that therefore this could be delegated to the State High Courts. The Chief Justices of the High Courts could constitute committees headed by a serving or retired judge of the High Court and include a retired DGP and another member from the civil society. This committee could monitor the implementation with reference to the ground realities and thereafter submit a report to the Chief Justice of the High Court, who would forward the same with his comments and recommendations to the Supreme Court. The suggestion was reiterated and endorsed by Raju Ramachandran, the amicus. The Court was however not impressed. Justice Thakur said that they would like to await the return of Salve and get his views also before deciding on further line of action.

The irony of the situation lay in the fact that the Court was under the impression that Salve was the amicus in the case, whereas actually it was Ramachandran who was the amicus. I was very surprised that neither Bhushan nor Ramachandran thought it proper to point this out to the Court and disabuse their mind of a factually wrong impression. That apart, I was even more disappointed that the progress in a case had to depend on the presence of a particular lawyer. I thought the course of justice should not depend on or be delayed for such a reason.

CONTEMPT PETITION AGAINST THE GOVERNMENT OF UP

A contempt petition against the Government of UP was also filed by me for appointing Directors General of Police for short durations. A.C. Sharma was DGP for about a year, Devraj Nagar for over eight months, Rizwan Ahmed for two months, A.L. Banerjee for 10 months, Arun Kumar Gupta for one month, Arvind Jain for two months which was extended by another three months, and now there was Jagmohan Yadav for six months.

The petition was filed before the summer vacation but somehow it was never listed. It came up for hearing on 14 July 2015. We expected the Court to issue a contempt notice. However, Justice Thakur took a very lenient view. He said that the Court would first like to know what difficulty, if any, the Government of UP had. Bhushan very politely conveyed that these postings were obviously for extraneous reasons and were in violation of the Court's orders regarding the appointment of DGP. Justice Thakur, however, decided that a copy of the petition be handed over to the Government of UP for its response. The matter was to be taken up on 25 August, but that did not happen.

Justice Thakur was elevated as Chief Justice of India on 3 December 2015. We were hoping that the PIL would now get an impetus. However, to our great disappointment and consternation, it was never listed during his tenure as Chief Justice. He retired on 3 January 2017. The PIL was first taken up by Justice Thakur on 15 July 2014. Thus, it was under his consideration for almost two and a half years, but unfortunately there was hardly any forward movement. Justice Thakur, to start with, took up what he thought was the simplest direction—separation of investigation from law and order—whose implementation could be followed up by the Court. However, he was derailed by leading advocates who suggested a vertical split in a manner which would have destroyed the cohesion of the department. It was very unfortunate that after his elevation as CJI, the PIL was never listed. Justice Thakur was well meaning and was keen on giving a push to police reforms. However, he would not be able to look back with any sense of pride or satisfaction on his contribution to police reforms.

JUSTICE KHEHAR: PERIPHERAL CONTRIBUTION

Justice Jagdish Singh (J.S.) Khehar took over as CJI on 4 January 2017. Surprisingly and disappointingly, the PIL was never listed during his tenure also. I made repeated requests to the advocates to get the matter listed, but somehow they were not keen on Justice Khehar taking up the PIL. The one silver lining during his tenure was that the Court took up the matter regarding large number of vacancies in the police ranks. It was brought to the notice of the Court through another PIL that there were 4.42 lakh vacancies in police department across India. The highest vacancies were in UP (1.15 lakh), West Bengal (37,325), Bihar (34,251), Jharkhand (26,303), Karnataka (24,399) and Tamil Nadu (19,803). A Bench of Chief Justice J.S. Khehar, Justices D.Y. Chandrachud and Sanjay Kishan Kaul passed an order on 18 April 2017 that either the Home Secretary or a Joint Secretary of these states should appear before the Court to assist the Bench in preparing a definite road map to fill up the vacancies. The state of UP promised to fill up the post of 3,200 sub-inspectors and 30,000 constables every year. Karnataka and Tamil Nadu also promised quick filling up of the vacancies.

The matter relating to filling up of vacancies later came up before the Bench of CJI, Ranjan Gogoi, with Justices Deepak Gupta and Sanjeev Khanna on 11 March 2019 in *Manish Kumar vs Union of India*. The Court held that 'in view of the factual matrix...the matter be sent to High Court(s) for effective monitoring.' It directed the Supreme Court Registry to transmit the records of the case to the respective High Courts while requesting the Chief Justices of the High Courts to entertain the matter on the judicial side by way of *suo moto* PILs.

The Supreme Court judgment of 2006 on police reforms did not touch upon the subject of police strength, but manpower requirement is an essential component of the full spectrum of police reforms. Actually, the sanctioned strength is itself inadequate. According to the *BPRD Data on Police Organization* (as on 1 January 2019), the country had 198 policemen per lakh of population as against the optimum of 222 per lakh of population. In actual fact, there were only 158 policemen per lakh on the ground because of the large number of vacancies. Filling up the vacancies would definitely improve the capacity of the police to deal with the multifarious problems it has to tackle.

CHIEF SECRETARY VIS-À-VIS DGP: THE SENKUMAR CASE

The Supreme Court of India, in a landmark judgment in Civil Appeal No. 5227 of 2017 in *Dr T.P. Senkumar IPS vs. Union of India & Ors*, delivered on 24 April 2017, set aside the judgment and order of the Central Administrative Tribunal and judgment and order of the Kerala High Court upholding the state government's removal of Dr T.P. Senkumar as DGP, and observed that he had been unfairly and arbitrarily dealt with. It went on to record the following significant observations:

> ... there is a difference in the role of the Chief Secretary as the chief executive of the State and the Director General of Police of a State—their roles cannot be equated. While the Chief Secretary can be removed if he or she does not enjoy the confidence of the Chief Minister or does not have a 'complete rapport and understanding' with the Chief Minister, the removal cannot be questioned, unless there is a violation of some statutory or constitutional provision. But that is not so with the State Police Chief. The reason is not far to seek—the Cabinet colleagues of the Chief Minister or senior bureaucrats (including the Chief Secretary) might need to be investigated in an appropriate case. Can the Chief Minister then remove the

State Police Chief on the ground that in such an event he or she does not enjoy the confidence of the Chief Minister or that there is no 'complete rapport and understanding' between the State Police Chief and the Chief Minister? The answer is quite obvious.[188]

The Court emphasized that 'the decision in *Prakash Singh* and the fashioning of the Act respect the necessity of the tenure appointment of the State Police Chief. *Prakash Singh* made sure that the removal of the State Police Chief is not a routine sort of affair.'[189]

JUSTICE DIPAK MISRA: ONE STEP FORWARD, TWO STEPS BACKWARDS

Justice Dipak Misra took charge as CJI on 28 August 2017. Immediately thereafter, on 29 August 2017, the petition was listed before the Bench of Justice Madan B. Lokur, Justice Sanjay Kishan Kaul and Justice Deepak Gupta. The matter could not be taken up in the forenoon. In the afternoon, before the proceedings could begin, I rose to request the Bench that the police reforms matter may kindly be taken up in view of its importance and the fact that it had been listed after about two years. Justice Lokur's response was: 'Mr Singh, we would definitely like to take up the case, but that may not be possible today.' Unfortunately, the case was never listed again before Justice Lokur. From whatever I knew of him, he was well disposed towards reforms in any branch of administration. Had the case been assigned to him, the police reforms matter would perhaps have made some headway.

The case was listed before the Bench of Chief Justice Dipak Misra, Justice A.M. Khanwilkar and Justice D.Y. Chandrachud

---

[188]Supreme Court judgment in *Dr. T.P. Senkumar vs. Union of India*, para 76.
[189]Ibid: para 73.

repeatedly on 11 December 2017, 12 February, 19 February, 2 April, 23 April, 3 May, 3 July and 30 July 2018. It was not that the Court monitored the implementation of its directions on these dates; it was preoccupied with disposing of IA No. 25307/2018 in Writ Petition (Civil) No. 310 of 1996 filed by the Government of India. The prayers in the IA were that the Hon'ble Court may be pleased to:

(a) direct that fixed tenure of two years of DGP should be made subject to the date of superannuation
(b) direct to carry out suitable amendment in the IPS (Cadre) Rules, 1954 to provide two years' tenure to IPS officers and to the effect that only such officers may be appointed as DGP (Head of Police Force [HoPF]) in the state/UT who have at least two years of residual service and have been empanelled to hold the DG's post in the state government by the empanelment committee.

It was obvious that the Government of India wanted to dilute the original mandate of the Supreme Court in its historic judgment of 22 September 2006, which clearly stated that the DGP of the state 'once he had been selected for the job, he should have a minimum tenure of at least two years irrespective of his superannuation'. The prayer that only such officers may be appointed as DGP, who have 'at least two years of residual service' was very unfortunate. The mandarins in the Home Department either did not realize or were callous about the implications of this prayer. It would mean that several officers, howsoever outstanding, would be excluded from consideration for promotion to the rank of DGP if they had, say, only one year of service or a few months left. I have a strong feeling that the case was listed with great frequency under some pressure from the government and, what was most unfortunate, the CJI was keen to oblige the establishment.

The following directions were given by the Bench on 3 July 2018:

(a) All the States shall send their proposals in anticipation of the vacancies to the Union Public Service Commission, well in time at least three months prior to the date of retirement of the incumbent on the post of Director General of Police;

(b) The Union Public Service Commission shall prepare the panel as per the directions of this Court in the judgment in Prakash Singh's case (supra) and intimate to the States;

(c) The State shall immediately appoint one of the persons from the panel prepared by the Union Public Service Commission;

(d) None of the States shall ever conceive of the idea of appointing any person on the post of Director General of Police on acting basis for there is no concept of acting Director General of Police as per the decision in Prakash Singh's case (supra);

(e) An endeavour has to be made by all concerned to see that the person who was selected and appointed as the Director General of Police continues despite his date of superannuation. However, the extended term beyond the date of superannuation should be a reasonable period. We say so as it has been brought to our notice that some of the States have adopted a practice to appoint the Director General of Police on the last date of retirement as a consequence of which the person continues for two years after his date of superannuation. Such a practice will not be in conformity with the spirit of the direction.

(f) Our direction No.(c) should be considered by the Union Public Service Commission to mean that the persons are to be empanelled, as far as practicable, from amongst the people within the zone of consideration who have two years of service. Merit and seniority should be given due weightage.

(g) Any legislation/rule framed by any of the States or the Central Government running counter to the direction shall remain in abeyance to the aforesaid extent.

There was justification for issuing the direction in Clause (d) because some states had adopted the questionable practice of appointing officers as Acting DGP, continuing him in that capacity for quite some time, and after satisfying themselves that the person chosen was politically convenient, confirming him in that assignment as regular DGP and giving him a two-year tenure thereafter. In actual practice, it meant an officer, at times, getting a three-year tenure or even longer. It happened in Telangana, where the DGP got a three-and-a-half-year tenure, and perhaps some other states also. The Hon'ble Judges, however, did not realize that there may be contingencies where a state would have no option but to appoint an Acting DGP. Thus, for example, if the incumbent DGP became incapacitated for some reason or he was removed by the Election Commission, the state would immediately have to appoint a person as Acting DGP.

What was worse, clauses (e) and (f) of the directions were contrary to the original order of the Apex Court, which clearly said that the DGP shall have 'a minimum tenure of at least two years irrespective of his date of superannuation.' The direction in Clause (e) aforesaid, on the other hand, talked of the extended term beyond the date of superannuation to be 'a reasonable period.' This was a vague expression which could be interpreted differently by the states. One state may say six months is enough; another state may say one year is reasonable, and so on. The interpretation would depend upon political considerations at state level. Clause (f) saying that officers should be empanelled, as far as practicable, 'from amongst the people within the zone of consideration who have got clear two years of service' was also against the spirit of Supreme Court's original order, apart from the fact that leaving out officers with less than two years of service from the zone of consideration would result in demoralization and frustration at the senior level in the department. Several officers thus excluded will have to face the grim prospect of either having to serve under an officer junior to them or seek voluntary retirement. These facts were brought to the notice of the Apex Court on 30 July 2018.

Meanwhile, in quite a few states the Court's order of 3 July 2018 were implemented in a manner which excluded police officers with less than two years of residual service from the process of empanelment. The UPSC, possibly under the influence of the Ministry of Home Affairs, misinterpreted the directions of the Court. The states of Punjab, Haryana, Bihar and some other states were affected. Senior officers with less than two years of service left, who were hoping to be elevated to the highest rank of DGP, were frustrated and demoralized. The dilemma before us was as to how to tell the Court that its judgment was flawed and that it was having an adverse effect on the morale of officers. CJI Dipak Misra was likely to be offended by any such presentation. After a lot of discussions with Prashant Bhushan, we ultimately filed an application with a very modest prayer that the Court may clarify that its directions of 3 July 2018 did not in any way dilute or modify the Hon'ble Court's original order of 22 September 2006 in Writ Petition (Civil) No. 310 of 1996 insofar as it related to the selection and minimum tenure of the DGP. The application was somehow never listed during Justice Misra's tenure.

CHIEF JUSTICE GOGOI: CLEARS THE FOG

Chief Justice Ranjan Gogoi took charge on 3 October 2018. The states of Punjab, Bihar, Haryana, West Bengal, Kerala and Bihar, which were affected by the Court's controversial order of 3 July 2018, had filed interlocutory applications. The state of Punjab was represented by Mr P. Chidambaram. On 12 December 2018, Mr Chidambaram argued that the power to enact legislation is a plenary constitutional power vested in Parliament and the state legislatures under articles 245 and 246 of the Constitution of India. Besides, police are a subject matter covered under Entry 2, List II of the Seventh Schedule of the Constitution and thus is under the exclusive legislative domain of the state governments. In the Prakash Singh case, there was express stipulation that the direction issued therein would cease to be operative once the legislation was framed by the state government. Regarding the role of UPSC, he argued that the Constitution has limited the functions of the UPSC only to the extent of 'consultation' on matters of 'suitability of candidates for such appointments, promotions or transfers'. He prayed that the state of Punjab be permitted to appoint the DGP in accordance with the Punjab Police (Second Amendment) Act, 2018. The state of Haryana also sought exemption from the operation of the 3 July 2018 order of the Court and prayed for permission to appoint the DGP in accordance with the Haryana Police Act, 2007. On 15 January 2019, the Secretary, UPSC, was asked to appear before the Court and explain the norms being applied for empanelment of officers.

The Ministry of Home Affairs supported the stand taken by the aforesaid state governments. Referring to the IA filed by the state of Punjab, it said that 'the contention of the applicant appears to be based on sound principles of administrative jurisprudence'. The MHA even suggested that the Court may consider directing each of the states to set up an 'Empanelment Committee' for the purpose of selecting the DGP. It was obvious that the Government of India was keen on diluting the Apex Court's direction of 2006 on the 'Selection and Minimum Tenure of Director General of Police'.

The Supreme Court disposed of the interlocutory application on 16 January 2019. Referring to the 2006 judgment in *Prakash Singh & Ors. Vs. Union of India & Ors*, it said that:

> On an in-depth consideration, we are left with no doubt that the said directions, keeping in mind the spirit in which the Court has proceeded to issue the same...are wholesome and if the same are implemented, it will subserve public interest until such time that the matter is heard finally...for the present, the directions in *Prakash Singh (supra)* read with the order of this Court dated 3.7.2018 would not require any correction or modification.

CJI Gogoi is to be given credit for having withstood the pressure from states to have complete freedom in the matter of appointment of DGP without any involvement of the UPSC. The Court, nevertheless, made it clear that this injunction is to hold good 'until such time that the matter is heard finally', that is, until the contempt petition, challenging the constitutional validity of the Acts legislated by the state governments, is decided.

The Court's order of 16 January 2019 was a reprieve for us in the context of pressure building up in the states. However, the more important issue now was UPSC's interpretation of Court's order of 3 July 2018, causing havoc in several states. The order, it may be recalled, had *inter alia* said that the UPSC should empanel persons 'as far as practicable, from amongst the people within the zone of consideration who have got clear two years of service'. The CJI, to the best of my understanding and information, had inserted this proviso under pressure from the Ministry. The UPSC, unfortunately, while preparing the panels for several states, excluded from consideration, all those officers who had less than two years of service. A number of meritorious officers were, as a consequence, not considered for empanelment. This caused huge demoralization among the top echelons of the service. The police reforms process was blamed by these officers for having ruined their careers at a very critical time when they were looking forward to occupying the top position. At one stage, I tried to get an appointment with the chairman, UPSC, with a view to discussing matters with him and sorting out the confusion. The good offices of DGP of a neighbouring state were utilized for the appointment. However, there was no response from the UPSC. I was then left with no option but to go to the Court against the UPSC's interpretation of the Court's orders. IA No. 24616/19 was filed.

We clearly stated that clauses (e) and (f) in the 3 July 2018 order of the Court were 'somewhat ambiguous and contrary', and that 'we were unfortunately beginning to see the unintended consequences of 03.07.2018 Court order'. It was brought to the notice of the Court that excluding all officers with less than two years of service would result in 'frustration and demoralization at senior level' and that senior officers not even considered for empanelment 'would be faced with the grim prospect of either serving under an officer junior to them or seeking voluntary retirement'. Hearing the case on 28 February 2019, the CJI wondered what the phrase 'as far as practicable' meant in the 3 July 2018 order. Obviously, he was not happy with the vague phraseology used by his predecessor. He then questioned as to why this matter was being raised after a lapse of about six months. Prashant Bhushan politely said that an application had actually been filed, but the same was never taken up for some reasons. It was also brought to the notice of the Court that while excluding IPS officers with less than two years of service for empanelment, the Ministry had not proposed a similar constraint for IAS officers. The case of Rajiv Mehrishi, who was appointed Home Secretary, Government of India, on the day of his superannuation, was mentioned. The CJI could see the confusion caused by a vague set of directions given by his predecessor and, possibly, also under pressure from the government through the UPSC to subvert the Court's original mandate. He decided to reserve the judgment and asked the amicus (Raju Ramachandran) to prepare a state-wise statement about the appointment of Directors General of Police in different states subsequent to the 3 July 2018 order.

The judgment on our interlocutory application was finally delivered on 13 March 2019. The relevant portions thereof are reproduced below:

> Having read and considered the decision of this Court in Prakash Singh (supra) we are of the view that what was emphasized in Prakash Singh (supra) is a minimum tenure of two years for an incumbent once he is appointed as the Director General of Police. The direction issued by this Court neither contemplated the appointment of a Director General of Police on the eve of his retirement nor the practice now adopted by the Union Public Service Commission in making the empanelment, i.e. empanelling officers who have at least two years of tenure...
>
> In the above conspectus the object in issuing the directions in Prakash Singh (supra), in our considered view, can best be achieved if the residual tenure of an officer, i.e. remaining period of service till normal retirement, is fixed on a reasonable basis, which, in our considered view, should be a period of six months...
>
> We, therefore, clarify the order of this Court dated 3rd July, 2018 passed in I.A. No. 25307 of 2018 in Writ

Petition No. 319 of 1996 to mean that recommendation for appointment to the post of Director General of Police by the Union Public Service Commission and preparation of panel should be purely on the basis of merit from officers who have a minimum residual tenure of six months i.e. officers who have at least six months of service prior to the retirement.

The above direction, naturally, will hold the field until the validity of the Police Acts in force which provides to the contrary are examined and dealt with by this Court in Writ Petition (Civil) No. 286 of 2013.

The judgment came as a relief to us and to the senior police officers in different states. A minimum of six months of residual service was considered a reasonable requirement for empanelment. The confusion caused by Justice Dipak Misra's vague order of 3 July 2018 and its interpretation by the UPSC was removed.

CONTEMPT PETITION

Contempt petitions had earlier been filed in the years 2007, 2010, 2013 and 2015. Unfortunately, none of those were taken up for one reason or the other. The petitions, with the passage of time, became infructuous also.

It may, however, be recalled that on 31 July 2013, in the context of writ petition (civil) no. 139/2013 which *inter alia* dealt with the Supreme Court's directions on police reforms also, Justice Singhvi had called the Chief Secretaries of Andhra Pradesh, Maharashtra and Tamil Nadu to appear before the Court, because, at that time, these were the most non-compliant states. The Chief Secretaries were given a dressing down whereupon they gave an assurance to the Court that its directions would be promptly responded to. This was the only occasion when the state governments were pulled up.

Another contempt petition was filed by me on 26 April 2019. It was stated therein that, of the states which had issued executive orders, none had fully complied with the directions of the Court. The petition described the position in the following words:

> Wherever the mandated institutions—State Security Commission, Police Establishment Board and Complaints Authorities—have been set up, their composition has been subverted, their charter diluted or their powers curtailed. There is arbitrariness in the appointment of Director General of Police (DGP) with most of the states not consulting the UPSC for the preparation of panel of officers suitable for promotion to the rank of DGP. Police officers on operational duties are shunted for all kinds of administrative reasons before the completion of two years. There is tardiness in the separation of investigative and law and order functions of the police.

The states of Jharkhand, Madhya Pradesh, Odisha, Uttar Pradesh and West Bengal were particularly non-compliant, and it was therefore prayed that contempt proceedings be initiated against these states for disobeying the orders of the Court while the remaining states which had only partially complied be directed to ensure full compliance of the directions by 30 June 2019.

JUSTICE BOBDE: LOCKED DOWN

Justice Sharad Arvind (S.A.) Bobde took charge as Chief Justice on 18 November 2019. As the case was not being listed during the pandemic, Prashant Bhushan reminded him about the importance of the matter on 28 February 2020. The case came up for hearing on 12 June 2020, though in a different context. Amicus Raju Ramachandran availed of the opportunity to suggest that monitoring the implementation of the Supreme Court's directions may be delegated to the jurisdictional High Courts. The Bench comprising CJI Bobde, Justice A.S. Bopanna and Justice Hrishikesh Roy recorded that this was a matter which required further consideration. Subsequently, the amicus filed an application with the following prayer on 6 July 2020:

> The jurisdictional High Courts constitute dedicated Benches to determine the extent to which compliance by executive orders has been made by the concerned States/ UTs. For this purpose, the High Courts would have to take the assistance of an Amicus Curiae and also appoint Expert Committees to verify compliance at the ground level. The High Courts may be requested to complete the exercise of determining compliance within a period of six months.

The suggestion was made because we found that even after 15 years of monitoring by the Supreme Court, there had been not much of progress. The petition has actually not been taken up by the Supreme Court during the last nearly three years (since March 2019).

There is perhaps better chance of state-wise compliance being monitored by the respective High Courts.

CONTRIBUTION OF JUDGES

It may be appropriate to place on record the contribution made by various judges to the cause of police reforms. Justice J.S. Verma was very keen on giving final directions in the matter, but it was too early and so he could not do that. Justice Bharucha was sympathetic to changes in the police and to him goes the credit of having suggested that the security of tenure should be given not only to the DGP but to all police officers holding operational assignments down to the level of SHO. Justice Sabharwal would be remembered with a sense of gratitude by the future generations of police officers for his landmark judgment. He understood the importance of police reforms and gave a comprehensive set of directions. One thing remarkable about him I noticed was that, while sitting in the Court, he completely dominated the proceedings. He was never overawed by any lawyer, howsoever formidable his reputation may be, and he would never let any lawyer hijack or derail the proceedings. I was witness to Justice Sabharwal snubbing some of the top lawyers of the country when, after the judgment, they came up with various pleas which amounted to seeking its review. Two judges who showed genuine seriousness in ensuring the implementation of Court's directions were Justice Kapadia and Justice Singhvi. Their handling of the matter raised our hopes, but unfortunately both of them gave up in the face of fierce resistance by the states. Justice Gogoi must be given credit for having clarified the directions regarding the appointment and tenure of the DGP.

A HISTORICAL PROCESS

The process of police reforms is moving slowly but surely. There have been—and there would be—attempts to dilute, delay, subvert or even sabotage the directions of the Supreme Court, but it is an inexorable historical process. Police reforms shall happen in the country one day or the other. The wheel has been set in motion and there could be no stopping it. The future of India is linked up with police reforms in the country. India cannot achieve political and economic progress without a sensitive and accountable police committed to upholding the rule of law.

'The longest day,' as Harriet Beecher Stowe said, 'must have its close—the gloomiest night will wear on to a morning.'

6

RESPONSE OF THE STATE GOVERNMENTS

The Supreme Court, in its judgment of 22 September 2006, had ordered that the directions shall be complied with by the central and state governments and the Union Territories on or before 31 December 2006 so that 'the bodies afore-noted became operational on the onset of the new year'. The Cabinet Secretary, Government of India and Chief Secretaries of state governments/Union Territories were directed to file affidavits of compliance by 3 January 2007.

The Supreme Court judgment caused quite a furore in government circles. The politicians and bureaucrats were taken completely by surprise. They never expected such an intervention by the Supreme Court, which would disturb the status quo and give police a certain degree of functional autonomy. Police had so far completely been at their beck and call. It appeared to them that they were now going to lose their hold over the police. The Home Secretary, Government of India, called a meeting of all the Chief Secretaries and Directors General of Police of all the states on 14 November 2006. This was followed by another meeting called by the home minister on 30 December 2006 of all the chief ministers of the country.

Several chief ministers are reported to have protested over the Supreme Court's directions on police reforms. They contended that these directions infringed on the powers of the states as per the Constitution, undermined the federal structure and eroded the authority of the legislature. Nitish Kumar (Bihar) was particularly vocal. He was supported by Mulayam Singh Yadav (UP). Both urged the Centre to file a review petition in the Supreme Court. Karunanidhi (Tamil Nadu) objected to the Supreme Court giving a minimum tenure of two years to the DGPs and said that the involvement of UPSC in the empanelment process, will 'neither be practical nor necessary as police is a State subject'. Buddhadeb Bhattacharjee (West Bengal), in a letter to the PM, wrote that 'maintenance of law and order including state police is a State subject and mandatory compliance of the Court's directions and acceptance of the Model Police Act appear to contravene this accepted position'. Shivraj Singh Chouhan (Madhya Pradesh) contended that the Supreme Court's directions relate to issues/subjects lying in the domain of executive powers of the state.[190]

At the next hearing on 11 January 2007, the Supreme Court found that there had been very little forward movement and that, barring Sikkim, all the other states had come up with arguments to explain the non-implementation of the Court's directions. The Court thereupon observed as follows:

> We wish to make it clear that by indirect method or in the garb of filing affidavits or I.A... we cannot permit review of our judgment and order dated 22nd September 2006. There is a proper procedure for seeking review on permissible grounds only. In this connection, it becomes important to again note that the matter was heard for [a] number of days and practically no state government /Union Territories objected to the suggestions contained in various reports.

---

[190]'Chief Ministers protest; order on police reforms violates Constitution,' *The Indian Express*, 3 January 2007.

The Court nevertheless extended the time limit for compliance till 31 March 2007.

The status of compliance in different states is summarized below.

ANDHRA PRADESH*[191]

The state government of Andhra took a defiant stand to start with. In its first affidavit dated 29 December 2006, it argued that the setting up of the SSC would mean that 'the state government would be denuded of its power of superintendence over the State Police, besides being contrary to the existing law'.[192] Regarding the selection of the DGP, the state took the stand that it was 'the prerogative of the state government since the police administration is under the control and superintendence of the state government'. The existing rules, besides, did not provide for sending the list of senior IPS officers to UPSC for the purpose of appointment of DGP. The state also expressed its opposition to giving a fixed tenure to police officers posting in the field. 'There may be emergent situations where the police officers may have to be transferred before completion of two years of tenure to meet the law-and-order situation even though one may not come within the eventualities mentioned by the Hon'ble Supreme Court.' On the question of separation of investigation from law and order, the state government submitted that this was being implemented 'to some extent', and expressed its commitment 'to take steps to entrust the investigation of all the cases to the separate investigating police and free law and order police from the investigation duties in a phased manner

---

[191]States bearing asterisk mark (*) are those which have passed Police Acts subsequent to the Supreme Court judgment.

[192]The state governments' views in the chapter, wherever quoted, are from affidavits filed in the Supreme Court.

as there are financial implications to create new posts and to provide infrastructure to implement the direction.' The state government also conveyed its willingness to set up a Police Establishment Board, though it expressed its reservation on the Board functioning as an appellate authority. Regarding setting up of Complaints Authority, the state government felt that such a step would amount to duplication of functions and would lead to demoralization in the force.

The next affidavit dated 8 February 2007 showed softening in the state government's attitude. While constituting a committee to draft a new Police Act for the State, the state government at the same time issued orders on 7 February 2007, fixing a minimum tenure of two years to police officers on operational duties in the field and another order constituting a Police Establishment Board comprising the DGP and four other Additional DGPs. Regarding selection and tenure of DGP, the state government said that it had addressed the Government of India to make suitable amendments in the All India Service Rules to enable it comply with the directions of the Supreme Court.

In the next affidavit dated 7 April 2007, the state government further clarified that it was implementing the direction regarding separation of investigation from law and order, and conveyed the government's commitment 'to take expeditious steps to implement the said directions in a phased manner as it involves recruitment of a large number of police officers and huge financial implications.' Regarding the Supreme Court's directions to set up a SSC and Police Complaints Authority, the state government submitted that it had filed a petition for review under Article 137 of the Constitution of India.

In 2014, the state passed the Andhra Pradesh Police Reforms (Amendment) Act.

State Security Commission: The Thomas Committee recorded that the state government had not constituted the Commission on the ground that law and order being a state subject this would weaken government's power of superintendence over the police department. Subsequently, however, the state government issued an order on 8 August 2013, constituting the Commission with the home minister, the leader of the Opposition, chief secretary, DGP and five independent members. There was an attempt to follow the Sorabjee Model. Significantly, the order said that the recommendations of the Commission would be binding. The procedure for selecting independent members was not clarified.

Selection and Tenure of DGP: The state government assured a two-year tenure to the DGP, though no order on the subject was issued. It contended that it is the state's prerogative to select the DGP. The state government sent a letter to the Government of India to amend the All India Service (DCRB) Rules, 1958 on the subject. It also filed an interlocutory application, seeking non-involvement of UPSC in the process.

Tenure of Field Officers: Government Order (G.O.) dated 7 February 2007 was issued on the subject. The Thomas Committee however found that transfer orders were being issued frequently in violation of the order.

Separation of Investigation from Law and Order: The state government conveyed that investigation of property crimes was being done by separate units in all major cities, and assured that it was committed to implementing the direction in full in a phased manner. On 8 August 2013, orders on the subject were issued.

Police Establishment Board: The Board has been constituted through an order passed on 7 February 2007. However, it is not authorized to make recommendations regarding postings/transfers of gazetted police officers, and it is not to function as a forum of appeal on representations from officers regarding their promotion/transfers, etc. or their being subjected to illegal orders. The Board is also not to review the functioning of the police.

Police Complaints Authority: The state government initially did not constitute Police Complaints Authority on the ground that adequate oversight fora like the NHRC and Lok Ayukta already existed, and that creation of another such body would mean unnecessary financial burden on the exchequer and adversely affect the working of police. Subsequently, however, it issued an order on 8 August 2013 constituting state and district-level authorities. Significantly, their recommendations will be binding.

ARUNACHAL PRADESH

Arunachal was one of the first states to comply with the Supreme Court's directions. In fact, it was interesting to see the north-eastern states as a whole showing greater respect for the Supreme Court's orders than several states in the heartland of the country. The state issued a number of notifications in compliance of the Court's directions.

State Security Commission: It was constituted through a notification issued on 27 February 2007. The model recommended by the Soli Sorabjee Committee was chosen. The Commission comprised six official and five independent members. There were, however, two significant deviations: instead of two official members (Chief Secretary and DGP), the state government added two more, namely, the Home Commissioner and the IGP, while there was no judicial component in the Commission. The recommendations of the SSC are not binding.

Selection and Tenure of DGP/Field Officers: The government also issued notifications dated 18 December 2006 on the lines of Court's directions regarding the selection of the DGP and a minimum tenure of two years for the DGP and other officers posted in the field. In actual practice, however, IPS officers in Arunachal Pradesh are posted by the MHA and as such the notifications are not really relevant except that they reflect the state government's willingness to comply with the directions of the Apex Court.

Separation of Investigation from Law and Order: This was implemented in nine police stations only which had crime figures of more than 100 IPC cases in a year.

Police Establishment Board: This was also constituted, vide notification dated 14 December 2006. There is, however, no mention of the Board reviewing the functioning of police in the state.

Complaints Authority: It was set up at the state level and its recommendations are binding. There are no district level Complaint Authorities.

ASSAM*

The state government of Assam, in its affidavit file dated 31 December 2006, pleaded that 'being an insurgency-affected state, Assom faces a peculiar situation of law enforcement, unlike most other States in India and hence, any mechanism for putting into place and implementing the directions of this Hon'ble Court in the Judgment and order dated 22 September 2006 need to be thoroughly examined in terms of any possible adverse impact on the ground, the various counterinsurgency operations, and more particularly, as a model working harmoniously with the Unified Command Structure in place in Assom.' On 7 February 2007, the state government issued three notifications: one dealing with selection and appointment of the DGP and his tenure of two years irrespective of the date of superannuation; the other dealing with the tenure of officers posted in the field, and the third dealing with the setting up of the Police Establishment Board. These were in compliance of the directions of the Apex Court. On 18 September 2007, the Assam Police Act was promulgated.

State Security Commission: Sections 34 and 35 of the Act provide for the setting up of the SSC. The leader of the Opposition was however not included in the body and the method of selection of non-official members was not spelt out. It was also not mentioned that the Commission would evaluate police performance or that the Commission's report would be placed before the state legislature.

Selection and Tenure of DGP/Field Officers: The empanelment of officers is to be done by the SSC rather than the UPSC. The DGP has been given a minimum tenure of one year only as against two years directed by the Supreme Court and this is also subject to superannuation. Besides, the DGP could be removed without any reference to the SSC. Among the field officers, only the district Superintendent of Police and station house officers were given minimum tenure of one year only and not two years as mandated by the Supreme Court.

Separation of Investigation from Law and Order: Section 55 of the Act deals with the separation of investigation from law and order, but its mechanism has not been spelt out.

Police Establishment Board: A Police Establishment Board was set up under Section 44 of the Act but it was not authorized to recommend postings or transfers of Additional SPs and above, and was not given the authority to review the performance of police.

Police Complaints Authority: Complaints authorities were constituted, but the methodology of selection of the chairperson and the members was not defined, and the recommendations of the authority are not binding.

BIHAR*

The state government, in its first response to the Supreme Court judgment on 30 December 2006, informed the Court that the State had constituted a committee headed by the Chief Secretary to examine the various reports and draft a Police Bill.

In its next affidavit dated 5 April 2007, the state government informed the Court that it had issued a notification on 7 February 2007 in compliance with three directions of the Supreme Court. The notification stated that the selection of DGP shall be made from a panel of three eligible and senior-most police officers prepared by the UPSC, and that the minimum tenure of the DGP shall be two years. The notification also gave a minimum tenure of two years to the Deputy Inspector General of Police, District Superintendent of Police and officer in-charge of the police station. It also provided for the setting up of a Police Establishment Board comprising the DGP, Additional DGP (HQ), one IGP, one DIGP and a senior officer belonging to the scheduled caste/tribe. It was, however, clarified that this was an interim arrangement and that as soon as the new Police Act was passed the arrangement will automatically be superseded. The affidavit also revealed that the state had enacted the Bihar Police Act, 2007, and that the same had been notified on 31 March 2007.

Interestingly, the Bihar Police Association filed a contempt petition on 5 September 2007 against the Government of Bihar 'for deliberately, intentionally and wilfully violating the order/ directions passed on 22.09.2006, by this Hon'ble Court, in the matter of writ petition (civil) no. 310/1996 titled *Prakash Singh and others Vs. Union of India and others,* being instrumental for drafting and inserting many erroneous provisions in the Bihar Police Act, 2007'. The Association alleged that the Bill had been drafted 'in a most hurried and hush-hush manner' and expressed its apprehension that the 'Police force organisation in the State would continue to be reduced to literally tool of the party in power instead of following rule of law and be people friendly'.

The provisions of the Bihar Police Act 2007 were examined in detail by the Thomas Committee. A synopsis of its observations is given below:

State Security Commission: The Act provides for the setting up of a State Police Board (Section 24) comprising the Chief Secretary as Chairman, DGP as Member and Secretary (Home) as Member Secretary.

(i) The composition of the Board does not conform to any of the three models suggested by the Supreme Court.
(ii) Its recommendations are not binding on the government.
(iii) Its report is not required to be placed before the state legislature.

Selection and Tenure of DGP: The Act (Section 6) states that the DGP shall be appointed from a panel of officers, which includes officers already working as DGP and contain such other officers who have been found suitable for promotion to the post of DGP. The tenure of DGP appointed in such a manner shall 'normally' be of two years.

(i) The Act does not provide for empanelment of officers by the UPSC or any other independent body.
(ii) The criteria for empanelment are not spelt out.
(iii) The minimum tenure of two years is not mandatory; it would 'normally' be so.

(iv)   Conditions for premature removal of DGP include subjective considerations such as incapacitation for 'any other reasons' and 'administrative grounds,' which are subject to misuse.

Tenure of Field Officers: The Act (Section 10) states that the tenure of officers posted as station house officers or in-charge of police circle or sub-division or Superintendent of Police of the district shall be minimum two years. Section 34 also says that the tenure of officers shall normally be of two years.

(i)   Condition for pre-mature removal includes subjective considerations such as incapacitation for 'any other reasons' or 'administrative grounds,' which are liable to misuse.

(ii)   Need to fill vacancies 'caused by transfers' is also violative of the Supreme Court guidelines.

Separation of Investigation from Law and Order: The Act (Section 36) states that the government shall constitute special investigation units in crime-infested areas which shall be headed by police officers not below the rank of sub-inspector.

(i)   These units will take up investigations only of specified crimes instead of all crimes, many of which will continue to be investigated by the staff handling law and order also.

(ii)   The provision does not satisfy the Supreme Court's direction.

Police Establishment Board: The Act (Section 10) provides for the creation of Transfer Committees for officers of the ranks of Constable to Inspector. For higher ranks of District Superintendent of Police, Range DIG and Zonal IG, there is no Board.

(i)   The Committees constituted under Section 10 will deal with only transfers and postings and not with other service-related matters.

(ii) Transfer and posting of officers of higher ranks will be governed by rules framed by the government from time to time.

(iii) The Committees are not departmental bodies in composition.

(iv) They are also not authorized to Act as forums of appeal for disposing of representations from police officers regarding service matters or being subjected to illegal or irregular orders.

(v)   They are not authorized to generally review the functioning of the State Police.

Police Complaints Authority: The Act (Section 59) lays down that the government shall set up a District Accountability Authority headed by the District Magistrate with Superintendent of Police and Senior Additional District Magistrate as members and Additional District Collector as Member Secretary.

(i)   There is no provision for state-level Complaints Authority.

(ii) The composition of the district-level authority does not conform to the Supreme Court's directive. It is headed by the District Magistrate; the other members are also all official with no representation of non-officials.

(iii) The recommendations of the Authority will not be binding on any administration authorities.

CHHATTISGARH*

The state government, in its first response dated 1 January 2007, hailed the Supreme Court directions as 'a path breaking judgement' and assured that it would soon bring out an appropriate legislation, and sought six months' time for the same. In its next affidavit dated 5 April 2007, the state government informed the Supreme Court that it had constituted a committee on 6 January 2007 headed by the Additional Chief Secretary (Home Department), the other members being Principal Secretary (Law), Principal Secretary (Home), Secretary (General Administration Department), DGP and IGP (Planning), to draft the Chhattisgarh Police Act. The state government also issued an order on 9 February 2007 that police officers posted in the field shall have a prescribed minimum tenure of two years. An Establishment Board was also set up on 9 February 2007 headed by the DGP and comprising Additional DGP, the IGP Raipur and the Senior Superintendent of Police, Raipur. Surprisingly, the order was silent on the powers or functions of the Board. Regarding selection and tenure of DGP, the state government argued that an amendment would be required in the All India Service Rules. The state expressed its own opinion that 'there is no basis or scientific reasoning in prescribing two years of minimum tenure for the DGP to function/perform effectively.'

The Chhattisgarh Police Act was notified on 28 September 2007. The latest position, as summarized by the Thomas Committee, is given below:

State Security Commission: The state government has set up a State Police Commission, but the composition does not fully conform to any of the three models suggested by the Supreme Court insofar as the leader of the Opposition is not included as a member. The Commission has no judicial member either. Besides, it has only an advisory role and its reports will not be put up before the state legislature.

Selection and Minimum Tenure of DGP: Section 12 of the Act, which deals with the subject, is silent about empanelment by

UPSC and the tenure of two years is subject to superannuation. The grounds for removal of DGP contain clauses like administrative exigencies which could be misused.

Tenure of Field Officers: Section 14 of the Act gives fixed tenure to station house officers and District Superintendents of Police, but does not extend the same benefit to DIG Range or IG Zone. Here also, the grounds of removal contain provisions which could be misused.

Separation of Investigation from Law and Order: Section 32 provided for the creation of 'Special Crime Investigation Units', but there is no specific provision for separation at the police station level in the urban areas.

Police Establishment Board: Section 22 of the Act limits the functions of the Police Establishment Board, which are advisory and recommendatory, in respect of transfers/postings of deputy superintendents of police (DySPs). The intra-District and intra-Range transfers of even subordinate ranks (Inspector and below) do not fall within the purview of the Board. The Act is silent on the Board making any recommendation to the state government regarding postings and transfers of officers of and above the rank of Superintendent of Police. There is no mention of the Board reviewing the functioning of the State Police.

Police Complaint Authority: Only state-level Police Accountability Authority has been set up. There is no clarity about the selection of head of this body or selection of its other members. Besides, the recommendations of the Authority will not be binding on the administration. The Act does not provide for any district-level authority.

DELHI AND UTS

The Government of Delhi, in an affidavit filed on 30 March 2007, argued that 'while some of the directions are possible of being complied with, several of the directions, having regard to their important Constitutional implications, particularly concerning the accountability of the executive wing of the government, required modification/clarification'. It prayed that in respect of the Union Territories, the Court may clarify/modify its orders on the following points:

   i.   creation of a SSC in each Union Territory;
  ii.   preparation of a panel of three senior-most officers for the purpose of selection of DGP by the UPSC;
 iii.   appointment of DGP for a minimum tenure of at least two years irrespective of his date of superannuation by clarifying that the DGP shall have, as far as possible, a tenure of at least two years subject to superannuation;
  iv.   minimum tenure of the Inspector General of Police and other officers;
   v.   vesting of appellate powers in Police Establishment Board; and
  vi.   creation of Police Complaints Authorities.

The latest position is summarized below:

State Security Commission: On 7 February 2013, an order constituting SSC for all the UTs (except Delhi) was issued. Home Secretary will be chairman of the SSC. The Commission is however dominated by government representatives. There is only one independent member, the other members, apart from Home Secretary, being the Chief Secretary/Administrator and Joint Secretary (UT) MHA.

Appointment and Tenure of DGP/Field Officers: Government of India is not in favour of involving the

UPSC in preparing the panel of officers for selection of DGP. Government also does not favour a fixed tenure and is opposed to giving that irrespective of superannuation on the ground that it would have legal and administrative repercussion. The Government agrees that senior level police functionaries should have a minimum tenure of two years but only 'as far as possible.'

Separation of Investigation from Law and Order: This is claimed to have been affected in Delhi.

Police Establishment Board: Boards have been set up in all the UTs 'as per availability of officers in a particular UT.' Government however does not favour these Boards being given appellate functions.

Police Complaints Authority: A notification was issued on 29 January 2018 constituting a single Police Complaints Authority for Delhi comprising the chairperson, who would be a retired High Court judge and three other members who would be selected from a panel prepared by the Chief Secretary, Delhi after consultation with the Lok Ayukta and the chairman, Public Grievance Commission. Its mandate would be to inquire into serious misconduct against any police personnel either *suo moto* or on complaint. Serious misconduct would include death, grievous hurt and rape or attempt to rape in police custody, arrest or detention without due process of law and extortion or land grabbing or any other incident involving serious abuse of authority. The recommendations of the Authority shall be 'ordinarily binding, unless for reasons to be recorded in writing, the government decides to disagree with the finding of the Authority.'

Earlier, authorities for all the UTs had been constituted through a notification issued in March 2010. PCAs for Daman and Diu, Dadar and Nagar Haveli and Lakshadweep had only one member who may be a retired District Judge or a retired civil service officer of the rank of Additional Secretary or above, or a person having 10 years of experience in law as a judicial officer, public prosecutor, lawyer or professor of law or a retired officer with experience in public administration. PCAs for Puducherry, Andaman and Nicobar Islands and Chandigarh comprised the chairperson and two members. The chairperson may be a retired High Court/District judge or a retired civil service officer of the rank of secretary.

The Government of India set up a Police Act Drafting Committee headed by Soli Sorabjee. It drafted a Model Police Act in 2006. Consultations were held at different levels by the chief minister of Delhi and the home secretary, Government of India. The Act has, however, yet to be passed.

GOA

Goa Police Bill, 2008 was introduced in the state legislature and a select committee was constituted to examine the bill. The bill however lapsed in 2012. The status of compliance in the state is summarized below:

State Security Commission: It was constituted through an order dated 3 April 2007 purportedly on the NHRC model, though there are deviations. The Lok Ayukta or a retired judge of the High Court or a member of the NHRC is not included in the body. It is also not clear that the recommendations of the Commission shall be binding on the authority concerned. In its latest affidavit (July 2013), state government took the stand that this direction 'affects the Constitutional distribution of powers.'

Selection and tenure of DGP/Field Officers: The state government has taken the plea that these appointments are done by the Ministry of Home Affairs and that therefore the state has no role to play in compliance with these directions.

The state sent a letter to the MHA to take 'appropriate and suitable measures' in compliance with these directions. Regarding field-level postings at junior levels, the state government assured that they will be given at least two years.

Separation of Investigation from Law and Order: The state does not have any town or urban area with a population of 10 lakh or above and, therefore, it sought exemption from the direction to separate investigation from law and order. It has nevertheless assured that separation would be done as far as possible.

Police Establishment Board: It was constituted through an order dated 15 February 2007. The order however does not specify that the recommendations of the Board regarding the posting and transfer of officers of and above the rank of Superintendent of Police shall be given due weightage by the state government and normally accepted.

State Complaints Authority: There is only state-level Complaints Authority. Need for a district-level authority was not felt as Goa is a small state.

GUJARAT*

In an affidavit dated 3 January 2007, the state government pleaded that the Supreme Court's directions needed 'further consideration' and requested for some more time to comply with those. The very next day, however, another affidavit was filed on 4 January 2007 and it was quite defiant in tenor. It said that the setting up of a SSC would 'undermine the jurisdiction and power of a constitutionally established government in a State and would work as a parallel body which is not answerable or accountable to the people of the State'. Regarding the selection and tenure of DGP, it said that there was no provision for the empanelment of officers by the UPSC and that any such arrangement 'would not be in conformity with the statutory provision.' Regarding fixed tenure to other officers on operational duties, it said that such tenures result in the 'creation of vested interests' and that such an arrangement would 'act against the public interest.' On the separation of investigation from law and order, the state government argued that it will have to incur extra expenditure and mobilize more resources which may not be feasible immediately. The setting up of a Police Establishment Board, according to the state government, would 'not only run contrary to the democratic functions of the government, but would result into creation of a separate power centre comprising bureaucrats who are neither answerable nor accountable to the people.' The Police Complaints Authority, the state government expressed its apprehension, 'may undermine the Constitutional role and functioning of democratically elected executive government in the state.'

The state government contended that the Supreme Court's directions are in 'direct contravention of constitutional scheme of allocation of powers as enshrined in the Constitution' and that they 'impinge on the federal structure of the Constitution and undermine its basic structure.'

The state government nevertheless passed the Bombay Police (Gujarat Amendment) Bill, 2007, which was subsequently modified on 23 March 2008. Its provisions are briefly summarized below along with the observations of the Thomas Committee:

State Security Commission: Section 32A of the Act stated that the Security Commission shall comprise the chief minister, who would be the ex-officio Chairperson, Minister in-charge of Home Department, Chief Secretary, Director General of Police and two non-official members. The composition did not comply with any of the models suggested by the Supreme Court; the leader of the Opposition in the State Assembly has no place in the Commission and, besides, it had no judicial element. The Commission's role is purely advisory and it has no power to make binding recommendations. Its annual report is also not required to be placed before the legislature; the report is only to be submitted to the government for 'consideration and appropriate action.'

Selection and Tenure of DGP: The panel for selection of officers of the rank of DGP shall be drawn up by a Screening Committee at the state level; there is no reference to the UPSC. Besides, the DGP will 'ordinarily' have a minimum tenure of two years, which implies that he could be removed before the completion of his tenure. There is no mention of consultation with the SSC before removing the DGP from his post.

Minimum Tenure of Field Officers: Section 5B of the Act says that police officers on operational duties in the field shall 'ordinarily' have a minimum tenure of two years. Here also, the term 'ordinarily' is violative of Supreme Court's direction.

Separation of Investigation from Law and Order: Section 7A of the Act mentions that the state government may, having regard to the population in an area or the circumstances prevailing in such area, by an order, separate the investigating police from the law-and-order police wing in such area, and that the investigating police shall investigate the serious crimes such as offences punishable under chapters XII, XVI, XVII of the Indian Penal Code and other offences like terrorist activities, cyber offences, etc. The modalities of separation are, however, not spelt out.

Police Establishment Board: The Board shall comprise the Director General of Police, the Additional Director General of Police (Administration), an officer not below the rank of Inspector General of Police to be nominated by the state government and an officer not below the rank of

Deputy Secretary. The Board is supposed to be entirely a departmental body; the inclusion of a Deputy Secretary in it is contrary to the direction of Supreme Court on this point. The powers of the Board are limited to the transfer of officers of the rank of inspector and sub-inspector only. There is no mention, as was mandated by the Supreme Court, that the Board would also function as a forum of appeal to dispose of representations from officers regarding their promotion/ transfer or their being subjected to illegal or irregular orders. The Board was also not authorized to generally review the functioning of the state police.

Police Complaints Authority: The composition of the authorities, both at the state and the district levels, is different from what was prescribed by the Supreme Court. The state-level authority could be headed by a retired Principal Secretary of the state government. The district-level authority could be headed by the Superintendent of Police or the Additional District Magistrate of the district; it has no non-official members and instead MLAs have been injected into the authority. These violate the Supreme Court's directions on the point. Besides, the recommendations of the state and the district-level authorities are not binding on the concerned administrative authorities.

HARYANA*

The state government first passed an ordinance on 20 December 2006 to comply with the directions of the Supreme Court as the state legislature was not in session. Later, the state government passed a Police Act which was notified on 2 June 2008. Its provisions and the critique of Thomas Committee are given below:

State Security Commission: Section 26 of the Act says that the Board shall comprise the chief minister as Chairperson, Home

Minister, leader of the Opposition, a retired High Court judge or Advocate General, Chief Secretary, Secretary in-charge Home Department, Director General of Police as Member Secretary and three non-political independent persons. The functions of the Board are to only 'aid and advise' the state government in the discharge of its functions and responsibilities. There is no mention that the Board's report on the performance of police shall be placed before the state legislature.

Selection and Tenure of DGP: The selection of DGP will be done by the state government; there is no role of UPSC in the preparation of panel for the selection of the top cop. Besides, his tenure is limited to one year as against two years prescribed by the Supreme Court. The DGP could be removed without any reference to the State Police Board.

Tenure of Field Officers: Section 13 of the Act dealing with the tenure of officers posted on operational duties in the field mentions only the IG in-charge Range and SP in-charge District. There is no mention of DIG in-charge Range or officer in-charge police station. Here also, the minimum tenure is limited to one year only.

Separation of Investigation from Law and Order: Section 43 of the Act says that the state government shall create in every district, a specialized crime investigation unit for investigating economic and heinous crimes and that the personnel posted to this unit shall not be diverted to any other duty except under very special circumstances, with the written permission of the DGP.

Police Establishment Board: The state has created a Police Establishment Committee for 'administrative matters'. However, Section 34 of the Act which deals with the subject, does not specify whether the Committee will have powers to decide transfers, postings, promotions and other service-related matters of the officers. The Section is also silent on the Committee making appropriate recommendations to the state government regarding postings and transfers of officers of and above the rank of Superintendent of Police. The Committee has further not been authorized to act as a forum of appeal to dispose of representations from police officers. It has thus a very limited mandate.

Police Complaints Authority: Section 59 of the Act provides for the setting up of a Police Complaints Authority at the state level. Its composition is, however, not in conformity with the directions of the Supreme Court. The Authority will be headed by a retired Judge or a retired civil servant or a lawyer. In any case, it will only 'communicate' its findings to the state government, which would consider the same and take appropriate action. The Act makes a very cursory reference to the District Police Complaints Authority in Section 68. These will be set up 'as and when required'. Their composition is not clarified.

HIMACHAL PRADESH*

In its affidavit filed on 2 January 2007, the state government conveyed that action had been initiated to draft a new Police Act based on the model prepared by the Sorabjee Committee. In the next affidavit dated 5 April 2007, the state government stated that it had set up a State Police Board, issued a notification regarding the tenure of officers posted in the field, and decided to constitute a State Police Establishment Committee. It added that the investigation wing had been ordered to be separated from law and order and that the task of Complaints Authority had been entrusted to the Lok Ayukta of the state. The state subsequently passed the Himachal Pradesh Police Act, 2007. Its provisions, as analysed by the Thomas Committee, are as follows:

State Police Commission: The Act provides for a State Police Board, but its composition does not conform to any of the models recommended by the Supreme Court. There is no judicial component in the Board and the numbers of officials (10) in it outweigh the number of independent members (three).

Selection and Tenure of DGP: The Act provides for a Screening Committee headed by the Chief Secretary to prepare a panel for selection of DGP. It does not envisage any role of UPSC in the selection process. The DGP has not been given any minimum tenure and the removal clauses include 'administrative exigencies in the larger public interest' which is likely to be misused. The Act is silent on consultation with the State Police Commission before removal of DGP from the post.

Tenure of Field Officers: Section 12 deals with minimum tenure for field officers, but the rule has not been made applicable to Zonal IGPs and Range DIGs. Besides, the removal clauses include 'administrative exigencies in the larger public interest', which is likely to be misused.

Separation of Investigation from Law and Order: Section 78 of the Act provides for creation of a Criminal Investigation Unit in every police station for investigation of only 'serious offences'. This would amount to only partial separation of investigation from law-and-order functions.

Police Establishment Board: Section 56 of the Act creates a Police Establishment Committee but it is authorized to approve postings and transfers 'with the prior approval of the government'. There is no provision for the Committee to act as forum of appeal to dispose of representations of police officers regarding service matters. The Committee is also not authorized to review the functioning of state police.

Police Complaints Authority: The authorities have been created under sections 93, 94 and 95 of the Act. The composition of the state-level authority is, however, not in accordance with the directions of the Supreme Court. Besides, powers of the authority have not been defined. The district-level authorities are to be headed by Divisional Commissioners, which is again contrary to the direction of the Supreme Court. The recommendations of the authorities will not be binding.

JAMMU AND KASHMIR[193]

The state government, in its affidavit dated 23 April 2007, initially took the stand that it would not be expedient to implement the directions of the Court relating to the setting up of the SSC, separation of investigation from law and order and setting up the Police Complaints Authority in J&K. There was however some forward movement subsequently. The present position is summarized below:

State Security Commission: It was argued that creation of the SSC at this juncture would amount to 'de-stabilizing this tested and tried set up of security in as much as State of J&K is concerned'. The state having become a Union Territory on 31 October 2019, it was indicated that the new UT will become part of the Union Territories Security Commission which is headed by the Union Home Secretary.

Selection and Tenure of DGP/Field Officers: The state has not issued any order regarding the procedure to be adopted for the selection of the DGP. However, considering that the DGP J&K is actually selected by the Government of India in consultation with the Intelligence Bureau, the state may not

---

[193]The assessment is for the State before its bifurcation on 31 October 2019 into two Union Territories of Jammu and Kashmir and Ladakh.

be faulted on this score. Regarding tenure of field officers, the state government has not issued any order following the direction of Supreme Court. It however drew attention of the Court to old Government Orders of 1978, 1988 and 1991 on the subject.

Separation of Investigation from Law and Order: It was said that such a measure may be counterproductive as 'it will disturb the existing security set up in the state', and suggested that it may be kept in abeyance 'till normalcy returns to the State'. In a subsequent affidavit, the state indicated that it had set up separate crime detection cells in all police stations within the municipal limits of Srinagar and Jammu only.

Police Establishment Board: The Board has been constituted; it has a DGP and nine other senior police officers as against only four recommended by the Court. However, the order is silent about the role of the Board in respect of posting/ transfers of officers above the rank of Superintendent of Police. The order also does not contain any instructions regarding the role of the Board in reviewing the functioning of the State Police.

Police Complaints Authority: It was said in the affidavit that 'many disruptive agencies are active in the State of J&K and that there are large groups of separatist organizations with their links with terrorist outfits who are on the look-out for excuses for complaints against the functioning of the police and security agencies' and that therefore 'at this juncture creation of police complaints authority would give fillip to their movement and there is every likelihood that the creation of such an authority would open a forum for them to lodge false and frivolous complaints against the police personnel to demoralize them as well as to create impediments in their work of tackling terrorism'. The state government's stand appears convincing.

JHARKHAND

The state government, in an affidavit filed on 26 July 2006, while expressing its commitments to have 'better organization and efficient management of the institution of police' submitted that they did not have a SSC and that appointment of the Police Chief was done after due consultation with the Home Secretary, Chief Secretary and the chief minister/departmental minister. There was no separation of investigation and law and order in the state either. Complaints against police officers were generally examined by the senior hierarchy of the police department.

In another affidavit dated 4 January 2007, the state government submitted that it has 'taken the order of this Hon'ble Court in right perspective and has implemented some of the directions of this Hon'ble Court for bringing reforms in the functioning of police in the state of Jharkhand'. In the next affidavit dated 9 April 2007, the state government informed the Apex Court about the setting up of SSC, sending letter to the UPSC for empanelment of officers for appointment to the post of DGP, grant of minimum tenure to IG Police and other officers, separation of investigation in specified towns, constitution of the Establishment Board and setting up of Complaints Authorities at the state and district levels. The government also conveyed that it had initiated steps for the enactment of a new Police Act and that a sub-committee headed by the Home Secretary was working on the draft.

The status of compliance is summarized below:

State Security Commission: The state government constituted a SSC through an order dated 31 December 2006. The Commission however does not have any judicial component and, besides, the order did not specify that recommendations of the Commission shall be binding.

Selection and Minimum Tenure of DGP: The state government initially expressed its view that the panel for eligible officers should be drawn by the SSC. Subsequently, however, in an affidavit filed on 14 December 2012, it stated that it was awaiting 'guidelines' from the UPSC.

Tenure of Field officers: The state government issued a notification on 27 February 2007 providing for a minimum tenure of two years 'generally' for police officers on operational duties in the field.

Separation of Investigation from Law and Order: The separation has been accepted in principle and ordered in the urban areas of Ranchi, Jamshedpur, Bokaro and Dhanbad. The order, however, does not give any details of how the separation would be affected.

Police Establishment Board: This was created through a notification dated 19 February 2007, and further reconstituted through a subsequent notification dated 9 October 2009. The notification is however silent on the Court's direction that the state government may interfere with the decisions of the Board only in exceptional cases and after duly recording its reasons. The Board is also not authorized to act as a forum of appeal by officers subjected to illegal or irregular orders. There is no mention of the Board reviewing the functioning of police either.

Police Complaints Authority: The state government initially wanted the discretion to appoint retired IAS officers of the rank of Chief Secretary/Secretary to head the state and district-level authorities. Subsequently, however, the state government, in its affidavit of 9 April 2007, agreed that the authorities will be headed as mandated by the Court. The recommendations of the authorities are, however, not binding.

KARNATAKA*

The state government, in its first affidavit dated 30 December 2006, drew the attention of the Court to the Karnataka Police Act, 1963 and said that it had since initiated steps to enact a comprehensive Police Act, and that a Committee of officers had been set up to examine the recommendations of various Commissions and Committees constituted by the Union of India and the State of Karnataka on police reforms. The state government however challenged the Court's directions regarding the setting up of a SSC and argued that 'since such [a] body will not be accountable to the State Legislature, giving it mandatory authority will infringe upon the constitutional jurisdiction of the elected executive'. On the appointment of the DGP, the state government contended that UPSC had no role, as it was not responsible for the empanelment of police officers borne on the state cadre under the All India Services Act. Regarding giving a fixed tenure to the DGP, the state expressed its view that any change in his tenure would require an amendment in the All India Services Act. Regarding the tenure of field-level officers, the state government stated that transfers and postings in the state are governed by government order no. DPAR 4 STR 2004 dated 22 November 2001 and argued that the procedure being followed was in consonance with the directions issued by the Court. Regarding the separation of investigation from law and order, the state government stated that such separation already exists in all the Commissionerate irrespective of the population. On setting up a Police Establishment Board, the state government's response was evasive; it stated that all service-related matters of the police department are being dealt with under the provisions of the Karnataka Police Act, 1963 and the Karnataka Civil Service Rules. The constitution of the Police Complaints Authority, it contended, would amount to the 'duplication of the functions and responsibilities' of the existing institutions and bodies which look into grievances against the police and police personnel. The state government submitted another affidavit on 4 April 2007 in which it informed the Court that the state had prepared a Bill to amend the Karnataka Police Act, 1963, and stated that the provisions of the Bill would amount to 'substantial compliance' with the directions of the Court.

The Karnataka Police (Amendment) Act, 2012 received the assent of the Governor on 8 August 2012. Its provisions are summarized below:

State Security Commission: The SSC will be headed by the Chief Minister and would include the Home Minister, Leader of the Opposition in the Assembly, a retired Judge of the High Court nominated by the Chief Justice of Karnataka, Chief Secretary, Additional Chief Secretary/Principal Secretary in-charge of Home Department and Director General of Police. The charter of the SSC is in keeping with the directions of the Supreme Court and its recommendations shall be binding on the government. However, the Commission is heavily tilted in favour of the government and therefore it is unlikely that it will function 'independent of government control.'

Selection and Tenure of DGP: The Director General of Police shall be selected by the state government from amongst officers of the Indian Police Service in the rank of Director General of Police. The UPSC has not been given any role in preparing the panel of officers suitable for the promotion to the rank of DGP. Besides, the DGP will have a tenure of not less than two years subject to superannuation. The Court wanted it irrespective of superannuation.

Tenure of Field Officers: Officers who are on operational duties and are in-charge of police station, circle, sub-division, district or range shall have a minimum tenure of one year against two years as recommended by the Court.

Separation of Investigation from Law and Order: Every police station shall have two units, one dealing exclusively with crime investigation and the other dealing with law and order. The police personnel assigned to either of the units may however be deployed for any other purpose with the written permission of the superintendent of police or the commissioner of police.

Police Establishment Board: The Police Establishment Board will be headed by the Director General of Police and will include three senior-most police officers not below the rank of Additional DG with Additional DG (Administration) as its Convenor. The Board has been authorized to decide on transfers, postings, promotions and other service-related matters of officers of and below the rank of Deputy Superintendent of Police, and also make recommendations to the government regarding postings and transfers of officers of and above the rank of Additional SP. The government may modify the decisions of the PEB in exceptional cases only after recording its reasons, and shall normally accept the Board's recommendations regarding the postings and transfers of officers of and above the rank of Additional SP. There is no mention, however, of the PEB acting as a forum of appeal.

Police Complaints Authority: The State Complaints Authority would be headed by a retired High Court Judge while the District Police Complaints Authority will be headed by the Regional Commissioner. The Court wanted the District Complaints Authority to be headed by a retired District Judge. There is no indication that the recommendations of the Complaints Authority shall be binding on the government.

KERALA*

The state government, in an affidavit filed in April 2007, stated that it had already implemented the direction regarding separation of investigation and law and order but submitted that 'it faces so many practical difficulties to implement the other directions of this Hon'ble Court'. A democratic government, it was argued, has 'obligations to common people and elected legislature and have the responsibility to maintain law and order in the State'. The government therefore sought clarifications and also more time to implement the directions of the Supreme Court. It also conveyed that the state was taking 'earnest steps' to enact a new Police Act and that a committee of senior police officers had been constituted for the purpose. Through another affidavit filed on 25 February 2008, the state government conveyed that the Kerala Police (Amendment) Bill 2007 had been passed by the legislative assembly on 19 September 2007. Later, the state government passed the Kerala Police Act in 2011.

State Security Commission: Sections 24 and 25 of the Kerala Police Act, 2011 deal with the Security Commission. The Commission consists of Minister in-charge of Home Department, who will be the chairperson, Minister in-charge of Law, leader of the Opposition, a retired Judge of the High Court, Chief Secretary, Secretary Home Department and State Police Chief, who would all be ex-officio members, and three non-official members of eminence nominated by governor of the state, one of whom shall be a woman. It was given the power to 'frame policy guidelines for the functioning of the police in the State' and 'to issue directions for the implementation of crime prevention tasks and service-oriented activities of the police'. The directions of the Commission shall be binding on the police department. The government may, however, for reasons to be recorded in writing, fully or partially, reject or modify any recommendation or direction of the Commission.

Selection and Tenure of DGP/Field Officers: Section 18 of the Act provides for the appointment of DGP from among those officers of the state cadre who have already been promoted to the rank of DGP, taking into account 'the ability to lead the Police Force of the State, the overall history of service, professional knowledge and experience'. It does not give any role to the UPSC in preparation of the panel. Besides, the tenure of the DGP is subject to superannuation. Section 97 of the Act gives a minimum tenure of two years to the DGP, Inspectors General in-charge of Ranges, Superintendents of Police or Commissioners in-charge of districts and station house officers.

Separation of Investigation from Law and Order: Separation is provided for in Section 23 of the Act for Kochi, Kozhikode and Thiruvananthapuram. The proposal to extend the same to other districts was under consideration.

Police Establishment Board: This was constituted under Section 105 of the Act. It has however no power to decide transfer/posting of officers of and below the rank of Deputy SP. The Board is not authorized even to make recommendations regarding posting/transfer of officers of and above the rank of Superintendent of Police. The appellate authority of the Board is limited to officers of and below the rank of Inspector.

Police Complaints Authority: Authorities at the state and the district level were constituted under Section 110 of the Act through a G.O. issued on 17 February 2012. The authorities however have bureaucrats and police officers which are contrary to the Court's directions.

MADHYA PRADESH

The state government, in its affidavits dated 29 March 2007 and 5 March 2008, claimed that the state had complied with the Court's directions regarding the selection and minimum tenure of the DGP, minimum tenure for field officers and setting up of the Police Establishment Board, and added that it was in the process of drafting the Madhya Pradesh Police Bill. The bill is yet to be passed. Meanwhile, the status of compliance is summarized below.

State Security Commission: The state government constituted a State Security Council through an order issued by the Home Department on 13 December 2011. It was claimed to be on the Sorabjee model. The Council however is an advisory body whose recommendations will not be binding on the state government. There is also no provision for the report of the Council being placed before the state legislature.

Appointment and Tenure of DGP: The state government issued an order on the subject on 14 February 2007. However, it does not envisage any role for the UPSC in the selection process. The circumstances under which the DGP could be removed include a clause which speaks of 'failure to provide leadership in a grave situation of general law and order'. This could be subjectively interpreted.

Tenure of Field Officers: An order on the subject was issued on 14 February 2007. Officers could however be prematurely removed for 'failure in controlling a grave law and order situation'. They could also be removed on 'becoming otherwise incapable of discharging official responsibilities' instead of 'becoming incapacitated' as per Supreme Court's direction.

Separation of Investigation from Law and Order: The state government, vide its order dated 27 August 2012, approved the appointment of 400 additional police officers in the metropolitan areas/districts of Bhopal, Indore, Gwalior and Jabalpur. The additional staff was however to be used for both investigation and law-and-order duties. Separate staff for investigation has not been provided for.

Police Establishment Board: A Police Establishment Board was created on 14 February 2007, but it was stipulated that all proposals of the Board regarding transfer and postings of officers up to the rank of Dy.SP shall be forwarded to the state government which will have the right to modify them. Regarding officers of the rank of Superintendent of Police and above, it was stated that the Board shall send its recommendations to the state government which would give them 'reasonable weightage'. Representation from police officers against transfer/posting, etc. and against being subjected to illegal or irregular orders is to be merely forwarded by the Board to the state government for decision.

Police Complaints Authority: The state government, vide their order dated 30 August 2010, constituted a Complaint Boards at the district level. These Boards are headed by Minister in-charge (District) instead of a retired district and sessions judge, as stipulated by the Supreme Court. The other members of the Board are also not as per the Court's directions. Besides, the recommendations of the Board will not be binding. There is no state-level Complaints Authority.

MAHARASHTRA*

The Government of Maharashtra was quite defiant in its affidavit of 9 January 2007. It 'clearly and unequivocally placed on record its disagreement with the suggestions of the Petitioners as regards police reforms' and submitted that 'where the aforesaid directions of this Hon'ble Court in this case are inconsistent with statutory provisions in existence, so long as the said statutory provisions remain in force and there is no legislative vacuum, the directions in question will not apply'. On the issue of the SSC, the state government expressed its view that the setting up of such a body 'may lead to the emergence of another power centre outside the Government to influence the working of the police'. The state government expressed its reservation on other directions of the Supreme

Court as well and stated that there are 'compelling legal and practical reasons why the implementation of the directions is not feasible.'

The state government filed Review Petition (C) No. 439 of 2007 in the Supreme Court, giving it grounds for review of the entire judgment. The Review Petition, along with similar petitions filed by some other states, were all dismissed by the Supreme Court on 23 August 2007.

The state government later passed the Maharashtra Police (Amendment and Continuance) Act 2014 in partial compliance of the Supreme Court's directions.

State Security Commission: The Commission was constituted as per the Sorabjee model. The Additional Chief Secretary (Home) was however included in the SSC. Regarding the non-official members (five), they were to be nominated by the state government. It is very doubtful if the state nominees would show the necessary objectivity. Besides, the recommendations of the Commission will be advisory in nature.

Selection and Minimum Tenure of DGP: The DGP shall be selected by the state government from amongst the four senior-most police officers of the cadre. UPSC was not given any role in the preparation of the panel. Besides, the DGP's tenure is subject to superannuation.

Tenure of Field Officer: The police officer shall normally have a tenure of two years. The state government however retained the power of mid-term transfer of officers in public interest and in administrative exigencies. These powers could always be misused.

Separation of Investigation from Law and Order: The Act is vague on this point. It merely says that local Crime Branch and Detection and Investigation cells in each police station shall concentrate on investigation of crimes and not be entrusted with law and order, security and other duties ordinarily. The separation arrangement is weak as it would apply 'ordinarily'.

Police Establishment Board: Two Police Establishment Boards were constituted at state level, one at the Range level and a fourth one at the Commissionerate level. The state-level Board, headed by the Additional Chief Secretary, is contrary to the Court's directions. The Court wanted it to be a purely departmental body. Besides, there should have been only one Board at the state level. The state government has the power to give overriding directions which will be binding on the Board. Besides, the Board has not been given any power to review the functioning of police in the state.

Police Complaint Authority: Complaints Authorities have been set up at the state and district levels. The composition of the authorities is however not in keeping with the Court's directions. Besides, the state government has the power to reject the report of the State Complaints Authority. The state government had earlier taken the stand that recommendation of any authority can never be binding on it and that such a direction is 'inconsistent with and contrary to the procedure laid down by the Constitution'. What is worse, there are provisions which could unduly penalize the complainants.[194]

MANIPUR

The north-eastern state of Manipur was prompt in reasonably complying with the Court's directions.

---

[194]I had an occasion to call on the chief minister of Maharashtra on 20 May 2015. I gave him a written representation, saying that the Act was against the letter and spirit of the Supreme Court's directions of 2006 and requesting him that the Act be suitably amended to bring it in conformity with the Court's directions. The chief minister, Devendra Fadnavis, was very courteous.

State Security Commission: The Commission was constituted through an order of the governor on 31 March 2007. The minister in-charge (Home Department) was made the ex officio chairperson. Other members included the leader of the Opposition, the chief secretary, five independent members and the DGP, who was made ex officio secretary. The state followed the model prescribed by the Sorabjee Committee.

Appointment and Tenure of DGP/Field Officers: The state government accepted the procedure prescribed by the Supreme Court. The police chief was also given a minimum tenure of two years 'except in those conditions where the officer is to retire within less than two years'. Police officers on operational duties were also given a minimum tenure of two years through the order of the governor dated 28 December 2006.

Separation of Investigation from Law and Order: The separation was not effected because the state does not have any town or urban area with a population of more than 10 lakh.

Police Establishment Board: The Board was authorized to decide transfers/postings of officers of the rank of DySP and below only. Regarding officers of the rank of SP and above, the Board would make recommendations. It was not explicitly laid down that the government will give due weight to those recommendations, as was desired by the Court. The Board was also not authorized to function as a forum of appeal for disposing of the representations of police officers subjected to illegal or irregular orders or to review the functioning of state police.

Police Complaints Authorities: Complaints Authorities were set up. The independent members of the state-level authority are however all bureaucrats. At the district level, the authority is headed by a retired district judge. The recommendations of the authorities are not binding on the government.

MEGHALAYA*

The Meghalaya Police Act, 2010 was notified on 7 February 2011.

State Security Commission: Section 36 of the Act deals with setting up of the SSC, which will function as a 'watchdog body'. Its composition is however heavily tilted in favour of the government and there is no judicial component in it. The recommendations of the Commission will be binding only 'to the extent feasible'.

Selection and Tenure of DGP/Field Officers: Section 6 of the Act deals with the selection/tenure of the DGP. It states that the state government shall appoint a DGP from amongst the five eligible senior-most officers of the cadre who have been empanelled for promotion to that rank by the SSC. The UPSC is not given any role in preparing the panel of suitable officers. Besides, the DGP has been given tenure of one year only and he could be shifted in 'public interest'. Field officers shall have a minimum tenure of two years.

Separation of Investigation from Law and Order: The state has no city with a population of 10 lakh or more.

Police Establishment Board: A PEB was constituted but it can only recommend transfer/posting of junior officers. There is a Review Committee headed by the chief secretary which will make recommendations about the transfer/posting of officers of the rank of IG/Additional DG.

Police Complaints Authority: There is a state-level accountability commission, but there is no mention of any district-level authority. The state-level authority is also not headed by a retired judge of the Supreme Court/High Court. It could be headed by a retired civil servant not below the rank of principal secretary or a retired police officer not below the rank of an IGP or a retired officer with experience in public administration.

MIZORAM*

The Mizoram Police Act was passed on 19 December 2001.

State Security Commission: The Commission was constituted but its composition is not as per the directions of the Court. There is no judicial element in it.

Selection and Tenure of DGP/Field Officers: The DGP was given a fixed tenure but it was not irrespective of superannuation. Field officers were also given a tenure of two years. Grounds for prematurely terminating the tenure include the need to fill up a vacancy caused by promotion, transfer or retirement.

Separation of Investigation from Law and Order: The state government sought exemption from this direction in view of its thin population and small police force.

Police Establishment Board: A Police Establishment Board was constituted under the chairmanship of DGP and including the IGP, DIG (Range), AIG I and AIG II. It was clearly laid down that the state government may interfere with the decisions of the Board in exceptional cases only after recording its reasons for doing so.

Police Complaints Authority: Complaints authorities have been constituted. However, the state-level authority has no independent members while the composition of the district-level authority is not in keeping with the Court's directions.

NAGALAND

The state may have witnessed the longest and the most threatening insurgency in the Northeast, but it showed the utmost respect to the directions of the Supreme Court. In its first affidavit filed on 3 January 2007, the state government endorsed the views of the Supreme Court on 'the requirement for reform in the functioning and administration of police and, in principle, agree that such reforms must be incorporated in the Police Act'. The state government however added that 'the peculiar conditions prevailing in the state of Nagaland deserve to be placed on record to highlight the various constraints faced by the state in complying with the directives of the Hon'ble Court'. Two other affidavits were filed on 10 April 2007 and 18 August 2007.

The status of compliance under different heads is as follows:

State Security Commission: The state government constituted a SSC on the model recommended by the Ribeiro Committee through a notification issued on 30 March 2007. The one minor flaw in the notification was that the Commission was not given the role to evaluate the performance of the state police or asked to prepare a report thereon to be placed before the State Legislature.

Selection and Tenure of DGP/Field Officers: Notifications regarding the selection and tenure of DGP and tenure of officers on operational duties are fully in keeping with the Court's directions.

Separation of Investigation from Law and Order: Orders were also issued to separate the investigating police from the law-and-order police with the proviso that this would be within available budgetary and manpower availability.

Police Establishment Board: The order regarding the setting up of Police Establishment Board was, however, flawed. A committee was constituted comprising the chief secretary, home commissioner, commissioner of Nagaland and the DGP through a notification dated 23 June 1998. Subsequently, through an order dated 17 January 2007, an Establishment Board was set up, but it was given power to post and transfer only sub-inspectors/assistant sub-inspectors (SIs/ASIs). Another order was issued on 23 June 2008 to cover the ranks of Superintendent of Police and above but it was not in keeping with directions of the Supreme Court, which mandated that the Police Establishment Board to be purely a departmental body. The Board was also not authorized to review the functioning of the police and is a recommendatory body only.

Police Complaints Authority: State-level authority was constituted, vide notification dated 30 March 2007. The notification was, however, silent on the recommendations of the authority being binding. District-level authorities were not constituted.

ODISHA

The state government had taken a very positive stand in the initial stages before the Court. It conceded that the police needed to be reformed and promised that the state government would carry out whatever directions were issued by the Court. After the judgment in 2006, however, there was a noticeable change in the response of the state government. It was cold and non-compliant, reflecting probably the change in the mindset of the executive at that time.

State Security Commission: The state government has not constituted the SSC which was essential to insulate the police from extraneous pressures. The Odisha Police Bill, which is yet to be passed, however, provides for SSC, though its composition does not conform to the Court's directions and the body is dominated by government officers.

Selection and Tenure of DGP/Field Officers: The state government issued a notification on 6 April 2007 regarding the selection of DGP, but it did not agree to officers being empanelled for the purpose by the UPSC. The notification said that the DGP shall continue in office as far as possible for a minimum period of two years. The state government conceded two-year tenure for officers on operational duties, but here also it said that the tenure shall normally be two years. Additional provisions were inserted to give the state government greater latitude in removing officers before the completion of their tenure.

Separation of Investigation from Law and Order: The separation is said to have been carried out in Cuttack and Bhubaneswar, though the notification of 6 April 2007 does not spell out the mechanics of separation.

Police Establishment Board: The Board was constituted, but was not given the authority to make any recommendation in respect of officers of the rank of Superintendent of Police and above, as stipulated by the Apex Court. The Board was also not authorized to act as a forum of appeal to dispose of representations from officers regarding their being subjected to illegal orders.

Police Complaints Authority: The Authority was constituted at the state level but powers were vested in the Lokpal. This was a deviation from the Court's directions. Besides, there was no provision for any independent members in the authority. The recommendations of the Authority will be dealt with in accordance with the procedure laid down in the Orissa Lokpal and Lok Ayukta Act, 1995. At the district level, no Complaints Authority was constituted.

PUNJAB*

The Punjab Police Act was passed in 2007.

State Security Commission: It was constituted but its composition does not conform to any of the three models prescribed by the Supreme Court. It comprises only government functionaries and there are no independent members in it. Besides, its recommendations will not be binding on the government.

Selection and Tenure of DGP: The procedure for appointment of DGP is silent on the criteria for selection and his tenure is subject to superannuation. Besides, the DGP could be removed prematurely for special reasons which are to be recorded in writing. On 21 September 2018, the state government passed an amendment to the Act, stating that it shall select the DGP from amongst the IPS officers from a panel of at least three eligible officers who would be having not less than 12 months of service left on the date of appointment. The panel shall be prepared by a committee comprising the chief secretary, principal secretary (Home) and the outgoing DGP or an expert in internal security. The DGP so appointed shall have a tenure of not less than two years, irrespective of his date of superannuation. The UPSC has not been given any role in preparing the panel, as was mandated by the Supreme Court.

Tenure of Field Officers: Police officers on operational duties are assured a minimum tenure of only one year which is extendable to a maximum of three years.

Separation of Investigation from Law and Order: The separation has been carried out in five districts of the state, namely, Jalandhar, Ludhiana, Amritsar, Patiala and Bhatinda. Recently, on 6 October 2020, the state government set up the

Punjab Bureau of Investigation to separate investigation from law and order.

Police Establishment Board: The Board has been constituted but it is not authorized to make any recommendations on the postings or transfers of officers of and above the rank of Superintendent of Police. It is also not authorized to function as a forum of appeal for disposing of representations from officers regarding their promotion, transfer or being subjected to illegal or irregular orders.

Police Complaints Authority: These have been set up, but their composition and functions have not been defined.

RAJASTHAN*

The state government set up a committee headed by the principal secretary (Home) to prepare a draft of Rajasthan Police Act. This was further examined by a high-level committee headed by the state home minister. The Rajasthan Police Act was passed in 2007.

State Security Commission: Sections 21 to 26 of the Act deal with the State Police Commission. Its composition does not conform to any of the models recommended by the Supreme Court. Besides, the Commission's role is limited to advising and assisting the state government and communicating its views periodically on the performance of the police. It is thus a toothless body and will not be able to ensure that 'the state government does not exercise unwarranted influence or pressure on the state police,' as was desired by the Court.

Selection and Tenure of DGP/Field Officers: The DGP shall be appointed from a panel, in the preparation of which the UPSC has no role. The parameters of empanelment are also not specified. The state thus wishes to keep its leverage in appointing the Police Chief. The Court's direction regarding tenure of field officers has, on the whole, been complied with in sections 14, 15, 16, 17 and 19 of the Act.

Separation of Investigation from Law and Order: The state government has been authorized, under Section 42 of the Act, to create in such police stations as it may decide from time to time, a separate Crime Investigation Unit headed by an officer not below the rank of sub-inspector of police. The state government's response on this point is rather half-hearted.

Police Establishment Board: Section 28 of the Act provides for the setting up of a Police Establishment Board. Its power of transfers and postings is rather vague insofar as the Board has been given power to transfer subordinate ranks from one Range to another only. The Board has no authority to make any recommendation regarding postings and transfers of officers of the rank of Superintendent of Police and above. Besides, the Board has not been authorized to function as a forum of appeal or to undertake review of police functioning.

Police Complaints Authority: Chapter IX of the Act deals with police accountability. Accountability committees have been set up at the state and district levels, though there are variations from the Court's direction in their composition. The State Committee will be headed not by a retired Judge of the Supreme Court or High Court, as was mandated by the Supreme Court, but by one of the independent members of the Committee. The selection of members of the accountability committees is left entirely to the discretion of the state government. Besides, the recommendations of the Authority will not be binding. The District Committee is also not headed by a retired district and sessions judge; it would comprise four persons of eminence and one officer of the rank of Additional Superintendent of Police, who would act as member-secretary. The government shall appoint one of the independent members as chairman of the District Committee. The Committee would merely send its recommendations to the disciplinary authority concerned.

SIKKIM*

The Sikkim Police Act was notified on 30 July 2008.

State Security Commission: Sections 39, 40 and 41 of the Act deal with setting up of the SSC. The body has a preponderance of official members and as such its composition is flawed.

Selection and Tenure of DGP/Field Officers: The DGP is to be selected by a Screening Committee comprising the chief secretary, additional chief secretary (Planning) and principal secretary (Personnel). The role of the UPSC in the preparation of a panel of suitable officers for elevation to the rank of DGP has not been recognized. Besides, the tenure of the DGP is subject to superannuation and he could be removed prematurely without any reference to the SSC. Section 11 of the Act gives two-year tenure only to the Superintendent of Police and the station house officer.

Separation of Investigation from Law and Order: Separation is dealt with in Section 97 of the Act, which creates a Special Crime Investigation Unit at the police station level in such crime-prone areas or urban areas as considered necessary.

Police Establishment Board: It is dealt with in Section 52 of the Act. The transfer or posting of Deputy Superintendents of Police are, however, kept out of the purview of the body which is also not authorized to function as a forum of appeal for disposing of representations from police officers regarding their being subjected to illegal or irregular orders. The Board is authorized to make appropriate recommendations to the state government regarding the postings and transfers of police officers of and above the rank of Deputy Superintendent of Police for due consideration only. There is no indication that the recommendations will be given due weightage.

Police Complaints Authority: There is only a state-level Complaints Authority in view of the small size of the state and the small number of complaints. The recommendations of the Authority are, however, not binding on the persons or institutions concerned.

TAMIL NADU*

The state government initially took a somewhat defiant stand. It argued in its affidavit dated 5 April 2007 that 'Courts have no power to pass directions by way of judicial order to affect the legislative autonomy of the State'. It expressed its reservations on the direction regarding setting up of SSC. Accepting the proposal in principle, the state argued that it is necessary to ensure that the composition and working of the Commission do not impinge upon the separation of power and accountability as envisaged under the Constitution. On the appointment of DGP, it said that fixing a statutory rigid tenure may lead to several practical difficulties and contended that the government needs to have absolute freedom in selecting the most suitable officers for the post of the DGP. Referring to the Court's direction that the panel of suitable officers for promotion to the rank of DGP shall be prepared by the UPSC, the state stated that this would seriously prejudice the autonomy of the state under the scheme of the Constitution which is federal in character. The state also disagreed with the Court's recommendations to set up Police Complaints Authority at the state and district levels on the ground that these will act as parallel authorities to the existing constitutional remedies.

In due course, however, the state government passed the Tamil Nadu Police (Reforms) Act in 2013.

State Security Commission: The Commission was constituted, vide sections 5 and 6 of the Act. However, its composition does not follow any of the three models prescribed by the Court. The SSC has chairpersons of the Tamil Nadu Public Service Commission, State Human Rights Commission, State Women's Commission, and State Minorities Commission as ex-officio members. They are all government nominees and therefore could not be considered independent. Besides, it is not clear if the recommendations of the government will be binding on the state government.

Selection and Tenure of DGP: The DGP will be selected from a panel of five officers prepared by the UPSC and will have tenure of two years. The Court had wanted the UPSC to prepare a panel of three officers only. The intention appears to be to give more latitude to the chief ministers. Besides, the grounds for removal of DGP include other administrative grounds to be recorded in writing. This provision could be misused.

Tenure of Field Officers: Officer in-charge of police station, Superintendent of Police in-charge of district and commissioner of police have been given tenure of two years under the Act, which is otherwise silent about the tenure of DIG in-charge Range or IG in-charge Zone. The officers may be transferred on administrative grounds to be recorded in writing.

Separation of Investigation from Law and Order: Section 9 of the Act provides for separation in every police station except those specifically designated as crime police stations. On 20 March 2019, the office of the DGP issued an order, clarifying the staffing pattern for Chennai and the other cities/districts. It was strictly laid down that police officers of the investigation wing shall not be diverted to any bandobast work except with the prior approval of the zonal inspector general of police/commissioner of police.

Police Establishment Board: The Act provides for several tiers of Police Establishment Board: one for officers of the rank of Superintendent of Police and above up to the rank of IG only, another for officers of and below the rank of Additional Superintendent of Police, and Boards at zonal, range, city and district levels. The DGP alone (and not the Police Establishment Board) will send proposals for officers of and above the rank of IGP. It is not clear if the recommendations of the Board will be given due weight by the government, which should normally accept them. The composition and functions of Police Establishment Committees at the four levels have not been clarified. The Board has also not been given the power to generally review the functioning of police in the state.

Police Complaints Authority: Complaints authorities have been established at the state and district levels. These authorities are however headed by bureaucrats—by home secretary at the state level and collector/DM at the district level. This is contrary to the Court's directions, which wanted them to be headed by retired judges. Besides, the authority will only make 'recommendations' to the state government for appropriate action.

TELANGANA

Telangana was carved out of Andhra Pradesh on 2 June 2014. The status of compliance in the state is summarized below.[195]

State Security Commission: The Commission has not been constituted so far.

Selection and Tenure of DGP: Telangana has passed the Telangana Police [Selection and Appointment of Director

---

[195]Based on information furnished by the office of DGP (Telangana).

General of Police (Head of Police Force)] Act, 2018. Section 3 of the Act says that the DGP shall be appointed by the state government from amongst the officers of the Indian Police Service in the rank of DGP 'on the basis of their length of service, very good history of service, professional knowledge and ability to lead police force in the State.' The DGP shall have a minimum tenure of two years subject to retirement in accordance with the rules under the All India Services Act, 1951. The role of the UPSC in preparing a panel of officers suitable for promotion is ruled out. Besides, the appointment is contingent on retirement and not irrespective of superannuation, as directed by the Court.

Tenure of Field Officers: Officers are being given a two-year tenure subject, however, for administrative reasons.

Separation of Investigation from Law and Order: In all urban police stations in major commissionerates, there are crime inspectors to deal with the investigation of crimes. The station house officer deals with law-and-order problems. In other districts, there is a separate central crime station to deal with the investigation of cases.

Police Establishment Board: Boards have been established at state/zonal/range/commissionerate/district levels.

Police Complaints Authority: Such authorities have not been constituted yet.

TRIPURA*

The Tripura Police Act, 2007 was passed 'to redefine the role, duties and responsibilities of the police service in the context of the emerging challenges of policing and security of the State, the imperatives of good governance, and respect for human rights.'

State Security Commission: Section 20 of the Act provides for a state police board. Its composition however does not conform to any of the models prescribed by the Supreme Court. The leader of the Opposition does not figure in the composition. Besides, the recommendations of the Board are not binding. Its report is also not required to be placed before the state legislature.

Selection and Tenure of DGP/Field Officers: The selection and tenure of DGP are dealt with in sections 5 and 6 of the Act. The UPSC has not been given any role in preparing the panel of officers, as was directed by the Apex Court. Besides, his tenure is subject to superannuation and the DGP could be removed without any consultation with the State Police Board. A minimum tenure of two years is given only to the station house officer, sub-divisional police officer and the Superintendent of Police in-charge district. It has not been extended to the DIG Range or the IG Zone.

Separation of Investigation from Law and Order: Chapter 7 of the Act provides for a crime investigation unit headed by an officer not below the rank of sub-Inspector in the police stations of crime prone areas.

Police Establishment Board: A Police Establishment Committee has been constituted, under Section 27 of the Act. Its powers are however limited. There is no indication that the Committee shall decide transfers, postings and other service-related matters of officers of and below the rank of Deputy Superintendent of Police. The Committee shall examine complaints from police officers regarding their being subjected to illegal orders, but it can only make appropriate recommendations to the competent authority for necessary action. There is no mention that the Committee would review the functioning of the state police.

Police Complaints Authority: Section 59 of the Act provides for the setting up of state-level police accountability commission. It is not mentioned that the chairperson would be chosen from a panel of names proposed by the chief justice of the High Court. Similarly, about the members also there is no clarity that they would be selected from a panel of names prepared by the State Human Rights Commission/Lok Ayukta/State Public Service Commission. The recommendations of the Commission are not binding. There is no provision for district-level accountability commissions.

UTTARAKHAND*

The Uttarakhand Police Act, 2007 was notified on 4 January 2008. The Uttarakhand Police (Amendment) Act was passed in 2018.

State Security Commission: Section 30 of the Act constitutes a state police board which is claimed to be on the model recommended by the Sorabjee Committee. Actually, however, it deviates from that. Apart from the chief secretary, the principal secretary (Home) has also been included in the Board and there are only two independent members as against the stipulation of five members. A police officer not below the rank of Additional Director General of Police has also been nominated as the secretary of the Board. There is thus a preponderance of official members. Besides, the State Police Board can only suggest and advise the state government on policy matters. Its recommendations will not be binding. The Supreme Court wanted the SSC to lay down the broad policy and give directions for the performance of preventive tasks and service-oriented functions of the police.

Selection and Tenure of DGP/Field Officers: The UPSC has not been given any role in preparing the panel of officers suitable for elevation to the rank of DGP. Besides, the DGP will have tenure of two years, subject to superannuation. The DGP could also be removed without any reference to the SSC. Officers in the field have been given a minimum term of two years except the station house officer who has been given a term of one year only. These officers could be removed, among others, on ground of public interest, a proviso which could be misused.

Separation of Investigation from Law and Order: The state does not have any town or urban area with population of 10 lakh or above and, therefore, the state government sought exemption from the direction to separate investigation from law and order. Section 50 of the Act nevertheless provides for the creation of special crime investigation units for a police district or a police station to investigate specified offences.

Police Establishment Board: Section 38 of the Act deals with setting up of Police Establishment Committee. It has however not been given power to function as a forum of appeal and also not authorized to review the functioning of state police. Besides, the state government has been authorized to alter or amend any decision of the Committee after recording its reasons for the same.

Police Complaints Authority: The Uttarakhand Police (Amendment) Act, 2018 constituted two District Police Complaints Authorities (DPCA)—one for the Kumaon region and the other for the Garhwal region. The DPCA will include a chairperson, who will be a retired district judge appointed by the state government from a panel of names proposed by the chief justice of the High Court or justice of the High Court appointed by the chief justice, and two members who will be appointed by the state government from amongst a panel prepared by the State Human Rights Commission, Lok Ayukta or State Police Service Commission. The DPCA shall inquire into complaints against officers of the rank of Deputy Superintendent of Police and below in cases of serious misconduct including death in police custody, grievous hurt or cases of rape and other instances of misuse of authority by police personnel.

Besides, there will be a State Public Complaints Authority headed by a retired judge of the High Court/Supreme Court and a maximum four other members. The state and district Police Complaints Authority shall have the power of a Civil Court. The recommendation made by the state/district Police Complaints Authority regarding disciplinary action against any police personnel, shall be binding on the state government.

UTTAR PRADESH

The attitude of the state government of UP was defiant from the very beginning. In an Interlocutory Application dated 21 December 2006, the state government took the stand that the establishment of the SSC 'would amount to a direct infringement of the rights of the state government and a dilution of the state government's authority.' Regarding Police Establishment Board, it argued that such a body would be 'against the established canons of the administrative system of the State.' Setting up of Complaints Authorities at the state and district levels, the Government felt, would be 'superfluous' and 'unwarranted.' The government expressed its objections on other directions of the Apex Court also.

A voluminous affidavit was submitted by the state government on 24 April 2007. The state government accused the Apex Court of issuing directions which are 'in direct contravention of the constitutional scheme of allocation of powers as enshrined in the VIIth schedule of the Constitution' and alleged that these would 'impinge upon the federal structure of the Constitution and undermine its basic structure'. The SSC would directly intervene in the day-to-day functioning of the state government; and amount to 'a direct infringement of the rights of the state government and a dilution of the state government's authority'. The state also expressed its opposition to the Court's directives on appointment of DGP, giving fixed tenure to officers performing operational duties, and separation of investigation from law and order. The Police Establishment Board, the state government contended, shall be 'totally against the established canons of the administrative system of the State' and that the Court's direction on this point was 'totally unworkable and may create chaos in administration'. Regarding complaints authorities, the state government argued that 'surfeit of statutory bodies to look into the complaints against the police is likely to result in adversely affecting the normal and routine functioning of the police'. The state government conveyed that it had, on 1 January 2007, constituted the UP State Police Reforms Commission to study different aspects of police administration and make recommendations for reforms.

The state of UP also filed a review petition, which was dismissed by the Supreme Court on 23 August 2007. Thereafter, on 29 August 2007, the state government submitted an application seeking six months' extension of time for complete compliance of the orders of the Court. It added that the state government had already constituted a Civil Services Board in 2001 and that, through an order dated 19 May 2007, it had been clarified that for police services the board shall comprise the principal secretary (Home) as chairman and principal secretary to chief minister and the DGP as members.

On 11 November 2008, the state government submitted for the first time its affidavit of compliance. The status, as summarised by the Thomas Committee in its final report, is enumerated below:

State Security Commission: The composition of the SSC does not follow any of the three models mentioned in the Supreme Court order. It does not include leader of the Opposition and a retired High Court judge. Besides, there is disproportionate representation of government functionaries (six) as against the non-officials (two) in the composition. The manner of selection of non-official members has also not been specified in the government order. The functions assigned to the Commission are at variance with the Supreme Court's directive. In any case, the Thomas Committee found that the Commission had not yet started functioning and that no meeting of the Commission had been held during the last two years ever since it was constituted. The state government subsequently, on 26 July 2013, reconstituted the Commission, accepting the Ribeiro model. The independent members of the Commission are however ex officio and therefore are not likely to be objective. It is unlikely that the commission would 'function independent of government control', as directed by the Supreme Court. The powers of the Commission are also very limited insofar as it would only lay down the guiding principles and not the broad policies. The Commission will give only suggestions and not directions for the preventive tasks and service-oriented functions of the police.

Selection and Minimum Tenure of DGP: The Committee found that no order had been issued on the subject, though the principal secretary (Home) had issued a letter to DGP indicating the selection procedure and tenure of DGP. The Committee, however, noted that the contents of this letter were at variance with the directive insofar as the DGP would be selected by a Committee comprising entirely of senior bureaucrats. The UPSC was not given the mandated role to prepare a panel of officers considered suitable for promotion to the rank of DGP. Besides, the letter did not spell out the process of empanelment or criteria for selection, and the minimum tenure of two years was subject to the incumbent's date of superannuation and not irrespective of it. The Committee also objected to 'failure of discharging his duties as DGP for any reason' being one of the conditions for premature removal of DGP.

Fixed Tenure of Field Officers: The state government had not issued any orders on the subject in compliance to the Court's directive. The state government had no reply to data pertaining to a two-year period from 1 June 2007 to 16 June 2009 furnished by the petitioner which showed that as many as 97 IPS officers were transferred at least five to 10 times each within that period in the state and that 144 of these transfers were effected within a month of posting of the officer. The state government has, in principle, not accepted the proposition of two-year tenure for the field police officers. It contends that it has to transfer officers in 'contingent circumstances and exigencies of ground situation.'

Separation of Investigation from Law and Order: The state government had not issued any order on the subject, though a letter had been sent to the DGP to separate crime investigation from law and order in inspector-level police stations by earmarking 4, 2 and 1 sub-inspector respectively for A, B and C category of police stations for investigation work. The state government argued that 'due to shortage of manpower it had not been possible to implement the system effectively in all the police stations.' However, the state government created 204,000 additional posts in the police department to augment its manpower. The Committee felt that 'the stated difficulty of the state government in effectively implementing this directive appears to be genuine and the steps taken by them to augment the police manpower are noteworthy.'

Police Establishment Board: The state government constituted four Police Establishment Boards: one each to deal with the state-level transfers of (i) assistant superintendent of police, (ii) deputy superintendent of police, (iii) inspectors and (iv) sub-inspectors and below. The Committee felt that the four Boards constituted by the state government would deal only with transfers and not with other service-related matters envisaged in the Supreme Court directive. Besides, the Boards were not authorized to function as a forum of appeal for police officers subjected to irregular or illegal orders, or to generally review the functioning of the state police. The government, through a GO dated 26 December 2010, constituted state-level Establishment Board to recommend transfers/posting of officers of and above the rank of Additional SP. However, there was no indication that the government will give due weight to these recommendations and normally accept them, as directed by the Court.

Police Complaints Authority: The state government has not taken any steps to constitute authorities at the state and district levels on the ground that there are a number of forums like the National Human Rights Commission, State Human Rights Commission and other national and state-level commissions which could be approached by the public with their grievances against the police.

The state government submitted two other affidavits, one on 5 December 2010 and the other on 4 January 2011. It argued that the SSC would function independent of government control, that the DGP will have a tenure of two years as far as possible, that the state government is sometimes constrained to transfer some police officer from one place to another having regard to contingent circumstances, that the GDP has been directed to initiate the process of separation of investigation from law and order, that Police Establishment Boards had been constituted at state, range and district levels and that constituting Police Complaints Authority in the context of existing internal and external review mechanisms would lead to uncertainties.

WEST BENGAL

The state government, in its first affidavit submitted on 2 January 2007, stated that they had set up a West Bengal Police Commission in 1996, and that the Commission had submitted its recommendations in two parts in 1998 and 2000. Out of the 83 recommendations of the State Police Commission, 69 had been accepted and 40 had been fully implemented, while the remaining 29 were in the process of being implemented. The state government assured the Court of its commitment to the cause of police reforms. In the context of Model Police Act drafted by the Sorabjee Committee, the state government set up a high-powered committee under the chairmanship of additional chief secretary (Home Department) to draft a new West Bengal Police Act and a new Kolkata Police Act.

The next affidavit was filed on 27 August 2007. The state government drew attention of the Court to its order of 30 March 2007 regarding the selection and minimum tenure of DG and IGP West Bengal. The order laid down that the DG and IGP West Bengal shall be selected by the state government 'from amongst the four senior-most officers of the state cadre of the Indian Police Service, who have either already been promoted to the rank of DG and IGP or are eligible to be promoted to such rank.' The order went on to add that 'once an incumbent has been selected for the above-mentioned post, he should have a minimum tenure of at least two years.' Regarding the minimum tenure of IG Police and other officers, the state government issued an order on 30 March 2007, which clearly stated that 'police officers on operational duties in the field...shall have a normal tenure of two years.' Regarding Police Establishment Board, the state government set up a West Bengal Police Establishment Board and a Kolkata Police Establishment Board through another order dated 30 March 2007. The former would be headed by the DG and IGP with three senior-most additional DGPs as members and the DIG

Police (Headquarters) as the convenor. This Board 'shall decide all matters of transfer, posting, promotion and other service-related matters of officers of and below the rank of Deputy Superintendent of Police'. The Board was also authorized 'to make appropriate recommendations to the state government regarding the posting and transfer of all officers of and above the rank of Additional Superintendent of Police' and it was clarified that the state government shall give due weight to these recommendations and normally accept them. The Police Establishment Board would also function as a forum of appeal. The Police Establishment Board for Kolkata Police would be headed by the commissioner of police and would comprise three-senior most additional commissioners of police as members and the deputy commissioner (Headquarters) as convenor.

The status of compliance, as summarized by the Thomas Committee in its final report, was as follows:

State Security Commission: The state government had issued a notification on 2 June 2010, constituting the West Bengal SSC with one year as its term of appointment. However, the Committee found that the composition of the Commission did not follow any of the three models mentioned in the Supreme Court order. The Committee was also surprised to find that the Commission was headed by the health minister and not by the chief minister, who held the Home portfolio.

Subsequently, through another affidavit on 24 December 2010, the state government conveyed that the SSC had been reconstituted with the chief minister as its head and included the leader of the Opposition in the State Assembly, a retired judge, a member of the West Bengal Human Rights Commission, the chief secretary and the DGP. The state government claimed to have chosen the NHRC model in the selection of members. Significantly, the recommendations of the SSC are to be binding on the state government.

Selection and Tenure of DGP: The state government issued a letter on 30 March 2007 to the DGP, intimating the 'principles to be followed' for the selection of DGP and prescribing minimum tenure for the incumbent. The order was silent about empanelment by the UPSC. Besides, the criteria for selection, as laid down in the letter, was found very sketchy and included a vague and subjective element like 'experience for leading the police force of the State'. The tenure of two years was also subject to superannuation. In the affidavit filed on 24 December 2010, the state government merely promised that it would issue appropriate order in compliance of the Hon'ble Court's direction.

Minimum Tenure for Field Officers: The state government issued a letter on 30 March 2007 to the DGP West Bengal and commissioner of police Kolkata, laying down the principles to be followed for the tenure of police officers on operational duties in the field. The Committee however found that conditions for premature removal of officers included vague and subjective elements. In the affidavit filed on 24 December 2010, however, the state government conceded that police officers on operational duties in the field shall have a prescribed minimum tenure of two years.

Separation of Investigation from Law and Order: The commissioner of police Kolkata had formed separate investigation wings in 10 police stations while the DGP West Bengal had formed separate investigation wings in 20 urban police stations in the first phase. The 24 December 2010 affidavit claimed that separation of investigation from law and order had been further extended in 10 more police stations under the jurisdiction of the Kolkata police and that steps were being taken for the constitution of separate investigation wings in all urban police stations phase-wise by sanctioning additional posts and filling up the vacancies.

Police Establishment Board: The state government set up a West Bengal Police Establishment Board and a separate Kolkata Police Establishment Board. The Committee found that the orders were 'broadly in consonance' with the directive, except that the Boards were not authorized to function as forums of appeal on representations from police officers on service matters (other than transfers/postings) and on their being subjected to illegal or irregular orders. The Committee found that both the state-level and Kolkata-level boards had become functional.

Through its affidavit filed in 2010, the state government pleaded that it may be allowed to set up Police Establishment Boards at district level also to decide posting, transfer and promotion of police officers below the rank of inspector, limiting the state-level board to decide on these matters in respect of police officers of and above the rank of inspector. The district level Board may be headed by the superintendent of police and two other senior officers of the district. It also expressed the view that the while the Police Establishment Board may function as a forum of appeal for disposal of representation of officers of the rank of superintendent of police and above regarding their promotion/transfer, the disciplinary matters be left to be dealt with under the existing set of laws, rules and regulations.

Police Complaints Authority: The state government, through a notification dated 2 June 2010, constituted a state-level Complaints Authority. The Committee however found that its composition did not conform to the Supreme Court directive. The term of the Authority was also one year only. Besides, the state government had not constituted any district-level Complaints Authority. Later, the state government informed, through its affidavit filed in 2010, that it had initiated action to reconstitute the state-level authority and constitute the district-level authority.

ASSESSMENT: DIRECTION-WISE

The states' compliance under different heads is summarized below[196]:

State Security Commission

i) Twenty-seven states have constituted SSC, either through Police Acts or government orders. Odisha is the only state which has not yet constituted the SSC.

ii) There are, however, sharp deviations from the Supreme Court's directions insofar as seven states have not included leader of the Opposition in the SSC and in 17 states there is no provision for an independent selection panel for the appointment of members who should function independent of government control. Bihar, Goa, Tamil Nadu and Punjab do not even provide for independent members in the SSC.

iii) The SSC recommendations are binding in only two states, Andhra Pradesh and Karnataka.

Selection and Tenure of DGP

i) Arunachal Pradesh and Nagaland are the only states which have fully complied with the judicial direction.

ii) Only five states (Andhra Pradesh, Arunachal Pradesh, Manipur, Nagaland and Tamil Nadu) have recognized the role of UPSC in preparing a panel of officers considered suitable for elevation to the rank of DGP.

iii) Only six states (Andhra Pradesh, Arunachal Pradesh, Madhya Pradesh, Nagaland, Tamil Nadu and Rajasthan)

---

[196]Based substantially on Commonwealth Human Rights Initiative's *Government Compliance with Supreme Court Directives on Police Reforms, An Assessment,* September 2021.

have given a minimum tenure of two years to the DGP. In 13 states, the tenure is subject to superannuation.

Tenure of Field Officers

i) Sixteen states (Andhra Pradesh, Arunachal Pradesh, Bihar, Gujarat, Himachal Pradesh, Kerala, Madhya Pradesh, Manipur, Meghalaya, Mizoram, Nagaland, Rajasthan, Sikkim, Tamil Nadu, Uttar Pradesh and West Bengal) have provided a minimum of two-year tenure to the field officers.

ii) Five states (Assam, Haryana, Karnataka, Punjab and Uttarakhand) provide only one-year tenure to some and not all ranks of officers on operational assignments.

Separation of Investigation from Law and Order

i) Seventeen states (Arunachal Pradesh, Assam, Bihar, Chhattisgarh, Himachal Pradesh, Karnataka, Kerala, Maharashtra, Meghalaya, Mizoram, Punjab, Rajasthan, Sikkim, Tamil Nadu, Tripura, Uttarakhand and Delhi) have taken measures to separate the investigative and law-and-order functions of the police.

ii) The remaining states are not opposed to this directive but have yet to initiate necessary steps for separation.

Police Establishment Board

i) Only two states (Arunachal Pradesh and Karnataka) have fully complied with this directive, though on paper all states have constituted Police Establishment Boards.

ii) Five states (Andhra Pradesh, Jharkhand, Manipur, Madhya Pradesh and Uttarakhand) have partially complied with the directive.

iii) The remaining states are non-compliant.

Police Complaints Authority

i) Twenty-three states have set up State Police Complaints Authority (SPCAs) while 18 states have constituted DPCAs.

ii) At the state-level, 10 states deviate from the requirement of a retired judge heading the Authority. At the district-level, 11 states do not provide for a district judge heading the Authority.

iii) Eight states (Arunachal Pradesh, Assam, Goa, Haryana, Kerala, Meghalaya, Mizoram and Uttarakhand) make SPCA recommendations binding. DPCA recommendations are binding only in four states (Haryana, Kerala, Mizoram and Uttarakhand).

iv) UP has not set up any complaints authority.

ASSESSMENT: OVERALL

An overall assessment of all the states was done, taking into consideration their response to the six directives of the Supreme Court. The states were given marks out of a total of 10.[197]

The results are categorized under the following heads (the score of each state is given in brackets):

Good (six states)
Andhra Pradesh (6), Arunachal Pradesh (6.5), Goa (6), Karnataka (6), Manipur (6.25) and Mizoram (6.25).

Satisfactory (three states)
Kerala (5.5), Nagaland (5.5) and Uttarakhand (5.5).

---

[197]The methodology adopted was to assign 2 marks each for compliance under State Security Commission, selection and tenure of DGP, Police Establishment Board and Police Complaints Authority while 1 mark each was allotted for compliance under tenure of field officers and separation of investigation from law and order.

Average (15 states)
Assam (4.25), Chhattisgarh (4.25), Delhi and UTs (4.75), Gujarat (4), Haryana (4), Jharkhand (4.75), Madhya Pradesh (4.5), Meghalaya (4.75), Odisha (4.5), Punjab (4.5), Rajasthan, (4), Sikkim (4.75), Tamil Nadu (4.75), Tripura (4.25) and West Bengal (4.5).

Poor (five states)
Bihar (3.75), Himachal Pradesh (3.75), Maharashtra (3.75), Telangana (3.75) and Uttar Pradesh (3.75).[198]

Fig. 1. Compliance Assessment (Overall)

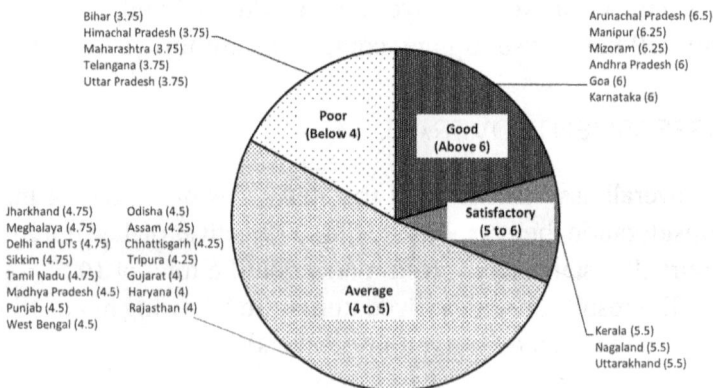

198 'Good' are states which have scored 6 or more marks, 'Satisfactory' are states getting marks between 5 and 6, 'Average' are states getting marks between 4 and 5 and those scoring less than 4 have been placed in 'Poor' category.

J&K has not been rated because the state government sought exemption from implementation of the directive regarding State Security Commission in view of the security situation in the state. It also argued that having State Police Complaints Authorities would lead to a flood of complaints by separatist elements against the police. Besides, the state DGP is selected by Government of India. In any case, the state was bifurcated into two Union Territories, Jammu and Kashmir and Ladakh, in 2019.

It would be seen that the smaller states (Arunachal Pradesh, Manipur, Mizoram, Nagaland, Goa and Uttarakhand) have shown better compliance than the larger states. Andhra Pradesh and Karnataka are the only big states which have shown reasonably good compliance. Kerala's compliance is also satisfactory. Significantly, all these three are southern states.

The majority of states (15) have shown just average compliance.

The states which figure at the bottom of the ladder are Bihar, Himachal Pradesh, Maharashtra, Telangana and Uttar Pradesh.

The assessment, it must be clarified, is based on affidavits given, orders issued by the state governments or provisions in the legislation on the subject. It does not reflect the ground situation.

7

RESPONSE OF GOVERNMENT OF INDIA

The response of Government of India left much to be desired.

RESPONSE TO NPC

In 1983, when the National Police Commission reports were forwarded to the state governments, they were asked merely to take appropriate follow-up action and told that:

> At some places in the 2nd Report (paras 15.24, 15.35 and 15.55) the Commission has relied on the observations and findings of the Shah Commission to arrive at certain conclusions. Government strongly repudiate all such conclusions. At several other places the Commission has been unduly critical of the political system or of the functioning of the police force in general. Such general criticism is hardly in keeping with an objective and rational approach to problems and reveals a biased attitude. Government are of the view that no note should be taken of such observations.

The hint was more than obvious, and it was not surprising therefore that the state governments conveniently put the major recommendations of the National Police Commission in cold storage.

SORABJEE COMMITTEE: MODEL POLICE ACT

As the PIL was making progress in the Supreme Court, the Ministry of Home Affairs, in an Office Memorandum dated 20 September 2005, recorded that 'it is necessary to replace the Police Act of 1861 in view of the changing role of police due to various socio-economic and political changes which have taken place in the country and the challenges posed by modern day global terrorism, extremism, rapid urbanisation as well as fast evolving aspirations of a modern democratic society.' A Police Act Drafting Committee (PADC) was, therefore, set up under the chairmanship of Soli J. Sorabjee in September 2005 to:

i) examine the Model Police Act prepared by the National Police Commission and other Draft Model Police Acts and suggest modifications as per the changing role/responsibility of police in view of the new challenges before it, especially growth and spread of insurgency/militancy/Naxalism, etc.

ii) suggest measures for attitudinal changes of police including working methodology, to elicit cooperation and assistance of the community rather than its distrust.

iii) emphasize the use of scientific investigation methods to strengthen the criminal justice system and enable the police tackle futuristic trends of organized crime including cyber crimes and technological advantages in the hands of criminals.

The new Police Act, it was emphasized, should 'reflect expectations of the people regarding the police in a democratic set up' and that the Act should address the concerns of 'human rights, weaker sections, women and the people belonging to scheduled castes/scheduled tribes.'

The Committee comprised six non-official members and four ex-officio members, besides a full-time secretary. The CHRI was invited to be a non-official member.

The Government of India perhaps wanted to demonstrate its commitment to police reforms and did not wish to be overtaken by a Supreme Court judgment on the subject. Two former prime ministers of India, V.P. Singh and I.K. Gujral, in a joint statement dated 10 November 2005, welcomed the Government of India's decision to constitute 'a national watchdog Committee for the expeditious implementation of police reforms.'

The Sorabjee Committee drafted the Model Police Act, 2006 which has 16 chapters comprising of 221 sections. The Committee was guided by the need to have a professional police 'service' in a democratic society, which is efficient, effective, responsive to the needs of the people and accountable to the rule of law. The Act provided for social responsibilities of the police and emphasized that the police will be governed by the principles of impartiality and human rights norms, with special attention to the protection of weaker sections, including minorities. It also contained a provision that the composition of the police will reflect social diversity.

The salient features of the Act are summarized below:

i)   The state government will ensure an efficient, effective, responsive and accountable police service for the entire state. It will lay down policies and guidelines so that the police performs its task in a professional manner, with functional autonomy.

ii) The state government shall appoint the DGP from amongst three senior-most officers of the State Police Service empanelled for the rank by the State Police Board. The DGP so appointed shall have a minimum tenure of two years, irrespective of his normal date of superannuation.

iii) An officer posted as station house officer in a police station or as an officer in-charge of a police circle or sub-division or as a superintendent of police of a district, shall have a term of a minimum of two years and a maximum of three years.

iv) The district magistrate will coordinate the functioning of the police with other agencies of district administration.

v) The primary ranks in civil police should ordinarily get three promotions on merit-cum-seniority criteria.

vi) The state government shall establish a State Police Board headed by the home minister as its chairperson and comprising the leader of the Opposition in the State Assembly, a retired High Court judge, the chief secretary, the home secretary, the DGP as member secretary and five non-political persons of proven reputation for integrity and competence. The Board will frame broad policy guidelines for promoting efficient, effective, responsive and accountable policing in accordance with the law.

vii) The state government shall constitute a Police Establishment Committee with the DGP as its chairperson and four other senior-most officers within the police organization of the state as members. The Committee shall recommend names of suitable officers to the state government for posting to all the positions in the ranks of assistant/deputy superintendents and above in the police organization of the state excluding the DGP.

viii) The role, functions and duties of the police were defined to include upholding and enforcing the law impartially and protecting the life, liberty, property, human rights and dignity of members of the public, promoting and preserving public order and protecting internal security.

ix) Each village in the district shall have at least one village guard enlisted by the district superintendent of police for a tenure of three years which may, depending on satisfactory performance, be renewed.

x) The state government shall appoint a commissioner of police for the metropolitan areas and other major urban areas with a population of 10 lakh or more.

xi) If and when the security of state in an area is threatened by insurgency, any terrorist or militant activity, or activities of any organized crime group, the Union government may, with the concurrence of the state government, declare such area as a Special Security Zone.

xii) The state government shall, in consultation with the DGP, issue guidelines with regard to constitution of Citizens' Policing Committees to promote community's participation in prevention and control of problems and for the protection of human rights.

xiii) There will be a Special Crime Investigation Unit in all urban police stations and crime-prone rural areas to investigate economic and heinous crimes.

xiv) The state government shall establish a state-level Police Accountability Commission and also District Accountability Authority to inquire into complaints or serious misconduct by police personnel.

xv) The state government shall take effective steps to ensure that the average hours of duty of a police officer do not normally exceed eight hours a day.

The recommendations were comprehensive. The Government of India should have, on the basis of Sorabjee Committee's recommendations, enacted the Model Police Act for Delhi and the Union Territories. That could have become the model for the other states, at least those where the same political party was in power. However, unfortunately, the

Model Police Act is yet to be legislated by the Government of India.

RESPONSE TO SUPREME COURT JUDGMENT

The Government of India's response to the Supreme Court's judgment on Police Reforms was lackadaisical.

The Cabinet Secretary, Government of India, in an affidavit filed on 3 January 2007, informed the Supreme Court as follows:

i) The Supreme Court judgment of 22 September 2006 had been sent to all the state governments and Union Territories on 26 September 2006 itself for information and further necessary action.

ii) The Model Police Act drafted by Soli Sorabjee Committee was presented to the Union home minister on 30 October 2006, and a copy of the Model Police Act had been sent to all the state governments for appropriate consideration.

iii) The Union home secretary had convened a meeting of all the chief secretaries and DGP of all the states on 14 November 2006 to discuss police reforms and all related issues.

iv) Another meeting had been held by the Union home minister with chief ministers of all states on 30 December 2006 to sensitize the state governments on police reforms, particularly in light of directions of this Hon'ble Court. The state governments, it was clarified, may bring in their legislations as expeditiously as possible since police is a state subject.

v) The Ministry of Home Affairs had considered the Model Police Act and was examining the same in consultation with other central ministries 'with a view to introducing in the current year legislation in the parliament for enacting a new Police Act applicable to the Union Territories.'

vi) A Committee called the Committee on National Security and Central Police Personnel Welfare, headed by the Union home minister, had been set up on 2 January 2007. It included the national security advisor, cabinet secretary, Union home secretary and director, Intelligence Bureau as members. Later, the Committee was enlarged with the inclusion of a retired Director General of a CPMF (Central Paramilitary Force) and a retired Chief Justice of a High Court.

Another affidavit filed by the Government of India on 12 February 2007 brought out the Government of India's reservations on the following points:

(a) Nomenclature: It was felt that it would be inappropriate to call the body 'National Security Commission' and preferred to call it the 'Committee on National Security and Central Police Personnel Welfare.'

(b) Composition: The Chiefs of the CPMF would be invited to the deliberations of the Committee if considered relevant or imperative. The government did not favour their being members of the Committee.

(c) Tenure: The government did not favour a tenure of two years to chiefs of Central Police Organizations and pleaded that 'flexibility needs to be made and maintained in the interest of the exigencies of service, morale of the senior officers and utilisation of special experience in specific circumstances.'

(d) Functions: The government also sought modification in the direction that the authority constituted will be required to review measures to upgrade the effectiveness of the Forces, ensure proper coordination amongst the various CPMFs on the ground that the existing institutions (Home Ministry, National Security Council, Cabinet Committee on Security, Cabinet Committee on Political Affairs and the Cabinet Committee of the Union Government) cater to these.

Yet another affidavit filed by the Government of India on 12 February 2007, in respect of the Union Territories, pleaded that the Hon'ble Court may be pleased to modify its directions relating to the creation of a SSC, preparation of a panel of three senior-most officers for the selection of DGP by the UPSC, giving a minimum tenure of two years to DGP irrespective of his date of superannuation, minimum tenure to the Inspector General and other officers, creation of a Police Establishment Board and Police Complaints Authority. In other words, the Government of India was not inclined to implementing any of the directions in the UTs.

The Cabinet secretary filed another affidavit on 29 March 2007, praying that the Court may be pleased to:

i)   clarify and modify the direction relating to creation of a National Security Commission, as envisaged in paragraph 31(7) of the judgment dated 22 September 2006;

ii)   modify the direction relating to the inclusion of the heads of the CPMFs as permanent members in any such authority;

iii) modify the direction relating to the tenure of Directors General of CPMFs;

iv)   modify the direction stipulating that such an authority will be required to review measures to upgrade the effectiveness of the Forces, ensure proper coordination amongst the various CPMFs and that the Forces are generally utilized for the purposes they were raised for.

It was claimed that 'there has been compliance with the directions issued by this Hon'ble Court' and that the government is fully committed to ensuring that all further and necessary steps shall continue to be taken with regard to the issues highlighted by the Hon'ble Court.

The Government of India's response thus has not been very positive. In fact, it had reservations on practically all the directions of the Apex Court. High-level meetings on 14 November 2006 by the Union home secretary and on 30 December 2006 by the Union home minister were held ostensibly to discuss compliance of the Supreme Court's directions, but it appears that the discussions were more on how to circumvent, or at least dilute, their implementation.

Briefly, the Government of India's response on the Court's directions was as follows:

State Security Commission: The Government of India was of the view that instead of setting up a SSC in each Union Territory, it shall create a Central Committee for the Union Territory Police (CCUTP). The government's argument was that there are only two UTs with a legislature and that it would be difficult for the other UTs to comply with the mandated composition of the SSC. The composition of the CCUTP violated the directions of the Apex Court while its functions were not defined.

Selection and Tenure of DGP: The government did not favour the empanelment of officers by the UPSC and argued that this would require amendment in the UPSC (Exemption from Consultations) Regulations. It further stated that giving two-year fixed tenure to the DGP would require changes in the All India Services Rules. Besides, if the DGP was given two-year tenure, similar provisions would have to be made for the administrator/chief secretary to ensure equality before the law. The Government of India also did not agree to give two-year tenure to chiefs of Central Police Organizations; it merely said that their tenure was 'generally' two years.

Minimum Tenure for Field Officers: The Government of India took the stand that there is 'normally' a two-year tenure for police officers on operational duties and that this is prescribed in the existing guidelines. It also said that if police officers were given a fixed tenure of two years, it would amount to discrimination against IAS officers. The argument was quite unconvincing, apart from the fact that the word 'normally' could be stretched either way to suit the government's convenience.

Separation of Investigation from Law and Order: Some UTs approached the Government of India for additional police officers to be able to comply with the directive. Puducherry asserted that separation had already been implemented at major police stations.

Police Establishment Board: The Government of India argued that the Police Establishment Board cannot have the functions of an appellate authority as that would dilute the functional control of the police chief.

Police Complaints Authorities: The government is of the view that creating Police Complaints Authorities will only add to the number of complaint mechanisms without improving the effectiveness of the police.

The most disappointing part of the Government of India's response has been its failure to enact a new Police Act for Delhi and the UTs.

PRIME MINISTER MANMOHAN SINGH'S OBSERVATIONS

Addressing a conference of the senior police officers on 15 September 2009, Prime Minister Manmohan Singh expressed the urgent need of a 'new age policemen'. He said:

> We need a new age policeman who is more professional,
> better motivated, suitably empowered, well trained
> and one who places greater emphasis on technology
> for investigation and other tasks... Each police station
> should aim at being self-sufficient and needs to be
> given the required resources in terms of anti-riot gear,
> better weapons, the nucleus of a mobile forensic unit
> and be connected to a networked criminal database
> management system.[199]

P. Chidambaram, the then Union home minister, criticized the
states for transferring officers arbitrarily and said that many
officers had been reduced to 'a football, to be kicked around
here and there, from one post to another, without regard to
the damage done to the job as well as the officer'.[200] He also
exhorted the state police chiefs to assert their authority:

> Why do you remain silent when arbitrary postings and
> transfers are made by the state government? Is it not your
> duty, as the head of the state police, to raise your voice
> not only on behalf of your officers but also on behalf of
> the people that you are duty bound to protect?

The observations made by the then prime minister and the
home minister were pertinent. However, the fact remains
that neither the UPA nor the NDA government has shown
seriousness in introducing reforms at the Centre or in states
where their party (by itself or in alliance with others) was in
power.

---

[199] Vishwa Mohan, 'Urgent need for a "new-age policeman": PM,' *The Times
of India*, 16 September 2009.
[200] PTI, 'Chidambaram asks police chiefs to raise voice against arbitrary
transfers,' *The Hindu*, 14 September 2019.

THE DELHI POLICE (AMENDMENT) BILL

The affidavits submitted by the Cabinet secretary, Government of India, on 3 January and 29 March 2007 contained a specific assurance to the following effect:

> The Ministry of Home Affairs has already considered the Model Police Act...clause by clause, under the chairmanship of [the] Union Home Minister, and is now examining the same in consultation with other concerned central Ministries, with a view to introducing in the current year a legislation in the Parliament for enacting a new Police Act, applicable to the Union Territories (the Union Territories being under the administrative control of the Home Ministry).

The Ministry of Home Affairs, it must be said to its credit, sent a letter to the chief secretaries of all states on 1 September 2009, drawing their attention to the Supreme Court's landmark judgment and asking them to ensure that 'these are implemented both in letter and in spirit'. The letter was actually issued by Gopal K. Pillai as home secretary after I met him and followed that up with a letter dated 27 August 2009 addressed to him. I had, along with my letter, enclosed a chart showing how the Supreme Court, the Second Administrative Reforms Commission and the Sorabjee Committee had made similar recommendations on vital aspects of Police Reforms. Pillai was good enough to enclose this chart in the letter which he sent to the chief secretaries of all states. Pillai was, however, a lone angel in the ministry. His enthusiasm for police reforms was not shared by the members of his fraternity and certainly not by the other officers of the ministry.

A series of consultations were held at different levels to finalize the Delhi Police Act. I remember having attended two of these, one presided over by the chief minister of

Delhi (Sheila Dikshit) and the other presided over by the Union home secretary, G.K. Pillai in the India International Centre on 10 April 2010. In due course, the proposals were finalized. However, the amendments recommended by the Delhi government in the Delhi Police Act, 1978 were very disappointing insofar as they did not conform to the guidelines laid down by the Supreme Court or the pattern of the Model Police Act, 2006 drafted by the Sorabjee Committee.

The Delhi Police (Amendment) Bill, 2010 was carefully examined by Common Cause, a reputed NGO. In a letter addressed to the home secretary, they deplored that the amendments proposed 'fall woefully short' of the imperative of preparing Delhi Police for meeting the challenges of policing, and expressed the view that the inherent limitations of the Delhi Police Act, 1978 could not be overcome through the amendment route and that it would be more appropriate to draft a new Delhi Police Act based on the Model Police Act, 2006 and the Supreme Court's directions.

The CHRI, which had been campaigning for police reforms, also addressed the home secretary on similar lines. They also regretted that 'in no way does the Amendment address the fundamental problem of policing today' and urged the ministry to 'reject these kinds of piecemeal changes and review how the new policing for the Capital and in the Union Territories is to be governed through a comprehensive reform agenda moored in significant and purposive legislative changes.'

Common Cause, CHRI and the Foundation for Restoration of National Values, in fact, jointly formulated a Model Delhi Police Bill, 2010 based on the Model Police Act, 2006 drafted by the Sorabjee Committee and incorporated the Supreme Court's directions in *Prakash Singh case*. The formulation also took into account the relevant recommendations of the Second Administrative Reforms commission contained in its Fifth report titled 'Public Order'. These were submitted to the home secretary, Government of India on 30 April 2010. Unfortunately, however, there was no forward movement.

An analysis of the correspondence between the Lieutenant Governor of Delhi and the Ministry of Home Affairs during this period shows that the resistance to reforms was primarily from within the latter. Lieutenant Governor, Tejendra Khanna, in a letter dated 22 October 2012, strongly argued for a two-year tenure for the commissioner of police in the following words:

> Delhi Police with over 80,000 police personnel is the largest metropolitan police force in the country and perhaps in the world. Delhi being the nation's capital is the seat of power and a hub for commercial and economic activities which present complex and enormous policing challenges. Delhi faces constant threat from terror groups. To effectively counter these challenges, the Commissioner of Police requires security of tenure to work out and implement his strategies and tactics.
>
> Each Commissioner of Police brings with him the wealth of his experience and ideas and gives directions to the force which needs time for implementation. Achievement of any fundamental transformation in line with his vision and perspective requires a minimum gestational period. I would strongly recommend, therefore, that the tenure of the Commissioner of Police, Delhi should be fixed for a minimum period of two years.

In another letter which Khanna wrote on 8 March 2013 to the Union home minister, he deplored that 'some matters which had been settled in the earlier consultations during the tenure of the former Home Secretary, Shri Gopal Pillai and former Home Minister, Shri P. Chidambaram, are now proposed to be changed unilaterally by [the] MHA'. These changes related to the composition of the SSC, Police Establishment Board and the Police Complaints Authority.

It is a great pity that the central government has not enacted the Delhi Police Bill, even till August 2020. Ideally, soon after the Supreme Court's judgment, the Government of India should have enacted the Delhi Police Bill on the lines of the Model Police Act drafted by Soli Sorabjee. That would have become a template for the states to adopt. In the absence of any such legislation by the central government, the states passed their own Police Acts. The objective apparently was to show follow-up action on the Court's judgment. The real objective, however, was to legitimize the status quo. The judgment contained a proviso that these directions would be operative till the new legislation is enacted by the state governments. The clever politicians found in it, a convenient escape route. They did in great hurry, what they had not done for the last nearly 60 years—passed legislation for a new Police Act.

Delhi Police Bill not being passed is a sad commentary on the functioning of the Ministry of Home Affairs. Fourteen years have elapsed and the central legislation is nowhere in sight. Two anecdotes in this context would throw light on the seriousness of the Home Ministry in the matter.

G.K. Pillai was the home secretary, Government of India, from 30 June 2009 to 30 January 2011. He is a gentleman to the core and a straightforward officer. Hoping to get a good response from him, I called on him in his office sometime in August 2009. I requested, among other things, his intervention to push the Model Police Act for Delhi. Pillai was surprised and pleaded ignorance about the Bill. However, in my presence, he checked from the office and told me that the file was there but had not been put up before him. He promised to resurrect the file and give it the required push. He genuinely tried to push the matter forward but was thwarted by vested interests and, after his departure, the file was buried again.

Later, I had occasion to call on Sushilkumar Shinde, home minister, on 14 June 2013. Actually, I led a delegation of retired senior police officers to him. The delegation included Balwinder Singh, Rajan Medhekar, Sankar Sen, B.L. Vohra and Gautam Kaul. On the eve of the meeting, Julio Ribeiro wrote me a letter advising me to 'impress upon the Union Home Minister that what he urgently needed is a police force that obeys the law and enforces it irrespective of the persons involved in the criminal transaction.' We were encouraged to see Shinde because of his police background. Apart from other points, I raised the issue of Police Bill which was still on the anvil and was awaiting passage. The home minister knew nothing about the Bill. He asked me to give him a copy of the Model Police Act. My response was that he could get any number of copies from his own office. What he said in response flabbergasted me. 'Look, I don't trust these people. You send me a copy of the Model Police Act.' I had no answer to that. I felt that the home minister was either too naïve or he just wanted to shake us off. In any case, I had to comply with his direction. Once I reached home, I got photocopies of the Model Police Act made and sent him one copy by speed post. Needless to say, I never heard of any progress in the matter. The Model Police Act remains in deep freeze. The aforesaid two episodes illustrate how bureaucracy scuttles proposals.

The Ministry of Home Affairs, facing flak for not having finalized the Delhi Police Bill, constituted another committee in 2013 headed by Kamal Kumar, a former director of the Sardar Vallabhbhai Patel National Police Academy, to redraft the Bill. A revised draft of the Model Police Act was finalized in July 2014. It had only 98 sections as against 221 sections in the Model Police Act drafted by Soli Sorabjee. The Ministry of Home Affairs gave suggestions and raised objections from time to time. The committee finally gave its recommendations on 6 February 2018. However, there was no forward movement. Delhi Police Bill remains in a limbo.

Article 252 of the Constitution gives Parliament the power to legislate for two or more states by consent and it lays down that such an Act shall apply to the consenting states and to any other states by which it is adopted through a resolution passed on that behalf by the House or, where there are two Houses, by each of the Houses of the Legislature of that state. If the Government of India had been sincere about implementing the Supreme Court's directions, it could have passed the Model Police Act and thereafter, under Article 252 of the Constitution, legislated for at least the Congress-ruled states. That would have had a ripple effect on the other states. However, in the absence of any initiative by the Government of India, the states passed their own Acts. It is rather anomalous that while British India had one Police Act of 1861 for the entire country, we are confronted with a situation where every state has a different Act with sharp differences in essential features. It would have been far better if there was a central legislation and the same was *mutatis mutandis* adopted by the other states/union territories of the country.

The bureaucracy was not content with frustrating the Supreme Court's efforts to bring about reforms in the police. They saw to it that the executive orders issued purportedly in compliance of the Court's directions violated its letter and spirit. They ensured that the Acts passed by the state governments legitimized the status quo. Affidavits were submitted to the Supreme Court which amounted to throwing dust in the eyes of the judiciary. What was worse, they even tried to dilute the judicial directions by passing the IPS (Cadre) Amendment Rules, 2014.

IPS (CADRE) AMENDMENT RULES, 2014: CONTEMPT PETITION

The Government of India, on 28 January 2014, issued the Indian Police Service (Cadre) Amendment Rules 2014, laying down that all appointments of cadre officers shall be made on the recommendations of the Civil Services Board, which shall consist of:

1. Chief secretary (Chairman)
2. Senior-most additional chief secretary or chairman Board of Revenue or financial commissioner or an officer of equivalent rank and status
3. Principal secretary or secretary, Department of Personnel in the state government (Secretary)
4. Principal secretary or secretary, Home
5. DGP

The Amendment Rules were issued purportedly in compliance of the Supreme Court's judgment in Writ Petition (Civil) No. 82 of 2011 moved by T.S.R. Subramanian, former Cabinet secretary, and other officers which was essentially for IAS officers, seeking insulation from executive interference on the lines extended to police officers in the Police Reforms Petition of 1996. The Personnel Department took advantage of the Apex Court's judgment in the 2011 case to constitute a Civil Services Board in violation of the Court's earlier order of 2006 constituting a Police Establishment Board. The Board was dominated by bureaucrats. Accordingly, a Contempt Petition (Civil) No. 235 of 2014 was filed by me in the Supreme Court on 17 February 2014 against the Ministry of Personnel, Government of India. My contention was that the Indian Police Service (Cadre) Amendment Rules 2014 had been issued 'to subvert the process of Police Reforms and deny police officers the autonomy in personnel matters which was considered necessary and, therefore, accorded by this Hon'ble Court! The contempt petition was taken up by the Supreme Court on 29 April 2014. I had to argue myself as Prashant Bhushan was otherwise busy.

The Solicitor General, representing the Government of India, argued that there was no contempt because the Supreme Court order of 2006 on Police Reforms gave authority to Police Establishment Board in service-related matters to officers of and below the rank of deputy superintendent of police, while the IPS (Cadre) Amendment Rules dealt with IPS officers only. This was controverted by me. I drew the attention of the Court to the fact that the Supreme Court order of 2006 gave authority to the Police Establishment Board 'to make appropriate recommendations to the state government regarding the postings and transfers of officers of and above the rank of Superintendent of Police and the Government is expected to give due weight to these recommendations and shall normally accept it! Justice Chauhan agreed with my interpretation and said that under the amended Cadre Rules, the old Police Establishment Board would become irrelevant. The Solicitor General thereupon agreed to advise the government to modify the IPS (Cadre) Amendment Rules, 2014 to make them consistent with the Supreme Court order of 2006.

As I came out of the Court, I urged the Solicitor General not to defend the government in a matter where it was trying to subvert the Supreme Court order of 2006 on Police Reforms. I further said that there was no need for the IPS (Cadre) Amendment Rules, which may in fact be withdrawn. The SG did not disagree with me.

The matter again came up before the Supreme Court on 6 May 2014. The Solicitor General placed before the Court a letter received from the secretary (Personnel). The Court perused the letter. The secretary had given an assurance that 'this Department would consult the Law Ministry in this regard and make necessary amendments, if required, in the

IPS Cadre Rules'. The Court took exception to the expression 'if required' and, in fact, returned the letter to the SG, saying that such a letter was unacceptable. The SG gave an undertaking that he would advise the Government to reconsider the order and suitably modify that to make it in consonance with Supreme Court's directions of 2006.

At this stage, I got up and said that I wanted to make two points. First, the historical context had to be kept in view. The Hon'ble Court had given directions in 2006 and the central government, on the one hand, did not carry out the direction specifically given to it and, on the other hand, it did not exercise its authority and influence to prevail upon the state governments to comply with the Supreme Court's orders. What was worse, they were now pushing things in reverse gear and trying to sabotage the Court's orders of 2006. Second, the Court's orders in *TSR Subramanian vs Union of India* were meant essentially for IAS and other civil services and not the police service. A careful reading of the judgment clearly brought that out. The Court agreed with me but said that in view of the assurance of the Solicitor General, they would like to wait for a further response from the Government of India. I said that I trusted the Solicitor General but could not trust the bureaucracy, and insisted that the impugned order be quashed. The Court however said that they would like to wait. I then fired my last salvo, and said that several states had constituted Boards in compliance with the Ministry's order and that this was causing havoc with two Boards functioning in some states: one Police Establishment Board and another Civil Services Board (CSB). The Supreme Court saw the force behind my argument and issued the following order:

> It appears prima facie that rule, as it exists on the statute book today, pursuant to an amendment made on 28 January 2014 insofar as it pertains to the cadre of Indian

Police Service does not appear to be in consonance with the earlier judgments of this Court (in *Prakash Singh and Ors. Vs. Government of India & Ors. 2006*).

In such circumstances, pending consideration by the Government of India about the amendment of the Rule, we direct the Government of India as well as all the state governments not to take any proceedings in pursuance of the rules referred to above.

The operation of the impugned Rules was thus stayed.

SEEKING PRIME MINISTER'S INTERVENTION

As the states were dragging their feet in implementing the Supreme Court's directions, I thought of seeking Prime Minister Manmohan Singh's intervention in the matter. There was a background to it. I had never served with Dr Singh nor had I ever met him. However, at a reception on the Special Protection Group's Raising Day in 2011, I had occasion to see him. I politely introduced myself whereupon he remarked: 'You are an icon, you have done so much for the country's security.' I was completely bowled over. I did not expect the Prime Minister to even know me, but here was a man who seemed to have followed my efforts to bring about changes in the police. I was emboldened to approach him.

A letter, seeking an appointment, was sent to the Prime Minister's Office on 20 April 2013 in which I wrote that the purpose was to 'plead with him to use the influence of his office to bring greater pressure on the MHA and the state governments to implement the Supreme Court's directions on police reforms'. It was indicated by me that I would be accompanied by two other persons, a retired police officer and a social activist (Vikram Lal). There was no response. Later, an officer posted in the Prime Minister's Office told me that the then NSA (M.K. Narayanan) had shot down the request for meeting.[201]

About three years back, a retired DGP (B.L. Vohra) once asked me, 'Sir, what has been the contribution of the present NSA (Ajit Doval) to police reforms?' I had no answer to that. The problem with the NSAs of police background has been that, notwithstanding their brilliance and tremendous contribution to national security, they never understood the angst of the police, having served all their lives in the Intelligence Bureau. Another reason could be that they were perhaps not prepared to risk the displeasure of their political bosses. In any case, their indifference to the cause of police reforms was extremely unfortunate—not only for the police but for the country as well.

NATIONAL POLICE MISSION

Prime Minister Manmohan Singh announced the setting up of a National Police Mission (NPM) in his address to the DGPs/IGPs Conference held on 6 October 2005.[202] He declared:

The Mission will seek to transform the police forces in the country into effective instruments for maintenance of internal security and facing the challenges of the next century by equipping them with the necessary material,

---

[201]Arvind Verma, a former IPS officer who is presently Prof. Criminal Justice in Indiana University (USA) has, in his book *The New Khaki* (Routledge; 2011) documented many individuals and their innovations to argue that one person can make a difference. Elsewhere, he says: 'Mr Narayanan was in the position where visible difference in improving policing in the country could have been made; he had the authority, clout, access and even time to undertake reforms. Alas!'

[202]Bureau of Police Research and Development, Ministry of Home Affairs, https://bprd.nic.in/content/42_1_Genesis.aspx, accessed on 26 December 2021.

intellectual and organizational resources. The Mission should be charged with the responsibility of creating a new vision for the Police. It could decide proper time frame in which to accomplish this task. The Mission would need to pay special attention to empowering the police force at all levels; to appropriate decentralization and delegation of powers; to enhancing the skills and competency levels at the grassroots; to the promotion of a culture of excellence in police organizations; to enhance accountability to the people; to meet new challenges such as asymmetric warfare, new trends in urban unrest and disorder, and new forms of social unrest.

The Police Mission differs from other missions insofar as while the other missions dealt with development themes, the NPM is the first Mission in the field of regulatory and enforcement administration. It was clarified that the NPM shall not be a substitute for the various committees or commissions set up on police reforms, but would rather equip the police to think creatively and help it to transform itself from a reactive to a proactive organization.

The BPR&D has developed seven micro missions in this context.[203] These relate to human resource development, community policing, communication and technology, infrastructure, new processes, proactive policing and visualizing future challenges and gender crimes and gender-related issues.

'SMART' POLICE

Addressing the 49th Annual Conference of Directors General of Police/Inspectors-General of Police and heads of all central police organizations at Guwahati on 30 November 2014, Prime

---

[203]Micro Mission: Seven micro missions have been formed to develop projects for achieving the objectives, https://bit.ly/3H3AUZt, accessed on 26 December 2021.

Minister Narendra Modi gave a call for making the police 'SMART'—strict and sensitive, modern and mobile, alert and accountable, reliable and responsive, techno-savvy and trained. 'Today's police have to be SMART. Only then will there be a new and big awakening among the huge police force we have,' he said.

The announcement raised great expectations. It was felt that the government would soon take measures which would bring about transformational changes in the police in tune with the directions given by the Supreme Court in 2006. We were all very hopeful that the Ministry of Home Affairs would issue some advisory to all the state governments and insist on their compliance at least in those states where the BJP, by itself or in alliance with its partners, was in power. However, nothing of the kind happened.

The Ministry of Home Affairs merely organized regional workshops on SMART policing in Bengaluru, Bhopal, Guwahati and Chandigarh during April/May 2015. The best practices of the state governments were compiled by the BPR&D and these were circulated to the DGPs during the next conference at Bhuj in December 2015. No doubt, some of the best practices are innovative and deserve to be replicated, with necessary modifications, in different states. Some of these best practices are: 'Project Prahari', a community policing initiative by Assam Police for conflict resolution; 'Himmat', for the safety of women in Delhi; 'Student Police Cadet Project' to educate and empower the youth to be responsible, law-abiding citizens, in Kerala; Hawk Eye, a mobile app to provide location-based services to the citizens especially women, in Telangana; and 'Women Powerline' to encourage young girls and women to speak up and not tolerate crimes against women, in UP.

It must also be said to the credit of Prime Minister Narendra Modi that he is the only PM who has been attending all the sessions of the annual conferences of DGPs and interacting with the senior police officers on subjects relevant to improvements in policing.

CONCLUSION

Summing up the Government of India's response, it has been disappointing to say the least. Once the Supreme Court had given its directions in 2006, the Government of India should have promptly introduced the Model Police Act and prevailed upon the states where also it was in power to adopt the legislation under Article 252 of the Constitution. The remaining states would have probably followed suit. However, the central government did not show any commitment to police reforms and it has not, even after more than 14 years, enacted the Delhi Police Bill. No wonder, the states took advantage of the Government of India's dithering in the matter to pass their own laws or issue executive orders which were not in conformity with the letter and spirit of the Supreme Court's directions.

What is worse, the Government of India even tried to subvert the Supreme Court's directions regarding the Police Establishment Board and appointment of DGP. Fortunately, the Supreme Court stayed the government's order undermining the authority of the Police Establishment Board. Regarding appointment of DGP, Justice Dipak Misra's order of 3 July 2018 based on arguments put forward by the Ministry of Home Affairs created enormous confusion among those eligible to be promoted to the rank of DGP. A large number of officers retired without even being considered for elevation to the highest post even though they were eligible for the same. The confusion was fortunately cleared by Justice Ranjan Gogoi on 6 January 2019.

The National Police Commission is a laudable initiative. Its implementation however requires greater push. SMART police was an excellent concept, but unfortunately there was hardly any follow-up action.

8

SUPPORTING EFFORTS

OPEN LETTER TO POLICEMEN

In the wake of Supreme Court's judgment on police reforms, I issued an *Open Letter to Police Officers of India* in 2007.[204] I felt that the judicial directions must be backed by internal reforms within the police—reforms which police officers could initiate on their own, reforms which would not require any financial allotment or legislative approval and which would generally not be opposed by any section or group of people. I wrote that while the Court battle will go on, we should see that an atmosphere in favour of police reforms was built up. The letter further stated:

> There is another area where all of you must contribute. You have to demonstrate not only your willingness but keenness to change. There are many aspects of police functioning which could be improved by your personal initiative and interest. You should do whatever is possible within the existing framework. These may appear small matters to you, but from the point of view of the people, they are very important.

---

[204]Copies of the letter were sent to the DGPs of all the states for being disseminated to all the SPs in-charge districts. The letter was also published in *G-files* Vol. I, 7 October 2007. Copies of the journal were also sent to all superintendents of police of the country. Full text of the letter may be seen in Appendix D.

I highlighted the following aspects of police functioning which could be improved upon by the officers at their own level:

1. Reception: A complainant should be properly received and his problem listened to with patience and understanding.
2. Behaviour: Police should behave politely and courteously with all the complainants.
3. Reporting: Registration of cases calls for improvement. Officers should have the moral courage to justify the increase in figures to the executive.
4. Women/Tribals/SCs/Poor People: These sections of people deserve special consideration.
5. Uphold the rule of law: This should be the paramount consideration and officers should be willing to pay the price today rather than risk prosecution at a later date for doing something which was wrong or illegal.

I emphasized that whatever contributions the officers make in the aforesaid areas would go a long way in generating public opinion in favour of police reforms.

26/11 TERROR ATTACK

Eminent Citizens Call for Police Reforms

On 26 November 2008, in the wake of the terrorist attack in Mumbai, a number of eminent citizens including I.K. Gujral, former prime minister of India; J.S. Verma, former CJI; Soli Sorabjee, former attorney general; Dr Abid Hussain, former ambassador to the US; Lalit Man Singh, former foreign secretary; Leila Seth, former chief justice, Himachal Pradesh High Court; Kuldip Nayar, columnist; B.G. Verghese, chairperson, CHRI and several others (including the author) issued a joint appeal for police reforms in the country on 12

December 2008. It was said that 'fighting terrorism and other crime is not possible on the basis of a foundationally weak and compromised police service that is used as a handmaiden rather than as a truly independent public service.' Referring to the Supreme Court's directions, the eminent citizens deplored that 'neither the Centre nor the states have complied with these directions and indeed most governments have subverted, diluted or disobeyed them.'

The joint statement urged that:

- All political parties immediately agree that police reforms and independent policing be treated as a bipartisan issue above the compulsions of competitive politics;
- All political parties in power—at the Centre and in the states—take immediate and effective action towards demonstrable police reform;
- All national parties, in advance of the next national election, declare in their manifestos the practical steps they commit to take on police reforms during their first 100 days of office.

The eminent citizens felt that these suggestions will ensure that the police are more responsive and better prepared to deal with security threats and that they are allowed and compelled to do their job professionally. The statement, however, made no impact on the government.

SORABJEE'S PETITION

Soli Sorabjee, who was the attorney general of India during 1989–90 and again from 1998 to 2004, filed Writ Petition (Civil) No. 591 of 2008 in the Supreme Court of India in the context of 'the recent horrific terrorist attacks in Mumbai which have disclosed several deficiencies and lapses in the existing systems and counter-terrorism measures' and to ensure that 'the police departments and security forces across the country are properly equipped and trained to handle situations of terrorism'.

It must be placed on record that the Government of India (GoI) did undertake quite a few measures to strengthen the capabilities of the police and the central armed police forces to meet any terrorist threats in the future. Some of these are:

- NSG hubs were set up at regional centres (Hyderabad, Kolkata, Mumbai and Chennai)
- Counter-insurgency and anti-terrorism schools were started
- National Investigation Agency was established
- Multi-agency centre was carved out within the IB for effective intelligence sharing, and
- Coastal security was beefed up

CORPORATE GROUPS

At this stage, I tried to garner support from the country's leading corporate houses for the cause of police reforms. A letter was sent on 4 May 2009 to several leading industrialists, including Ratan Tata, Mukesh Ambani, Kumar Mangalam Birla, Laxmi M. Mittal, Amit Mitra (FICCI), D.P. Jindal and others, highlighting the fact that the threat of terrorism persists and emphasizing that 'if there is one single measure which is going to determine the success or failure of our efforts to combat terrorism, it would be our commitment to and implementation of specific measures to insulate the police from political influences and transform it into a professional body accountable to the laws of the land [and] the constitution of the country'. Unless that happens, I cautioned, 'any cosmetic changes by way of giving additional weapons or equipment to the police would not take it far'. I suggested that a meeting may be called at Mumbai or Delhi of the leading corporate houses of the country, where they could discuss the issue threadbare and throw the weight of their opinion in favour of police reforms. Sadly, there was no response.

The **Confederation of Indian Industry (CII)** was, however, sensitive to the need for police reforms. The CII National Council meeting, held on 29 November 2008, at Chandigarh, deliberated on the subject of terrorism and identified it as a serious threat to the nation and its economy, and further emphasized the need to think differently to deal with such threats in the future. It constituted a national task force on internal security which, at a meeting held in New Delhi on 10 June 2009, made *inter alia* the following recommendations on police reforms:

1. Political parties must view police as a non-partisan subject.
2. Political parties and governments must give clear undertakings about the specific actions they mean to take to improve policing in light of Supreme Court directives and provide a timeline for this.
3. Governments must involve citizens in developing policing plans and priorities in consultation with local populations.
4. To remove undue and illegitimate interference in all aspects of policing.

The Confederation stated that 'the brazen attack on Mumbai on 26 November 2008 was a grim reminder of the threats our country is facing' and emphasized that 'the attack was not only on Mumbai but also on the economy of the country and the ideals of democracy that India holds dear'.

The **Federation of Indian Chambers of Commerce and Industry (FICCI)** also showed interest in police reforms. On 10 July 2015, they organized a policy round table on

'SMART Policing: India's Growth Imperative' in New Delhi in collaboration with the Indian Police Foundation and the IPS (Central) Association. It emphasized that it is imperative to build a robust criminal justice system which should be supported by a strong internal security infrastructure. Its recommendations included implementation of all pending reforms, particularly the directives given by the Supreme Court of India, equipping the police forces with state-of-the-art weapons, sharpening intelligence, strengthening police infrastructure with cutting-edge equipment and technology, etc.

FICCI has also been preparing for the last few years, a Compendium of Best Practices in SMART Policing and giving SMART Policing Awards under different heads such as community policing, cyber-crime management, human trafficking, women's safety, training and capacity building, emergency response, counterinsurgency, etc.[205]

DHARNA AT JANTAR MANTAR

At one stage, in 2012, I was very frustrated with the progress in the implementation of the Supreme Court's directions. I was beginning to lose my faith in the judiciary. In a communication to the top cops, I made the following observations:

> There is only one hope left—that is, if the people in general become interested in police reforms and agitate for it. I made sincere efforts to convince Anna Hazare that police reforms were an essential pre-requisite to anti-corruption. Unless the police were reformed and

---

[205]FICCI Compendium of Best Practices in SMART Policing 2019, https://bprd.nic.in/WriteReadData/Bannerpdf/FICCI%20Compendium%20of%20Best%20Practices%20in%20SMART%20Policing%202019.pdf, accessed on 12 February 2022.

cleansed, anti-corruption mechanisms would never function effectively. However, Anna was not impressed and, unfortunately, members of Anna team also were not enthusiastic.

Under the circumstances, with the other options gradually fading, I am now seriously thinking of sitting on a *dharna* at Jantar Mantar on 22 September 2012, the day we complete six years of the Supreme Court judgment. The *dharna* could be for three days from 22 to 25, September. May be, a couple of other people including perhaps some police officers would also join in the protest. The idea would be to focus public attention on the need and urgency of police reforms, and highlight that reforms are essential to uphold the democratic structure of the Republic and revive the momentum of economic progress.

It would be great if sympathetic *dharna* could be organised at other state capitals also simultaneously.

I must admit that my mind is full of misgivings. Would there be any response? Besides, people might say that I am behaving like a politician, or that perhaps I am seeking publicity. Such ideas are far, far from my mind. Actually my thoughts—desperate thoughts, perhaps—are the outpourings of a man keen to give as much push as he possibly can to the cause of police reforms within his life-time.

Before I finalise the plan and decide to take the plunge, I want frank and honest opinion of the senior police officers.

The majority of senior officers, however, opposed the idea. Julio Ribeiro did not approve of it. B.S. Das was of the opinion that it would damage the achievement so far, apart from upsetting the Supreme Court to an extent. Ashwani Kumar was vehemently against it. A.B. Tripathy had reservations. Anil

Chowdhry thought it would be 'demeaning' to my stature. Gautam Kaul thought it will be 'setting a wrong precedent for a good cause'. Balachandran, my batchmate, advised me against it. Vaidyanathan, another batchmate of mine, asked me not to rush into the dharna programme. Satish Sahni conveyed his sense of dismay over the proposal. Sankar Sen conveyed on behalf of the Association of Retired Senior IPS Officers (ARSIPSO) that the dharna will be counterproductive and ill-timed and would also set a wrong precedent.

The only support I got was from some young serving officers. Taking the totality of circumstances into consideration, particularly the strong opinion to the contrary of the senior officers, and the fact that inadequate and divided support from the police fraternity may perhaps weaken the cause of police reforms, I abandoned the idea of sitting on dharna at the Jantar Mantar.

MOVEMENT FOR PEOPLE'S POLICE

One of the criticisms I was facing was that the Supreme Court's directions on police reforms dealt with only the officer cadre and that the non-gazetted ranks, especially the constabulary, had been neglected. It was not a valid criticism because the State Security Commission was to insulate police at all levels from external pressures. Fixed tenure to officers on operational duties included the SHO and sub-divisional officers also, and the Establishment Board's charter covered specifically the lower ranks. Nevertheless, I felt that the movement of police reforms should cover a much wider area than stipulated in the judicial directions. It was, therefore, decided to give it the character of a Movement for People's Police with the following demands:

1. What we have today is 'Ruler's Police'. It must metamorphose into 'People's Police'.
2. The executive stranglehold over the police must go.

The police should have freedom to act as per the law of the land.

3. Upholding the rule of law should be the supreme objective of the police.

4. Registration of cases must improve. Assessment of crime situation should not be based on statistical figures.

5. Police behaviour towards the common man must improve; it should be marked by empathy and respect for human rights.

6. The police must extend appropriate legal protection to the weaker sections of society, especially the scheduled castes, scheduled tribes, women and the minorities.

7. Police infrastructure—manpower, transport, communications and forensic support—must improve substantially. Housing of the subordinate ranks must receive special attention.

8. Any police officer, whether starting as a constable, sub-inspector or deputy superintendent of police should be able to earn at least three promotions in his service career.

9. A policeman should not be on duty for more than 12 hours, which may in due course be brought down to eight hours.

10. The Supreme Court's orders regarding police reforms must be implemented. Acts legislated by state governments should conform to the Court's directions in letter and in spirit.

Fali Sam Nariman, after reading the above-mentioned 10 points, observed that it was interesting to see that the Court's directions were now only one of the points in the overall scheme of police reforms.

A letter indicating the shift in the movement was sent to

all the DGPs of the country on 4 September 2012, seeking their cooperation and active involvement in the movement to the extent possible. 'We need a better police, a reformed police sensitive to the problems and aspirations of the people,' I said while concluding the letter.

LETTERS TO PARTY PRESIDENTS

I sent letters to the president, All India Congress Committee (Sonia Gandhi) and the president, Bharatiya Janata Party (Rajnath Singh) on 4 June 2013. It was when general elections were round the corner and the parties would have started working on their manifesto. I drew their attention to the Court's directions and urged upon the parties to 'incorporate Police Reforms in their election manifesto with a promise that the party shall pass a central legislation on the subject on the lines of the Model Police Act drafted by [the] Soli Sorabjee Committee, including therein the directions of the Supreme Court, and persuade the state governments to implement the mandatory directions of the Supreme Court or pass laws under Article 252 of the Constitution on the lines of the central legislation on the subject.'

Significantly, the Congress manifesto, while acknowledging that the judiciary had made suggestions (for police reforms), stated that 'we will accord the highest priority to instituting these reforms'. The BJP promised to 'roll out a comprehensive strategy for bringing the Indian Police at par with international standards' and to modernize the police force, equipping it with the latest technology.

On the eve of the general election in 2019, the Indian Police Foundation, through a press note, appealed to all the national and major political parties to declare the commitment to police reforms in their election manifestos. They were particularly requested to commit that 'Supreme Court's directions on police reforms would be implemented in letter and spirit to meet the democratic aspirations of the people.'

The Indian National Congress did include police reforms in its manifesto. The relevant paragraph read as follows:

> [The] Congress promises to consult state governments and reach a consensus on the police reforms directed by the Supreme Court in the *Prakash Singh case*. Based on the consensus, [the] Congress will pass a Model Police Act that the states will be advised to adopt and enact in the state legislatures.
>
> The objective of the Model Police Act will be to make the police forces technology-enabled, people-friendly, and upholders of human rights and legal rights.

The BJP manifesto talked of securing India and, in that context, expressed its resolve to continue its policy of zero tolerance towards terrorism and extremism, and empowering the security forces to combat terrorism. Subsequently, the government introduced a scheme to release funds to the states which had taken initiatives to implement specific items of police reforms such as filling up of vacancies, using technology in tackling crime and trying to achieve welfare of police personnel.[206]

This is, however, not to suggest that the aforesaid entries were made in the party manifestos because of the letters we sent them. There must have been other forces at work too. It is necessary, however, that the citizenry builds pressure on all the major political parties to include police reforms in their agenda.

---

[206]The Centre, in 2019, released ₹7.69 crore each to 10 states which had taken initiatives in these areas. These states included Andhra Pradesh, Gujarat, Punjab, Telangana, Tamil Nadu, Odisha, Rajasthan, Madhya Pradesh, Uttarakhand and Uttar Pradesh.

NGOS' CONTRIBUTION

Several NGOs contributed to the cause of police reforms. Out of all these, the Commonwealth Human Rights Initiative (CHRI) played a very significant role. It organized a series of conferences, seminars and round table discussions on the subject in different parts of the country to educate the people about the need and relevance of police reforms. Some of these were held on 22 August 1998, 20–21 May 1999, 17–18 August 1999, 16–17 December 1999, 4 October 2002, 23–24 March 2005, 7 December 2005, 23–24 March 2007 and 31 October–1 November 2009. Workshops and meetings on the Madhya Pradesh Police Vidheyak were held at Indore, Bhopal, Raisen, Vidisha and Itarsi in the second half of 2001. Maja Daruwala of the CHRI played a stellar role in educating the people on the importance of police reforms.

The CHRI was permitted to file suggestions and furnish documents in the Supreme Court subsequent to the judgment. On 27 April 2008, it submitted a note to the Supreme Court on the status of compliance in different states. In another affidavit, also filed in 2008, commenting on the bills/statutes passed by the states, it stated that the legislation reveals 'the subtle erosion of this Hon'ble Court's order, to the point where the directives have been rendered devoid of any substantive meaning'. It went on to say that 'a review of the statutes notified and bills drafted leads to the inescapable conclusion that both the letter and spirit of this Court's ruling of 22.9.2006 has been undermined'.

Common Cause was one of the petitioners. As mentioned earlier, H.D. Shourie had signed the petition, though neither he nor any member of the Common Cause executive took any interest in the progress of the petition. Subsequent to the judgment, however, Common Cause has been taking active interest in police reforms. It brought out two excellent reports on *Status of Policing in India* in 2018 and 2019. The NGO has also been actively associating with the Indian Police Foundation to promote the cause of police reforms.

The Foundation for Restoration of National Values (FRNV) and Public Concern for Governance Trust also supported the cause of police reforms. The FRNV organized a workshop on the subject in Delhi on 30 June 2009, which was attended among others by E. Sreedharan.[207]

INDIAN POLICE FOUNDATION

The Indian Police Foundation and Institute, a multidisciplinary think tank, which was inaugurated by the Union home minister in 2015, has been systematically working for reforms in policing and focusing on raising the ethical values and service delivery standards of the police. The Foundation has been observing 22 September every year as 'Police Reforms Day' to commemorate the Supreme Court verdict on police reforms in the *Prakash Singh case*. This annual programme has been attended by several eminent personalities, including the vice president of India, Union ministers, retired chief justices of the Supreme Court, Home Secretaries and directors of the IB, among others.

The IPF has been spearheading an ambitious project involving nationwide stakeholder consultations on the safety of women and children. It has been collaborating with the BPR&D and the state police in the exercise with a view to understand the current levels of preparedness and response systems, identify the good practices and the practical challenges involved in preventing and combating crime and sexual violence against women and children.

---

[207] I was asked to address the workshop on 'The Background and the Supreme Court Judgment.'

POLICE REFORMS DAY FUNCTIONS

In 2012, it was decided that 22 September should be observed every year as 'Police Reforms Day'. A function was held at the India International Centre. It was attended by police officers, lawyers, activists, journalists and representatives of reputed NGOs such as CHRI, Common Cause, FRNV and India Rejuvenation Initiative. Fali S. Nariman, noted constitutional jurist, presided over the deliberations. It was resolved that the movement for police reforms should be transformed into a Movement for People's Police.

In 2013, an impressive rally in support of police reforms was taken out in Lucknow on 25 September. About 2,500 students of universities and colleges participated. The rally started from the Varsity Union building, marched through Hazratganj, the heart of the city, and terminated near Mahatma Gandhi's statue opposite the GPO. Distinguished citizens present in the rally included two retired judges: Justice Kamleshwar Nath and Justice S.C. Verma. About a hundred placards were carried by the participants. These read: 'We want People's Police, Not Rulers' Police', 'Implement Police Reforms', 'Supreme Court Directions are for Good Policing', 'Police Badlo, Samaj Badlo', etc. A rally was taken out in Bhopal on 22 September, which was attended by about 2,000 people. NDTV highlighted the need of police reforms in their programme *We the People* on Sunday (22 September).

In 2014, the Adarsh Bharat Abhiyan (ABHA) organized a satyagraha at Rajghat on 20 September in support of police reforms. The programme was endorsed by Shri Justice Lahoti, Justice Teotia, Ram Jethmalani, Prashant Bhushan, J.F. Ribeiro, T.S.R. Subramanian, Bhure Lal and several others. We assembled at the Samadhi, sat in silence there for about 10 minutes and thereafter the gathering was addressed by me and also by Abha Singh, advocate, and Ashwini Upadhyay of ABHA.

About 20,000 pamphlets on police reforms were distributed across the country to mobilize the support of people to the cause of police reforms. Aamir Khan Productions' *Satyamev Jayate* devoted one full episode to police reforms.[208]

The Indian Police Foundation (IPF) and the Indian Police Institute were inaugurated by Union Home Minister Rajnath Singh at the India International Centre, New Delhi on 2 October 2015. Eminent speakers included Kiren Rijiju, Minister of State for Home Affairs, Soli Sorabjee, Dilip Padgaonkar, G.K. Pillai, Praveen Swami and Patricia Mukhim. The home minister expressed the hope that the Foundation and Institute will work closely with the institutions of government and police training institutions while working for raising the professional competence of police personnel and bringing about positive and transformative changes in the Indian Police. The programme was attended by a galaxy of dignitaries including serving and retired police officers, civil society leaders and high-level government officials. The movement for police reforms was henceforth spearheaded by the IPF.[209]

On 23 September 2016, the IPF organized a seminar on 'Whither Police Reforms: Ten Years after the Supreme Court Verdict', in the Constitution Club of India, New Delhi. It was presided over by former Chief Justice R.C. Lahoti. At the end of the deliberations, the IPF, the CHRI and several distinguished citizens including Chief Justice R.C. Lahoti, Kiran Rijiju, Union state minister for home, Veerappa Moily, former law minister, Fali Nariman, noted Jurist, Praveen Swami and others passed a unanimous resolution which read as follows:

i)   That it is a matter of serious concern that even 10 years after the Supreme Court's judgment on police

---

[208]The participants included Prakash Singh, Jacob Punnoose, Abhinav Kumar and others, vide https://yhoo.it/3h8UHwo.

[209]Author was Chairman, IPF, from 2015 to 2021.

reforms delivered on 22 September 2006, progress in the implementation of judicial directions had been tardy and that the states had either passed laws which were against the letter and spirit of Court's directions or issued executive orders which diluted or modified the directions;

ii) That the Apex Court be requested to ensure effective compliance of its directions on the subject in larger public interest and to improve governance in the country failing which a wrong message would go that states could defy the directions of the highest Court of the land and get away with it;

iii) That the GoI should convene a Conference of the Chief Ministers of States, along with Chief Secretaries and Directors General of Police of the States, not only to discuss the issue of implementation in letter and spirit of the Court's directions but also to adopt an INDIA-CENTRIC Policy on Police Reforms, and adopt measures to transform the existing police into an instrument of service to the people, upholding the rule of law.

The IPF, in partnership with Common Cause, organized Police Reforms Day on 22 September 2017. The function was presided over by Justice G.S. Singhvi, former judge of the Supreme Court. Those who addressed it included R.K. Singh, minister of Power, New and Renewable Energy, GoI; Jairam Ramesh, Member of Parliament; and Sitaram Yechury, general secretary, Communist Party of India (Marxist) (CPI [M]).

A conference on 'Future of Policing: Vision 2025' was held on 22 September 2018. The function was presided over by Justice Balbir Singh Chauhan, former judge, Supreme Court of India. The speakers included Dr Satyapal Singh, minister of state, Ministry of Human Resource Development, GoI; Amitabh Kant, chief executive officer (CEO), NITI Aayog; Rajiv

Gauba, Union home secretary; and Rajiv Jain, Director, IB.

A national seminar on 'Realization of the SMART Policing Vision of the Prime Minister' was held at the India International Centre on 5 October 2019, where Vice President of India Shri Venkaiah Naidu was the chief guest. Besides, two law colleges of repute in the National Capital Region (NCR) organized functions to observe Police Reforms Day. Lloyd Law College in Greater Noida observed the programme on 5 September. The Faculty of Law of the University of Delhi also organized a seminar on 23 September.

The IPF organized an online lecture on 22 September 2020 on 'Reforms in Police and Criminal Justice System Are Crucial to Safeguard the Democratic Rights of Citizens' by Justice Madan Lokur. Referring to the present state of criminal justice system, Justice Lokur said: 'Police Reforms are the answer.' This was followed by a dialogue on '14 Years after the Police Reform Judgment by the Supreme Court, Where Do We Stand?'[210]

An appeal was also issued on 22 September 2020 by 32 distinguished citizens and NGOs of the country, at the initiative of the IPF. They included: Justice R.C. Lahoti, lawyers Fali Nariman, Dushyant Dave and Prashant Bhushan, journalist Shekhar Gupta, seven retired IPS officers including Julio Ribeiro, five retired IAS officers including Madhav Godbole and the NGOs Common Cause, CHRI, Association for Democratic Reforms, FRNV and Citizens' Forum India. The appeal deplored that 'none of the major parties of the country have shown interest in police reforms' and it seemed that 'they all find it convenient to use this instrument to subserve their political agenda'. The appeal emphasized that police reforms are directly linked with the progress of the country

---

[210]The participants were Prakash Singh, chairman, IPF and Maja Daruwala, senior advisor, CHRI. The programme was anchored by Faye D'Souza, senior journalist.

and stated that 'we cannot have a modern Indian state unless the police, which is the kingpin of the criminal justice system, is reorganized and restructured'. The appeal even warned that 'the democratic structure of the country itself may be in jeopardy if we do not arrest the criminalization of politics and politicization of crime'. It went on to say that 'good law and order is the *sine qua non* for economic progress' and that 'the dreams of more than a billion people for better life would not be fulfilled unless we have a professional police upholding the rule of law'.

In 2021, Justice Kurian Joseph, former judge of the Supreme Court of India, addressed the police fraternity online. On 23 September, he spoke on the 'Role of the Police in Securing Citizens' Rights and Strengthening India's Democracy'. Earlier, on 22 September, there was a panel discussion on 'Generating Public Awareness and a Groundswell of Public Demand on Police Reform'; the panellists were Raghu Raman, former CEO National Intelligence Grid (NATGRID); Vipul Mudgal, director, Common Cause and Prakash Singh. Lokmanya and Synergia Foundation—two online platforms—published articles and organized discussions on police reforms. The Symbiosis Law School, Pune and the Public Concern for Governance Trust (Pune chapter) jointly organized the B.G. Deshmukh Memorial Lecture on 'The Need of the Hour: Police Reforms' on 28 September; it was addressed by Prakash Singh.

9

POLICE REFORMS
IN OTHER COUNTRIES

It would be of interest to study, even if very briefly, the process of police reforms in some of the major countries of the world. There are countries where the police have a good image, thanks to the constitutional and administrative arrangements, which enable it to function independent of external pressures.

UNITED KINGDOM

The first professional police in UK was set up in the city of Glasgow through an Act of Parliament in 1800. The next significant step was setting up a centralized police force in Ireland, then a part of UK, in 1814, following the Peace Preservation Act.

Sir Robert Peel, as home secretary, introduced the concept of professional policing in 1822. The Metropolitan Police Act, 1829 established a full-time professional and centrally organized police force for the metropolitan area of Greater London. Gradually, policing was extended to the boroughs and counties and, by the 1850s, police set-up was established all over the country.

Sir Robert is credited with the following ethical principles which were to be the working philosophy of the police: every police officer should be issued an identification number to ensure accountability for his actions; whether the police are effective or not would be measured not by the number of arrests but by the control over crime; and 'the police are the public and the public are the police.'

Subsequently, the 'Nine Principles of Policing' were enunciated in 1829:

1. The basic mission for which the police exist is to prevent crime and disorder.
2. The ability of the police to perform their duties is dependent upon public approval of police actions.
3. Police must secure the willing co-operation of the public in voluntary observance of the law to be able to secure and maintain the respect of the public.
4. The degree of co-operation of the public that can be secured diminishes proportionately to the necessity of the use of physical force.
5. Police seek and preserve public favour not by catering to public opinion but by constantly demonstrating absolute impartial service to the law.
6. Police use physical force to the extent necessary to secure observance of the law or to restore order only when the exercise of persuasion, advice and warning is found to be insufficient.
7. Police, at all times, should maintain a relationship with the public that gives reality to the historic tradition that the police are the public and the public are the police; the police being only members of the public who are paid to give full-time attention to duties which are incumbent on every citizen in the interests of community welfare and existence.
8. Police should always direct their action strictly towards their functions and never appear to usurp the powers of the judiciary.
9. The test of police efficiency is the absence of crime

and disorder, not the visible evidence of police action in dealing with it.

These principles, according to an author, are 'unique in history and throughout the world because it is derived not from fear but almost exclusively from public cooperation with the police'.[211] This approach to policing came to be known as 'policing by consent'.

The Police Act, 1946 amalgamated the smaller borough police forces with the county constabularies in England and Wales. In 1960, a Royal Commission was appointed under the chairmanship of Henry Willink in the wake of high-profile scandals involving borough police forces. Its principal recommendations were as follows:

1. No single national force was to be formed, but central government should exercise more powers over local forces;

2. Retention of small police forces of between 200 and 350 officers 'justifiable only by special circumstances such as the distribution of the population and the geography of the area';

3. The optimum size for a police force was more than 500 members with the police area having a population of at least 250,000;

4. There was a case for single police forces for major conurbations.

The Police Act, 1964 was passed on the basis of the Royal Commission's recommendations. The old county and borough police authorities were replaced with police authorities composed of two-thirds elected representatives and one-third magistrates.

Lord Denning's statement of the doctrine of police

---

[211]Charles Reith, *New Study of Police History*, Oliver and Boyd, 1956.

independence has effectively become the *locus classicus* on the subject in common law countries around the world. A policeman in UK (England and Wales) has an original power vested in him and once a law is passed by Parliament, no one can tell any policeman how he should act in upholding it. As stated by Lord Denning in the case of *R. v. Metropolitan Police Commissioner ex parte Blackburn* in 1968:[212]

> I have no hesitation, however, in holding that, like every constable in the land, [the Commissioner of the London Metropolitan Police] should be, and is, independent of the executive. He is not subject to the orders of the Secretary of State, save that under the Police Act, 1964; the Secretary of State can call upon him to give a report, or to retire in the interests of efficiency.
>
> I hold it to be the duty of the Commissioner of Police of the Metropolis, as it is of every chief constable, to enforce the law of the land. He must take steps so as to post his men that crimes may be detected; and that honest citizens may go about their affairs in peace. He must decide whether or not suspected persons are to be prosecuted; and, if need be, bring the prosecution or see that it is brought.
>
> But in all these things he is not the servant of anyone, save the law itself. No Minister of the Crown can tell him that he must, or must not, keep observation on this place or that; or that he must, or must not, prosecute this man or that one. Nor can any police authority tell him so. The responsibility for law enforcement lies on him. He is answerable to the law and the law alone.

---

[212]Philip Stenning, 'The Idea of the Political "Independence" of the Police: International Interpretations and Experiences,' Ipperwash, http://www. archives.gov.on.ca/en/e_records/ipperwash/policy_part/meetings/pdf/ stenning.pdf, accessed on 14 February 2022.

In 1984, the Police and Criminal Evidence (PACE) Act attempted to strike 'a balance between the powers of the British Police and the rights of members of the public'.

In 1985, the Police Complaints Authority was set up. It was, however, superseded by the Independent Police Complaints Commission in 2004 and again by Independent Office for Police Conduct in 2018.

London's Metropolitan Police Commissioner, for historical reasons, has been responsible directly to the home secretary, i.e. the central government and not to the local authorities. At the local-government level, there are committees of local councillors and magistrates. The committee's duty is to secure the maintenance of an adequate and efficient police force for the area. The Police Authority is a committee of the council though its decisions generally do not require to be ratified by the council and a member of the Authority is designated to answer questions from and provide information to meetings of the council. The Authority could not be instructed by the council what it should do, but may be called upon to explain its actions through its spokesman. The chief constable had complete independence in operational matters.

The Police Reform and Social Responsibility Act, 2011 has brought about radical changes in important policy areas: police accountability and governance; alcohol licencing; regulation of protests around Parliament Square; and issue of arrest warrants in respect of private prosecutions for universal jurisdiction offences. The Act has transferred the control of police forces from local authorities to elected police and crime commissioners in areas outside London.[213] The first police commissioner elections were held in November 2012. The police and crime commissioners have the power to appoint

---

[213]'Police Reform and Social Responsibility Act 2011,' Legislation.gov. uk, https://www.legislation.gov.uk/ukpga/2011/13/contents/enacted, accessed on 14 February 2022.

and, if necessary, even suspend or dismiss the chief constable of the police, who has otherwise control over all the other police officers. The Metropolitan Police Authority has been replaced by Mayor's Office for Policing and Crime, though the Queen continues to appoint the metropolitan commissioner and deputy metropolitan commissioner on the advice of the home secretary.

THE UNITED STATES

The American police, although modelled on the British pattern, was influenced by short-term crises, ethnic rivalries and local politics. Like the growth of America itself, the growth of its police department was rapid and haphazard. American police institutions largely reflected the qualities of local governments. According to historian Robert Fogelson, the police were accountable neither to the courts nor to their fellow citizens but to the political machines that dominated urban America.

During the 1960s, the propriety of police policies and activities came under intense public scrutiny. Questions were raised, particularly by minority groups, about the structure and functions of the police organizations and quality of police training, and the proper use of police discretion. President Lyndon B. Johnson thereupon set up a President's Commission on Law Enforcement and Administration of Justice (also known as the Katzenbach Commission, after its chairman, or the National Crime Commission). Its final report, which came out in 1967, was described as the most comprehensive evaluation of crime and crime control in the US at the time. It recommended reorganization of the police department and suggested a slew of reforms.

A series of US's Supreme Court's decisions under the Warren Court led to important changes in policing with respect to civil rights and constitutional law. In due course, several commissions, such as the Knapp Commission in New York City during the 1970s were used to bring about changes in law-enforcement agencies. These reforms improved matters and, as stated by Jerome H. Skolnick and Candace McCoy, 'in general, political machines can no longer control the working of [the] American police department nor can they protect police departments from public scrutiny.'[214]

The Violent Crime Control and Law Enforcement Act passed in 1994 sought to curb abuse of power by the police and hold the agencies accountable.

In the early 2000s and 2010s, there was emphasis on de-escalation as a method of conflict resolution. There was also emphasis on community policing, evidence-based policing and civilian oversight of police work.

In the 2010s, there were a number of incidents of the police shooting unarmed individuals. An investigation into the shooting of Michael Brown in Ferguson in August 2014 by the United States Department of Justice came to the conclusion that members of the police department were 'routinely violating the constitutional rights of its black residents.'[215] In April 2015, Baltimore went up in flames with thousands of protestors taking to the streets after Freddie Gray, a 25-year-old African-American, who had not been accused of any crime, died in police custody. Six officers were found responsible for his death caused by severe injuries to his neck and spine. It was another episode in the 'long history of mistrust between

[214]Cited in Vinod Tiwari, Sanjoosh Bhadauriya and Shweta Saxena, 'Rendering Criminal Justice System in India', Rajeev Gandhi Law College, Bhopal.
[215]Matt Apuzzo, 'Ferguson Police Routinely Violate Rights of Blacks, Justice Dept. Finds', The New York Times, 3 March 2015, https://www.nytimes.com/2015/03/04/us/justice-department-finds-pattern-of-police-bias-and-excessive-force-in-ferguson.html, accessed on 14 February 2022.

police officers and black people in the United States.'[216]

US president Barack Obama, responding to the Baltimore protest, said that 'it is in the interest of police officers to root out the police who are not doing the right thing, to hold accountable people when they do something wrong instead of just the closing-ranks approach that all too often we see that ends up feeding greater frustration and ultimately, I think, putting more police officers in danger.'[217] He went on to say that 'unfortunately, we have seen these police-related killings or deaths too often now, and obviously everybody is starting to recognize that this is not just an isolated incident in Ferguson or New York, but we have got some broader issues.'[218] Police leaders thereafter issued a new set of guidelines in 'Use of Force: Taking Policing to a Higher Standard', in which they laid down higher standards for the use of force than those prescribed by the US Supreme Court.

On 7 July 2016, there was a change in the complexion of events. A number of police officers were shot and killed in Dallas, Texas. Again, on 17 July, multiple officers were shot and killed in Baton Rouge (Louisiana). President Obama condemned these attacks saying that 'there is no justification for violence against law enforcement.'[219]

There was a strong demand for police reforms with emphasis on police ranks being made more representative

[216]Joshua Serrano, 'Five Reforms Every Police Department Should Make', Institute for Policy Studies, https://ips-dc.org/five-reforms-every-police-department-make/, accessed on 14 February 2022.

[217]Nedra Pickler, 'Obama: police must hold officers accountable for wrongdoing', AP News, 29 April 2015, https://apnews.com/article/b0c194f48d174ed28afcadcd6b1ad059, accessed on 14 February 2022.

[218]Ibid.

[219]Tanya Somanader, 'President Obama on the Attack on Law Enforcement in Baton Rouge', 17 July 2016, The White House, https://obamawhitehouse.archives.gov/blog/2016/07/17/president-obama-attack-law-enforcement-baton-rouge, accessed on 14 February 2022.

of different sections of society and humane treatment of the minorities. The Institute for Policy Studies, a US-based think tank, suggested the following five reforms in 2016: [220]

1. Community policing with a view to optimizing positive contacts within police officers and community members;
2. Demilitarize the police which has been found to be using military grade weapons and vehicles against non-violent protestors;
3. Appoint independent prosecutors so that the police officers are held more accountable for their actions;
4. Set up civilian complaint review boards to empower members of the community to seek their own evidence in cases of police violence;
5. Provide racial-bias training so that the African-American and Latino people do not feel discriminated at different levels of the criminal justice system.

Recently, on 25 May 2020, George Floyd, an African-American, died in Minneapolis after a white police officer pinned him to the ground with his knee during an arrest until he suffocated to death. There were protests across nearly 30 cities in the US. The White House went into a temporary lockdown and the CNN headquarters in Atlanta was vandalised. The military was asked to be on standby. The police officer, Derek Chauvin, was arrested and charged with third-degree murder and manslaughter, but that did not satisfy the people. Racial discrimination continues to be an issue in US policing. *The New York Times,* in an editorial on 1 June 2020, admitted that racial inequality was 'rampant' in

---

[220]Joshua Serrano, *Five Reforms Every Police Department Should Make*, Institute for Policy Studies, 3 June, 2016, available at https://ips-dc.org/five-reforms-every-police-department-make/, accessed on 8 March 2022.

the enforcement of law.[221] There is a strong demand that the 'use of force policy' needs to be redefined. This policy varies from jurisdiction to jurisdiction. The type of 'neck restraint' or chokehold that Chauvin used on Floyd has been banned in New York City since 1993. The city of Baltimore revamped its policy in 2019 as a part of its consent decree with the US Department of Justice after the death of Gray. The new version requires officers to report use-of-force incidents and compels them to intervene if they see another officer improperly using force.

President Donald Trump, responding to the widespread demand for police reforms, signed an executive order on 16 June 2020 to establish a database which would track police officers with excessive use of force complaints in their records. It would also give the police department a financial incentive to adopt best practices and encourage co-responder programmes in which social workers would join the police when they respond to non-violent calls involving mental health, addiction and homeless issues. Trump also said that, as part of the order, the use of chokeholds would be banned 'except if an officer's life is at risk'.[222] The demand to 'defund the police' was slammed by Trump as radical and dangerous.[223] He said: 'Without police there is chaos.

---

[221]Nikole Hannah-Jones, 'What Is Owed?', *The New York Times*, 30 June 2020, https://www.nytimes.com/interactive/2020/06/24/magazine/reparations-slavery.html, accessed on 14 February 2022.

[222]Jack Brewster, 'Trump Signs Executive Order Banning Choke Holds "Unless an Officer's Life Is at Risk"', *Forbes*, 16 June 2020, https://www.forbes.com/sites/jackbrewster/2020/06/16/trump-signs-executive-order-banning-chokeholds-unless-officers-life-is-at-risk/?sh=152594392f8b, accessed on 14 February 2022.

[223]Lauren Gambino, 'Trump and Republicans use calls to "defund the police" to attack Democrats', *The Guardian*, https://www.theguardian.com/us-news/2020/jun/08/trump-republicans-defund-the-police-george-floyd, accessed on 14 February 2022.

Without law there is anarchy and without safety there is catastrophe.'[224]

JAPAN

In Japan, there is a National Public Safety Commission (NPSC) at the apex which comprises a chairperson, who is a minister of state, and five other members who are appointed with the consent of both the Houses of the Diet. The national police force is known as the National Police Agency (NPA); its chief is appointed by the NPSC with the consent of the prime minister. At the local level, police affairs are dealt with by the Prefectural Police Forces and the Tokyo Metropolitan Area. There is a Prefectural Public Safety Commission (PPSC) consisting of three to five members depending on the size of the prefecture. The members are appointed by the governor of each prefecture with the consent of the prefectural assembly from among the residents of the area, ensuring that members affiliated with a particular party do not constitute a majority in the Commission. The Metropolitan Police Department is given a special status and is headed by a superintendent general.

Both the NPSC as well as the PPSC are insulated from political pressure and neither the prime minister nor the prefectural governor has the power to give them any directions.

A significant feature of the Japanese police is the great emphasis they place on maintaining good relations with the community. The Koban System[225] performs this vital role.

---

[224]Reuters, 'Trump signs order on police reform after weeks of protests', 17 June 2020, https://www.thehindu.com/news/international/trump-signs-order-on-police-reform-after-weeks-of-protests/article31848455.ece, accessed on 14 February 2022.
[225]Under the Koban System, police stations divide their precincts into beats, and a Koban is the operating base for police officers assigned to each beat.

The Japanese police was involved in a series of scandals at the end of the twentieth century. The NPSC thereupon constituted a Police Reforms Committee in March 2000, which recommended the following eight reforms:

1. Transparency in operations;
2. Complaints by citizens to get a positive response;
3. Inspections to be effective;
4. Democratic control over local police should be reflected in the functioning of PPSCs;
5. The police should be citizen-friendly;
6. Discipline must be maintained;
7. There should be dialogue between the police stations and members of the community;
8. The police should adapt to social changes.

The NPSC and the National Police Agency (NPA) thereafter codified the Charter of Police Reforms. The Charter had four major sections dealing with: (1) enhancement of transparency, self-improvement, disclosure, affirmative responses to citizen's complaints, strict inspection, as well as enhancement of the control by the PSC over the police; (2) the establishment of 'Police for the People', i.e. the police should listen to citizens' needs and respond to those, reinforce activities to ease citizens' fears about crime and support the victims of crime; (3) strong measures against organized crime groups, and enhancement of international cooperation to cope with transnational crime and cyber-crime; and (4) development of human resources including education and training as well as burden reduction through new technologies and increase in personnel.[226]

---

[226]Taisuke Kanayama, 'A Decade from Police Reforms in Japan, Has a Police for the People Been Realized?', Police Policy Research Center, National Police Agency of Japan, http://www.npa.go.jp/english/keidai/Guidelines_of_Police_Policy/A_DECADE_FROM_POLICE_REFORMS_IN_JAPAN.pdf, accessed on 14 February 2022.

In 2016, far-reaching reforms were introduced in the criminal justice system following a scandal involving prosecutors fabricating evidence in a case. The Ministry of Justice constituted a special committee whose recommendations formed the basis for amendment of several laws including the Criminal Procedure Code. The five major reforms approved by the Diet related to: mandatory video recording of interrogation in certain types of crimes; introduction of bargaining between the defendant and the prosecutor; widening the scope of wiretapping as an investigative tool; expanding of the scope of evidence that must be disclosed in trials; and victim protection.[227]

SOUTH AFRICA

The South African Police Service was known for its brutality, corruption and inefficiency. Investigations were not given much importance and the police relied more on extracting confessions. However, with the end of apartheid, the process of reforms was initiated. The Strategic Plan, 1991 of the South African Police Service highlighted the following features:

1. De-politicization of the police force;
2. Increased community accountability;
3. More visible policing;
4. Establishment of improved and effective management practices;
5. Reform of the police training system with racial integration; and
6. Restructuring of the police force.[228]

---

[227]Legal Reports (Publications of the Law Library of Congress), https://www.loc.gov/law/help/criminal-justice-system-reform/japan.php, accessed on 14 February 2022.

[228]Second Administrative Reforms Commission, Fifth Report on *Public Order*, June 2007, p. 55.

An ombudsman was also appointed in 1991 to look into allegations of the police's misconduct. In 1992, the police was reorganized into a three-tier force: a national police responsible for internal security and major crimes; autonomous regional forces responsible for prevention of crime and maintenance of law and order; and municipal police responsible for minor local crimes.

The South African Police Service Act, 1995 sought to transform what was a repressive police into a democratically controlled police service. The salient features of the Act were:

- The South African Police Service shall be structured at both national and provincial levels and shall function under the direction of the national and provincial governments.
- The 'Secretariats for Safety and Security' would monitor the adherence of the police to promotion of democratic accountability, transparency, and evaluate its performance.
- 'Independent Complaints Directorate' will be established which will investigate the public complaints of police misconduct. It would report directly to the minister of safety and security.
- Local governments were empowered to establish municipal or metropolitan police service.[229]

'An important component of the new South Africa is the transformed South African Police Service (SAPS). From a history of brutal and indiscriminate violence, the new police system is attempting to transition into a responsible democratic police organization.'[230]

---

[229]Ibid. 56.

[230]William R. Pruitt, 'The Progress of Democratic Policing in Post-Apartheid South Africa', *African Journal of Criminology and Justice Studies*, Vol. 4, No. 1, June 2010.

AUSTRALIA

The Police Regulation Act, 1862 amalgamated the several independent police units in the country into one police force. It was replaced by another Police Regulation Act, passed in 1899. A comprehensive Police Act was promulgated in 1990. Under it, commissioner of police, appointed by the governor on the advice of the concerned minister, was the head of the police force.

Complaints of corruption led to the setting up of a Royal Commission in 1994, which found systemic and entrenched corruption in the police. The Commission's recommendations led to the passage of the Police Integrity Commission Act, 1996. Its objectives were:

- to establish an independent, accountable body whose principal function will be to detect, investigate and prevent police corruption and other serious police misconduct;
- to provide special mechanism for the detection, investigation and prevention of serious police misconducts;
- to protect public interest by preventing and dealing with police misconduct; and
- to provide for the auditing and monitoring of particular aspect of the operations and procedures of the New South Wales Police.[231]

The Police Integrity Commission is in addition to the Independent Commission Against Corruption as well as an ombudsman. It has been laid down that, to prevent any overlap, any complaint made to the ICIC or the ombudsman shall be referred by them to the Police Integrity Commission

---

[231]Second Administrative Reforms Commission, Fifth Report on *Public Order*, June 2007, p. 59.

if it is related to police misconduct. There is an intricate web of accountability.

In the wake of the 'Black Lives Matter' and 'Stop First Nations Deaths in Custody' protests across Australia in 2020, there is a strong demand to make police officers[232] and prison guards[233] responsible for deaths in custody and put an end to racial police violence.

UN: CODE OF CONDUCT FOR POLICE

The UN Code of Conduct (1979) for law-enforcement officials specifically requires that: 'Law enforcement officials shall at all times fulfil the duty imposed upon them by law, by serving the community and by protecting all persons against illegal acts, consistent with the high degree of responsibility required by their profession.'[234]

It goes on to say that: 'In the performance of their duty, law enforcement officials shall respect and protect human dignity and maintain and uphold the human rights of all persons.'[235]

The emphasis is on enforcing the law and serving the community. There is no reference anywhere in the Code to carrying out the dictates of the executive.

---

[232]Paul Gregoire, 'After being vindicated by the state, the family of Tanya Day are fighting on', *The Big Smoke*, 26 April 2020, https://thebigsmoke.com.au/2020/04/26/after-being-vindicated-by-the-state-the-family-of-tanya-day-are-fighting-on-tanya-day/, accessed on 14 February 2022.

[233]Lachlan Harper, 'Over 82,000 call for charges over David Dungay Jrs death in custody', *Port News*, 18 June 2020, https://www.portnews.com.au/story/6797204/82000-want-charges-laid-over-dungay-jnrs-death-in-custody/, accessed on 14 February 2022.

[234]'UN Code of Conduct for Law Enforcement Officials', 19 November 2013, https://www.facing-finance.org/en/database/norms-and-standards/un-code-of-conduct-for-law-enforcement-officials/, accessed on 14 February 2022.

[235]Ibid.

10

THE WAY AHEAD

It is one of the ironies of modern India that while we are capable of sending a mission to the moon, while there has been a revolution in information technology, while there has been vast improvement in the rail and road network across the country, while we have taken a quantum leap in nuclear science, while we are capable of firing missiles across continents, we are yet saddled with a colonial police with a feudal mindset. There have been any number of Commissions, both at the state and central levels—State Police Commissions, National Police Commission, Gore Committee, Ribeiro Committee, Padmanabhaiah Committee and Malimath Committee, to name only a few, which made recommendations for reforms. However, these received no more than cosmetic treatment at the hands of the government, with the result that there has been hardly any change in the colonial policing which we inherited from the British. The common man does not feel secure or protected—on the contrary, he may be harassed or even persecuted by the police if he dares take a stand against the establishment.

There are about 26,000 police stations and outposts across the length and breadth of the country, and their working impinges on the life of the common man, from Srinagar to Kanyakumari and from Ahmedabad to Aizawl, irrespective of whether he has a complaint or not. It is a sad commentary on our republic that we have not been able to transform this police into an instrument of service upholding the rule of law and inspiring confidence among the people.

It needs to be emphasized that police reforms are absolutely essential if India is to emerge as a great power. Economic progress cannot be sustained if we are unable to generate a safe and secure environment. The democratic structure may also crumble if we do not arrest the trend of criminals gaining ascendancy in public life.

The three greatest problems in the area of internal security confronting us are: the separatist or secessionist movements in Jammu and Kashmir, the multiple insurgencies in the Northeast and the Maoist insurrection across vast stretches of central India. If we are to tackle these problems effectively, there is no getting away from having a professional police force that is well trained and equipped, motivated, and committed to upholding the laws of the land and the Constitution of the country. The police are the first responders in the event of any terrorist attack, insurgent onslaught or Maoist violence.

The prime minister, while addressing the Directors General of Police (DGPs) in Guwahati on 30 November 2014 enunciated the concept of SMART Police—police which should be strict and sensitive, modern and mobile, alert and accountable, reliable and responsible, techno-savvy and trained. The Ministry of Home Affairs subsequently organized regional workshops on SMART policing in Bengaluru, Bhopal, Guwahati and Chandigarh during April/May 2015. The best practices being followed by some state governments were compiled by the BPR&D and circulated to the DGPs during the next conference at Bhuj (Gujarat) in December 2015. These were, at best, half-hearted attempts to implement a concept which actually required systemic changes in the functioning of the police.

What is the state of policing in the country today? It would be in the fitness of things that we get a clear picture of that.

STATUS OF POLICING IN INDIA

A comprehensive report on the subject was prepared by Common Cause[236] and Lokniti programme of the Centre for the Study of Developing Societies (CSDS). The salient findings of the *Status of Policing in India Report 2019*[237] are summarized below:

1. The police in India work at 77 per cent of its sanctioned strength or just three-fourth of its required capacity. These personnel work for 14 hours a day on an average. Three out of four personnel believe that this workload is affecting their physical and mental health.

2. Training of personnel is abysmal. Over the last five years, on an average, only 6.4 per cent of the police force has been provided in-service training.

3. Police infrastructure is poor:
   i. Across 22 states, 70 police stations do not have wireless devices
   ii. Two hundred and fourteen police stations do not have access to telephones
   iii. Twenty-four police stations have access to neither wireless nor telephones
   iv. Two hundred and forty stations have no access to vehicles

4. There are inadequate facilities at police stations:
   i. Twelve per cent personnel reported that there is no provision for drinking water
   ii. Eighteen per cent said there are no clean toilets
   iii. Fourteen per cent said there is no provision for seating area for the public

---

[236] Author is member of the governing body of Common Cause.
[237] *Status of Policing in India Report 2019: Police Adequacy and Working Conditions* by Common Cause, Centre for the Study of Developing Societies, Lokniti, Tata Trusts and Lal Family Foundation.

5. Housing facilities are unsatisfactory. Nearly three out of five respondents from the families of personnel were dissatisfied with the quarters provided by the government.

6. Technology support leaves much to be desired:
   i. Eight per cent personnel said that functional computers are never available at their police stations
   ii. Forty-two per cent said that forensic technology is never available at the police station

7. The premature transfer of SSPs and DIGs in less than two years has significantly declined since 2007 (post the *Prakash Singh* judgment). However, at the all India-level, 12 per cent officers of the ranks have been transferred in less than two years.

8. Three out of five personnel reported transfer as the most common consequence of not complying with external pressures.

9. Twenty-eight per cent police personnel believe that pressure from politicians is the biggest hindrance in crime investigation.

10. Women police personnel are more likely to be engaged in in-house tasks. One in five female personnel reported absence of separate toilets for women at their police station or workplace.

11. Three-fifth of the civil police personnel believe that no matter how serious a crime, there should be preliminary investigation before registering a FIR.

12. Three out of four personnel feel that it is justified for the police to be violent towards criminals. Four out of five personnel believe that there is nothing wrong in the police beating up criminals to extract confessions. One out of five police personnel feel that killing dangerous criminals is better than a legal trial.

The report emphasized that 'India's future as a democracy and an economic powerhouse cannot be secured by an obsolete criminal justice system' and that it was necessary therefore to improve the working conditions of policemen and orient the police to 'a more sophisticated, democratic and humane work ethic.'

The *India Justice Report 2019*[238] also states that 'the police's capacity is severely curtailed by its structural frailties' insofar as 'the police remain inadequately staffed, poorly representative and inaccessible to a majority of the population.'

RULE OF LAW: WHERE DO WE STAND?

Rule of law, according to A.V. Dicey, is 'the absolute supremacy and predominance of regular law as opposed to the influence of arbitrary power, and excludes the existence of arbitrariness, of prerogative or even wide discretionary authority on the part of the government.' It should be the cardinal principle guiding the actions, investigative or relating to enforcement of law and order, of any police.

Where does India figure in the rule of law Index? The *World Justice Project* for 2021[239] measured 139 countries' performance across eight factors. These are shown below together with India's ranking under the different heads:

- Constraints on Government Powers   52/139
- Absence of Corruption   95/139
- Open Government   40/139
- Fundamental Rights   93/139

---

[238]The Report is supported by Tata Trusts in partnership with Centre for Social Justice, Common Cause, CHRI, DAKSH, Tata Institute of Social Sciences (TISS)-Prayas and Vidhi Centre for Legal Policy.

[239]'WJP rule of law Index 2021', https://worldjusticeproject.org/sites/default/files/documents/WJP-INDEX-21.pdf, accessed on 8 March 2022.

- Order and Security   121/139
- Regulatory Enforcement   78/139
- Civil Justice   110/139
- Criminal Justice   86/139

The countries with the highest ranking are Denmark (1), Norway (2) and Finland (3). India's overall global rank is 79. Among the other Asian countries, Nepal (70) is followed by Sri Lanka (76), China (98), Bangladesh (124) and Pakistan (130).

It is definitely not a happy situation and underscores the need for comprehensive reforms. 'Effective Rule of Law,' according to the *World Justice Project*, 'reduces corruption, combats poverty and disease and protects people from injustices large and small. It is the foundation for communities of justice, opportunity and peace—underpinning development, accountable government, and respect for fundamental rights.'[240]

POLICE REFORMS FOR A PROGRESSIVE MODERN INDIA

Police reforms are going to be a long haul. It is necessary to clarify at this stage that police reforms are not just about implementing the directions of the Supreme Court. No doubt, they touch the core of police functioning, but police reforms cover a much wider spectrum and include the entire gamut of its functioning. It is not possible to cover the entire canvas; some of the more prominent aspects of reforms are discussed below. These reforms are categorized under three heads: short term, medium term and long term.

The short-term reforms are in the nature of low-hanging fruits and it should not be difficult to implement them.

---

[240]World Justice Project, Rule of Law Index, 2021, p. 13, https://worldjusticeproject.org/sites/default/files/documents/WJP-INDEX-21.pdf, accessed on 8 March 2022.

The medium-term reforms would require some effort. The long-term measures would involve changes in policy or amendment in the Constitution and would therefore require popular backing and political support.[241] Let us discuss these three categories in detail.

Short-Term Reforms

Human Resources

According to the *Data on Police Organizations* (as on 1 January 2020),[242] the total sanctioned strength of state police forces in the country was 26.23 lakh. Out of these, 16.70 lakh are civil police, 2.82 lakh are district armed reserve police and the remaining 6.71 lakh are state special armed police. The actual strength on ground, however, was 20.91 lakh, which included 13.34 lakh civil police, 2.25 lakh district armed police and the remaining 5.33 lakh state armed police. Uttar Pradesh has the largest police force (3.03 lakh) in the country.

There is an overall vacancy of 5,31,737 police personnel: 3,36,044 in civil police, 56,797 in district armed police and 1,38,896 in state armed police. These vacancies should be filled up at the earliest. There is no justification for keeping so many vacancies, especially when we have such a large number of unemployed youth.

The total police personnel sanctioned per lakh of population at the all-India level works out to 195.39. The boots on the ground are, however, only 155.78. The lowest number of policemen per lakh of population are in Bihar (115.26) followed by Andhra Pradesh (141.06), Rajasthan (142.14) and

---

[241]A note incorporating the suggestions in the paragraphs which follow was given to the NITI Aayog on 30 March 2017.
[242]Published by the Bureau of Police Research and Development (BPR&D), Ministry of Home Affairs, Government of India.

Odisha (146.36). These figures compare unfavourably with the international figures.[243]

The most recent figures of police-population ratio are given by Eurostat, which mentions the average for the years 2017–19 for European countries only. The relevant figures of policemen per 100,000 population of some countries are as follows:Italy (413.6), Spain (363.4), France (322.2), Germany (297.4) and (Sweden) 198.4. In the US, it is 247.39.[244]

The total population which a policeman has to look after is 511.81. Considering the vacancies, however, it works out to a population of 641.93, which is quite a high number. In Bihar, which has the worst police–population ratio, a policeman's responsibility actually extends over a population 1,312.39 persons. Area-wise, according to sanctioned strength, a policeman is responsible for 1.25 sq. km; in actual conditions, it works out to 1.57 sq. km.

The total strength of women police in the country is 2,15,504; the maximum number are employed in Uttar Pradesh (29,112). Their percentage in total police force works out to 10.30. The GoI is committed to a target of 33 per cent women in the total

---

[243]There is a general impression that the United Nations has recommended a proportion of 222 policemen per lakh of population. However, in spite of my best efforts, I could not locate any such UN reference. According to my batchmate, Vappala Balachandran, this misconception arose out of a misreading of a Wikipedia entry, vide his article, 'Forget UN standards, think of better policing', published in the NewsX bulletin of 30 July 2021. The number of policemen required in a country would depend on a number of variable factors: the ethnic, caste, class or communal fault-lines in the country, the number of people living below the poverty line, availability of drugs and arms, cultural background of the people, rural–urban divide and a whole range of other factors. There cannot be a uniform standard for all countries of the world. The 'one-size-fits-all' formula would just not apply. In fact, even within a country, if it has a large territory and massive population, there will have to be different yardsticks for different regions.
[244]https://datausa.io/profile/soc/police-officers. The figures may be rounded to the nearest whole numbers because you can't have mutilated policemen.

police force. Available data show that the number of women police personnel is steadily increasing every year. The number was 1,22,912 in 2015; 1,69,550 in 2017 and 2,15,504 as of 2020.

There are large numbers of vacancies even in the Indian Police Service, India's premier police service, whose officers hold leadership positions at different levels across the country. As on 1 January 2020, only 4,074 officers were available as against the sanctioned strength 4,982.

The difficulties arising out of shortage of manpower get aggravated with a sizeable chunk of police force being diverted on unauthorized duties. VIP security is one such area. It was estimated by the BPR&D that, in 2020, a total of 66,043 police personnel were deployed for the protection of ministers, MPs, MLAs, judges and bureaucrats, etc. as against the sanction of 43,566 personnel only.

Infrastructure

The shortfalls at the state level in respect of the following elements of infrastructure need to be made up:

  i) Transport
  ii) Communications and
  iii) Forensics

There are a total of 2,02,925 vehicles available with the states and UTs. Their break-up is as follows:

Heavy duty vehicles	11,956
Medium duty vehicles	19,536
Light duty vehicles	81,099
Very light vehicles (two-wheelers and three-wheelers)	87,586
Special vehicles (Riot-control vehicles, mine-protected vehicles, forensic vans, prison vans, etc.)	27,248

The numbers look impressive, but considering the total strength of police personnel in the country, it works out to only 7.74 vehicles per 100 policemen. The states which are better off are Tamil Nadu (15.38), followed by Andhra Pradesh (13.10), Telangana (12.77) and Karnataka (12.16). The need for the police to have a good fleet of vehicles which meet the law-enforcement challenges of present times cannot be overemphasized.

Communication facilities need to be substantially upgraded. It is ironic that while technology has made such advances, there are still 143 police stations in the country which have neither wireless nor mobile connectivity.[245] The position is worst in Assam, which has 141 police stations without telephones. Tamil Nadu has the best connectivity among the states.

Forensics is essential for good investigation. There are a total of 530 forensic science laboratories in the country. Out of these, 32 are main laboratories, 80 are regional laboratories and the remaining 418 are mobile laboratories. The forensic support should have a broader base, considering the huge population of the country and the large number of cases which are registered.

The GoI, therefore, set up a National Forensic Sciences University in 2020, the first of its kind in the world, with the status of an 'Institution of National Importance' to fulfil the acute shortage of forensic experts in the country. The university has campuses in Gandhinagar and Delhi, where training programmes are conducted for in-service personnel on the subjects of forensic science, cyber crime investigation, digital forensics, cyber security and fraud investigation. The university has already trained more than 19,500 Indian officials and more than 2,800 foreign officials.[246]

---

[245]These are BPR&D figures.

[246]https://www.nfsu.ac.in/about-training, accessed on 14 February 2022.

Housing

The NPC recommended that 100 per cent family accommodation should be provided to all ranks of non-gazetted police personnel. According to information available with the BPR&D, as on 1 January 2020, only 6,47,977 family quarters were available for the police personnel of the country. Out of these, 6,42,027 quarters were for non-gazetted staff, whose actual strength in the country stands at 20,74,162. It means, the satisfaction level in respect of housing for non-gazetted staff was only 31.24 per cent. This is far below the ideal recommended by the NPC way back in 1979. Housing has a direct impact on the welfare and morale of police personnel. There are numerous instances of policemen living in miserable sub-human conditions. A national daily[247] carried a news item under the caption *Delhi cops live in these hellholes*. This has to end. The police personnel must have decent accommodation commensurate with their rank and the onerous duties they perform.

Working Hours

A police officer, under Section 22 of the Police Act of 1861, is 'always on duty', which means he could be put on duty for any number of hours or any number of days at a stretch. This is humanly not possible. The policemen are nevertheless made to put in long hours. The NPC, in its first report (1979), mentioned that 'a job analysis conducted by the National Productivity Council has shown that the working hours of the subordinate police officers range from 10 to 16 hours every day of seven days in a week'. It went on to say:

> Long and arduous hours of work without facilities for rest and recreation, continuous employment on jobs under

[247]Nitisha Kashyap/TNN, *The Times of India*, 3 August 2015.

extreme conditions of stress and strain, both mental and physical, prolonged stagnation in the same rank without even one rank promotion throughout their service for a majority of them, constant exposure to criticism and ridicule by a demanding public, a totally inadequate pay structure with no compensation for the handicaps and privations they undergo in their jobs, low status and lack of involvement in planning and executing field jobs with a full understanding of the objectives set by the police organisation, etc., have all had their telling effect on the morale of the constabulary throughout the country.[248]

A survey conducted by McKinsey & Co. in 2003 identified long working hours (average 14 hours per day) as one of the prominent factors responsible for low motivation and high stress levels. A recent study (2014) sponsored by the BPR&D on the 'National Requirement of Manpower for 8-Hour Shifts in Police Stations' brought out the following picture of long hours of work for policemen[249]:

Staff members of their police stations have to remain on duty for 11 hours or more per day. 27.7 per cent SHOs and 30.4 per cent supervisory officers even reported that their staff worked for more than 14 hours a day.

As if this is not enough, 73.6 per cent of police station staff indicated that they were not able to avail weekly offs even once a month... What makes the situation even worse is that most (over 80 per cent) of the staff are commonly recalled to duty during their off time, to deal with emergencies of law and order, VIP *bandobust* or other works. Nearly a half (46.7%) of staff reported that they were called in for duty, on an average, for 8–10

---

[248]First Report of the National Police Commission (NPC), p. 18.
[249]Rakesh Dubuddu, '90% of the Police Force in the Country works more than 8 hours a day', *Factly*, 4 May 2015.

times in a month. A majority of SHOs also confirmed this trend.

The situation of inordinately long and irregular working hours for police station staff is, thus, quite serious. Long and irregular work hours have multiple negative impacts on efficient policing, since weary, overworked and exhausted personnel cannot be expected to put in their best in their work.

Fig. 2. Average Working Hours

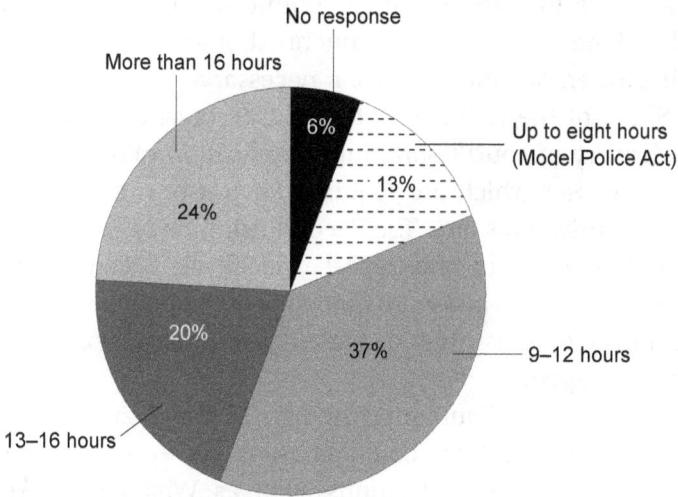

Source: Status of Policing in India Report, 2019, p. 46.

Kerala was the first state which tried to introduce eight-hour duties. Haryana tried to introduce the shift system. UP announced that it would be giving one day off to the policemen every 10 days. The change-over would require an increase in manpower. The BPR&D study referred to above, projected the requirement of additional manpower as 3,37,500 only for introducing eight-hour shifts in all police stations of the country. This is not a large number. To start with, we may have 12-hour shifts and, in course of time, move to eight-hour duties.

Reducing Police Workload

The police perform a number of functions which do not require special knowledge or skills associated with the functioning of the police. These could be outsourced to either government departments or private agencies so that the police are able to concentrate on its core functions. It has been seen that the excise, forest, transport and food departments lean on the state police to discharge their routine functions. This must end and the concerned departments should be asked to have their own enforcement wings, if necessary.

Some of the duties which could be outsourced include the delivery of court's summons, verification of antecedents and addresses which are required for passport applications or job verifications, etc. The Second Administrative Reforms Commission, in its fifth report, specifically recommended that some of these non-core functions of the police should be outsourced or redistributed to other government departments or private agencies.[250]

The Supreme Court suggested on 10 July 2020 that court summons and notices could be sent via e-mail, fax and instant messaging applications such as WhatsApp during the pandemic. Considering that India has about 448 million mobile phone internet users, embracing technology even in normal times would be good idea.

Training

Training remains a neglected area which calls for comprehensive improvement. During 2019–20, an amount

---

[250]Fifth Report of Second Administrative Reforms Commission (Public Order), June 2007, p. 103.

of ₹1,566.85 crore was spent on police training at the all-India level out of the total police expenditure of ₹1,38,794.32 crore, which works out to merely 1.12 per cent. A total of 203 training institutes are being run by the state police forces across the country. These institutes generally have very poor infrastructure in terms of buildings, equipment, literature and facilities. The most unwanted police officers are quite often dumped in these institutions. Bereft of any motivation, they are unable to inspire or inculcate high values among the trainees.

The Second Administrative Reforms Commission recommended that the deputation to training institutions must be made more attractive in terms of facilities and allowances so that the best talent is drawn as instructors. Besides, training should focus on bringing attitudinal change in police, so that they are more sensitive to citizens' needs. All training programmes should include a module on gender and human rights and should sensitize the police towards the weaker sections.[251] Police training or refresher courses should be mandatory for officers at different levels and made an essential precondition for their promotion. Army training institutes attract the best talent, and officers look forward to undergoing training. A similar environment needs to be created in the police force too. Another committee on the lines of Gore Committee should be appointed to go into the entire gamut of training and make appropriate recommendations.

Modernization

The Modernisation of State Police Forces scheme is a centrally sponsored scheme, which was initiated in 1969–70. Funds allotted under the scheme are generally used for improving police infrastructure through construction of police

---

[251]Ibid.120.

stations and provision of modern weaponry, surveillance and communication equipment. Upgradation of training infrastructure, police housing and computerization are also important objectives funded through the scheme. The cost-sharing pattern between the Centre and states is 90:10 for the north-eastern and Himalayan states and 60:40 for all other states.

The following amounts (in INR crore) were released under the modernization scheme during the last five years[252]:

Year	Allocation	Funds Released
2016-17	595	594
2017-18	769	452
2018-19	769	769
2019-20	811	781
2020-21	771	103

There is a gap between allocation and allotment in certain years because some states had unspent balances and had not submitted utilization certificates in respect of funds released during the previous year. Under-utilization of modernization grants has, in fact, been an endemic problem. There are bottlenecks which need to be removed; the government should consider direct allocations to the state police.

In February 2022, a total of ₹4,846 crore was allocated by the GoI for the modernization of state police forces for the period 2021–22 to 2025–26.

The states, unfortunately, accord very low priority to police while budgeting. According to the *India Justice Report 2019*,

---

[252]Ministry of Home Affairs, Standing Committee on Home Affairs (2022), https://prsindia.org/budgets/parliament/demand-for-grants-2022-23-analysis-home-affairs, accessed on 8 March 2022.

most large and mid-sized states spent only between 3 and 5 per cent of their total budget on policing.[253]

Registration of Cases

Non-registration of cases is a very sore point with the people. It is a fact that there is concealment and minimization of crime on a big scale. The political culture of the country is, to a large extent, responsible for it. In the state of UP, for example, oral directions were given by a chief minister in 2002 that crime figures be brought down by 50–70 per cent. There is no magic wand to bring down the crime figures, and so there was burking on a large scale all over the state. This was brought by me to the notice of the National Human Rights Commission through a letter dated 6 January 2003. It was stated therein that 'it is a case of human rights being denied on a huge scale to the largest segment of humanity in the second most populous country of the world'. The Commission, unfortunately, did not take any effective action in the matter. A number of senior police officers who could not meet the target were placed under suspension.[254]

The opposition parties make a lot of hue and cry if crime figures show an increase since this tarnishes the image of the government. The ruling party, under these circumstances, puts pressure on the police to doctor the figures. Society must accept the inevitability of increase in crime figures every passing year.

In some developed countries, the police take cognizance

---

[253]*India Justice Report 2019*, p. 30, https://www.tatatrusts.org/upload/pdf/overall-report-single.pdf, accessed on 14 February 2022.

[254]Officers suspended included DIG Kanpur Range and superintendents of police of Jaunpur, Basti, Mirzapur, Balrampur and Muzaffarnagar districts. IG Kanpur Zone was threatened with an adverse entry. DIG Chitrakoot Range and DIG Agra Range were given warnings.

of a criminal offence only after preliminary verification.[255] In India and countries with similar colonial systems of policing, such as Pakistan, Bangladesh and Sri Lanka, an FIR is supposed to be registered as soon as the complaint of a criminal offence is made. It is common knowledge that many of the complaints are false or highly exaggerated and are intended to harass an adversary. The existing arrangement leads to multiple abuses: there is tendency to conceal and minimize crime on the part of the police. In addition, there is corruption in both registration and non-registration of cases, and the system is saddled with false cases. It is, therefore, suggested that the Criminal Procedure Code, which mandates registration of cases on the bare narration found in a complaint, be amended to allow the police to make a preliminary verification. They would register all complaints, but register an FIR only when they find crime to have been committed after preliminary verification. It would require an amendment in Section 157 (1) of the Code of Criminal Procedure, which would then read as: 'If from information received or otherwise, an officer in charge of a police station, *after such preliminary verification as he deems necessary*, has reason to suspect the commission of an offence.'

The Supreme Court, in Writ Petition (Criminal) No. 68 of 2008 in *Lalita Kumari Vs State of UP & Ors*, laid down that while it is mandatory to register an FIR u/s 154 of the Code if the information discloses the commission of a cognizable offence, a preliminary inquiry may be conducted if the information does not disclose a cognizable offence. It

---

[255]Burking seems to be a universal phenomenon, only that the degree of it varies from one country to another. *The Guardian* (17 July 2018) reported that, according to Her Majesty's Inspectorate of Constabulary and Fire and Rescue Services, nearly 10,000 crimes including violent crimes, sexual offences and domestic abuse went unrecorded by a UK police force over the course of a year.

further said that preliminary inquiry may be conducted before registration of FIR in the following categories of (illustrative and not exhaustive) cases: matrimonial disputes or family disputes, commercial offences, medical negligence cases, corruption cases and cases where there is abnormal delay in initiating criminal prosecution.

It is high time that the existing provisions regarding registration of crime are reviewed and simplified in such a way that reporting becomes citizen-friendly and, at the same time, the police are not overburdened with false reports. Technology can play a major role in achieving this objective. In Delhi, Odisha, Rajasthan and UP, e-FIR facility has been introduced for property and vehicle theft cases where particulars of the accused are not known. Online registration would save people the hassle of running to police stations to lodge complaints. The MHA should work on the modalities of lodging e-FIRs in other non-heinous crimes as well, and advise the states to adopt them.

Separation of Investigation from Law and Order

The Supreme Court, in its judgment of 22 September 2006, directed *inter alia* that 'the investigating police shall be separated from the law-and-order police to ensure speedier investigation, better expertise and improved rapport with the people'. The Court emphasized that there should be full coordination between the two wings and that to start with, it may be carried out in towns or urban areas which have a population of 10 lakh or more. The separation, as clarified by the NPC in its sixth report, should be at the police-station level only and both the wings should remain under the SHO. Higher officers, that is, those above the SHO would remain territorially responsible for both law and order and investigation of crimes. Among all the Court's directions, it was the least controversial. The states have generally no objection to it. Their problem is that such a separation would require additional manpower for which, as some say, they do not have the funds. Finances should not be such a big constraint; in genuine cases, the GoI could assist them.

Delhi Police Bill

A Model Police Act was drafted by Soli Sorabjee as far back as 2006. It was expected that the GoI would be the first to enact the Delhi Police Bill and that the same would become a model for other states. However, the GoI dragged its feet in the matter and, in the absence of any initiative by the Centre, the states passed their own laws on the subject. Fifteen years have since gone by. It is high time that the Delhi Police Bill is legislated. There has been considerable discussion already at different levels on the bill. The state governments which have not passed any laws on the subject so far could thereafter be persuaded to adopt that law under Article 252 of the Constitution.

Commissionerate System

The NPC, in its sixth report, had recommended that in large cities, that is, those with a population of five lakh and above and even in places where there may be special reasons, such as speedy urbanization, industrialization, etc., the system of Police Commissionerate should be introduced. The commissioner should be a police officer of adequate maturity, seniority and expertise, and he should have complete authority over the force and be functionally autonomous. There has been fierce resistance to the Commissionerate system by the bureaucracy and it has been seen that even when the chief minister was agreeable to introducing the system, the bureaucracy managed to scuttle it. In UP, the state government announced in 1978 that they will have a Commissionerate in Kanpur. An officer was also designated to take charge as commissioner. However, the bureaucracy sabotaged the proposal. Another four decades had to elapse before UP could have the Commissionerate system in 2020. This executive resistance would have to be overcome in public interest. At present, 67 cities have police Commissionerate system in the country. Maharashtra (11) has the largest number followed by Telangana (9), Tamil Nadu (7) and West Bengal (7). Among the bigger states, there is no Commissionerate in Bihar, Chhattisgarh, Jammu and Kashmir, and Jharkhand.

The Parliamentary Standing Committee on Home Affairs, in a report submitted to Rajya Sabha on 10 February 2022, expressed its view that 'the police commissionerate system leads to faster decision-making to solve urban-centric issues' and that therefore 'the MHA may advise states to consider establishing police commissionerate system in cities having more than 10 lakh population.'

Internal Reforms

Apart from the above, which would require government support, there are a number of internal reforms which could be carried out by the police officers themselves. 'What changes police culture is leadership from within.'[256] These changes would not require any political support, legislative back-up or financial allocation. The ambience at the police stations must improve. A complainant walking into a police station should not have any misgivings or apprehensions about the treatment he will get. Just as a man, while walking into a hospital, feels assured that he will get some treatment which would relieve his pain, a man walking into a police station should also have the confidence that his problem would be looked into and that the police would make efforts to bring

---

[256]William J. Bratton, 'How to Reform Police from Within', *The New York Times*, 16 September 2016.

the culprits to book. It only requires an attitudinal change. There should not be any inordinate delay in the registration of cases and the officer on duty must ensure that there are no unreasonable demands on the complainant in the process. Police behaviour towards the weaker sections of society—women, scheduled castes and scheduled tribes, and the economically backward—should be more humane and sensitive. The policemen must invariably endeavour to uphold the rule of law. N.R. Madhava Menon suggested that the police must adopt 'fair, quick and responsible methods of redressal of complaints against the police' and that the system should be institutionalized and integrated with police role and responsibilities.[257] Unfortunately, these internal reforms have not received due attention from the departmental officers. The police need to set their house in order. Once they do that, they will find public support forthcoming, and once there is public support, it will be only a question of time that the government would be obliged to give police the required degree of autonomy.[258]

The Central Armed Police Forces

India has a formidable array of Central Armed Police Forces (CAPF). These were raised from time to time to meet the specific requirements of national security. International borders are guarded by the Border Security Force, Indo-Tibetan Border Police, Sashastra Seema Bal and Assam Rifles in different theatres. The CRPF looks after internal security while the Central Industrial Security Force is entrusted with the security

---

[257]N.R. Madhava Menon, *Police Reform: Imperative for Efficiency in Criminal Justice,* published in National Workshop on Public Order (2006) organized on behalf of Administrative Reforms Commission, Government of India by the S.V.P. National Police Academy, Hyderabad.

[258]A detailed letter was sent to police officers in the country on the subject soon after the Supreme Court's judgment, vide Appendix D.

of industrial installations and airports. The National Security Guard is an elite anti-terror outfit. The National Disaster Response Force was raised for the purpose of special response to a threatening disaster situation or disaster. The Railway Protection Force is entrusted with securing railway property.

As on 1 January 2020, the actual strength of the CAPF in India was as follows:[259]

Assam Rifles	60,524
Border Security Force	2,37,750
Central Industrial Security Force	1,41,650
Central Reserve Police Force	2,99,410
Indo-Tibetan Border Police	82,631
National Disaster Response Force	10,996
National Security Guard	9,857
Railway Protection Force	60,764
Sashastra Seema Bal	78,809
Total	**9,82,391**

The CAPFs have played a stellar role in dealing with internal security situations in different sectors: cross-border terrorism in Jammu and Kashmir, insurgent movements in the Northeast, Maoist insurrection in parts of central India and in defending the international borders, particularly against Pakistan and China.

During the last few decades, there has unfortunately been a lopsided expansion of the police forces. There has been exponential growth of CAPFs, while growth of the state police forces has been at a slow pace. This has been mainly because the state governments, while not investing adequately

[259]*Data on Police Organisations* (As on 1 January 2020), Bureau of police Research and Development, MHA, Government of India, p. 139.

in their own police forces, have been extravagant in placing demands for CAPFs to deal with the law-and-order situations in the states from time to time. The Centre has been indulgent towards the states in this regard and was therefore compelled to increase the strength of its armed police forces from time to time. This trend must be arrested. A group of experts should study the deployment of forces and work out their optimum strength. The CAPFs have developed a lot of flabs and need to be pruned. The GoI could offer to transfer some manpower from the CAPFs to the states. CAPF personnel who have crossed 50 years of age could be given the option to migrate to the armed police of any state of their choice. This would reduce attrition from the CAPFs as well.

Certain other measures are also called for: the deployment of CAPFs needs to be rationalized; it should be ensured that training companies are not sent on duty under any circumstances; legitimate grievances of cadre officers should be addressed; and stringent norms laid down for the selection of chiefs of the CAPFs, who should also be given a fixed tenure of two years.

Medium-Term Reforms

Implementing Supreme Court's Directions

The Supreme Court's directions on police reforms touch the core of police functioning and are therefore very vital. Eighteen states have passed laws and the rest have issued executive orders purportedly in compliance of the Court's orders. The states have, however, not complied with the letter and spirit of the Supreme Court's directions, which have been modified, amended or diluted. The Centre should put pressure on the state governments to comply, in a transparent and sincere manner, with the Court's directions regarding:

- The setting up of the State Security Commission
- Police Establishment Board
- Police Complaints Authorities
- Selection and tenure of DGP
- Fixed tenure of officers on operational duties, and
- Separation of investigation from law and order.

The GoI could convene a conference of chief ministers, home ministers and home secretaries of the various states for this purpose and impress upon them the need and urgency of implementing the Supreme Court's directions in letter and spirit. The NITI Aayog has, in a paper *India: Three Year Action Agenda (2017-18 to 2019-20)*, suggested that 'states should be encouraged, with fiscal incentives, to introduce critical legislative reform to their police acts, most of which are still based on the police act of 1861.'

The Malimath Committee

The Committee on Reforms of Criminal Justice System headed by Justice V.S. Malimath, constituted on 24 November 2000, submitted a comprehensive report in 2004. It expressed the view that the present Adversarial System could be improved by adopting some useful feature of the Inquisitorial System such as the duty of the courts to search for truth. It therefore recommended that 'Quest for Truth' should be the guiding star of the entire criminal justice system. Regarding the standard of proof, the committee was of the view that we should have a standard higher than 'preponderance of probabilities', and lower than 'proof beyond reasonable doubt'. It should be 'clear and convincing' standard of proof. The committee suggested a number of amendments in the existing criminal laws. Thus, it suggested that Section 25 of the Evidence Act should be amended so that confession recorded by the superintendent of police or an officer above him is admissible in evidence. It also gave suggestions to expedite the disposal of cases, saying that all cases in which punishment is three years or less should be tried summarily, vacations for high courts and Supreme Court should be reduced, etc. The Malimath Committee recommendations, unfortunately, did not get the attention they deserved, mainly because the report was severely criticized by human rights groups, especially the Amnesty International. The recommendations need to be revisited and implemented to the extent they are pragmatic.

Combating Terror

Terrorism, international as well as domestic, is a formidable problem. According to the *Global Terrorism Index 2020*, India is the eighth-most affected country by terrorism (after Afghanistan, Iraq, Nigeria, Syria, Somalia, Yemen and Pakistan). 'Compared to other countries amongst the ten most impacted, India faces a wider range of terrorist groups with Islamist, Communist and separatist groups active across the country.'[260]

Terrorist attacks happen at regular intervals in the states of Jammu and Kashmir, the Northeast and parts of central India. In August 2019, the GoI amended the Unlawful Activities Prevention Act to allow for the designation of individuals as terrorists. The National Investigation Agency (NIA) Act of 2008 was also amended to give the NIA the ability to investigate terrorism cases overseas.

It is absolutely essential that the capabilities of the state police are raised to a level where they are able to deal with the threat of terror emanating from any source, on their own, except in extreme cases, where central help may be sought. For this, the following measures are considered essential:

---

[260]https://visionofhumanity.org/wp-content/uploads/2020/11/GTI-2020-web-1.pdf, accessed on 14 February 2022.

- Every state should have, on the lines of the National Security Guard (NSG), its own State Security Guard (SSG). Its strength could range between 100 to 300 depending on the size of the state and the gravity of the likely threat.
- The country must have a stringent anti-terror law.
- The National Counter Terrorism Centre (NCTC) should be put in place with such modifications as may be considered necessary.

Central Bureau of Investigation

The Central Bureau of Investigation (CBI) was set up by the GoI through a resolution passed on 1 April 1963, and it derives power to investigate from the Delhi Special Police Establishment Act, 1946. It is an anomalous arrangement. The L.P. Singh Committee recommended as far back as 1978 the 'enactment of a comprehensive central legislation to remove the deficiency of not having a central investigative agency with a self-sufficient statutory charter of duties and functions.' In 2007, the 19th report of the Parliamentary Standing Committee also recommended that a separate Act should be promulgated for the CBI 'in tune with the requirements of the time to ensure credibility and impartiality.' In 2008, the 24th report of the Parliamentary Committee emphasized that 'the need of the hour is to strengthen the CBI in terms of legal mandate, infrastructure and resources.' It is high time that the CBI is given appropriate statutory support.

Organized Crimes Act

The United Nations (UN) views organized crime as a large-scale and complex criminal activity carried out by groups of persons, however loosely or tightly organized, for the enrichment of those participating and at the expense of the community and its members. Such crime is frequently accomplished through ruthless disregard of any law including offenses against the person, and frequently in connection with political corruption.[261]

Organized crimes include crimes of money laundering, arms trafficking, drug trafficking, terror networks, trafficking in women and girls, etc. These are assuming dangerous proportions today. Organized criminals have spread their network across the country and have linkages with crime syndicates beyond the borders. It is a pity that the GoI has not enacted any law so far to deal with organized crimes. Maharashtra, which is the epicentre of organized crimes in India, enacted a special law called the Maharashtra Control of Organised Crime Act (MCOCA), 1999. The statement of objects and reasons of MCOCA mentions the following:

> Organized crime has been for quite some years now a very serious threat to our society. It knows no national boundaries and is fuelled by illegal wealth generated by contract killing, extortion, smuggling in contrabands, illegal trade in narcotics, kidnappings for ransom, collection of protection money and money laundering, etc. The illegal wealth and black money generated by the organized crime being very huge, it has had serious adverse effect on our economy. It was seen that the organized criminal syndicates made a common cause with terrorist gangs and foster narco-terrorism which extend beyond the national boundaries. There was reason to believe that organized criminal gangs have been operating in the State and thus, there was immediate need to curb their activities.[262]

---

[261]Fifth Report of the Second Administrative Reforms Commission (Public Order), p. 229.

[262]*Zameer Ahmed Latifur Rehman ... vs State of Maharashtra & Ors* on 23 April 2010, https://indiankanoon.org/docfragment/37174/?

Several states have passed laws on the lines of MCOCA. What is needed is a central legislation to deal with the menace. The Second Administrative Reforms Commission felt that 'provisions as contained in MCOCA can be a major tool in the fight against organized crime' and recommended that 'it is now essential to have a central law' to deal with these crimes. India is party to the UN Convention against transnational organized crimes. There is thus international obligation also to enact a pan-India legislation on the subject.

Prosecution

The NPC emphasized the need to 'mesh the prosecuting agency set up with the police set up to ensure active cooperation and coordinated functioning'. It recommended that the Director of Prosecution at the state level should be placed under the administrative control of the DGP. The Malimath Committee recommended that the Director of Prosecution should be selected from among suitable police officers of the rank of DGP. It went on to say that 'all prosecutors should work in close cooperation with the police department'. The present trend however is to the contrary. Prosecution has been separated from the police at the state level and the Centre also favours such an arrangement. The results of separation have not been in the best interests of criminal justice administration. Conviction rates have fallen drastically. It is time that we revisit the existing arrangement. The US follows the integrationist approach regarding the police and prosecution with complete synergy between the two. In the UK, with the passing of the Criminal Justice Act 2003, the prosecutors function from the police stations as part of the Criminal Justice Unit.

---

formInput=kidnapping%20%20%20doctypes%3A%20supremecourt, accessed on 14 February 2022.

Technology

There is enormous scope for technological inputs into the functioning of police in the country. These inputs would act as a force multiplier. Addressing the police chiefs of the country on 15 September 2009, the then prime minister, Dr Manmohan Singh, emphasized the importance of new technology and said that these would go a long way in improving our performance in all dimensions of the internal security challenges.[263] Prime Minister Narendra Modi, while addressing the DGPs/IGPs conference at Lucknow on 21 November 2021, called for the setting up of a high-powered technology mission to adopt future technologies for fulfilling grassroots policing requirements.[264]

A number of initiatives have already been taken in this direction. There is a national Emergency Response Support System (ERSS) with telephone number 112. Control rooms are being modernized. Dial 100 in UP has been a great success. CCTV cameras are being installed at all police stations. The IIT Mumbai has set up the National Center of Excellence in Technology for Internal Security (NCETIS), which is funded by the Government of India.

Some major initiatives are discussed below:

Crime and Criminal Tracking Network and Systems

The Crime and Criminal Tracking Network and Systems (CCTNS) is an ambitious project to network all police stations across the country. The project was sanctioned as far back as 2009 and funds to the tune of ₹2,000 crore were allocated for the purpose; as on 11 August 2021, ₹1,949 crore had been

---

[263]'PM calls for new-age policeman to combat new-age terror', *Hindustan Times*, 15 September 2009.

[264]'PM seeks adoption of future tech for grassroots policing', *The Times of India*, 22 November 2021.

spent. The CCTNS is a very useful project as it would enable the police stations exchange information on a whole range of subjects related to crime and criminals. The project is being implemented by the National Crime Records Bureau (NCRB). FIRs are now being registered electronically in 16,074 police stations across the country.[265]

The scope of the CCTNS project has since been extended with the setting up of the Interoperable Criminal Justice System (ICJS) by integrating data from police, prosecution, courts, prisons, and forensics with a view to facilitate integration of all the pillars of criminal justice and make the justice delivery system more transparent. On 18 February 2022, the Centre approved the implementation of Phase II of the ICJS at a total cost of ₹3,375 crore during the period 2022–26. The ICJS would work through a dedicated and secure cloud-based infrastructure with high speed connectivity.

NATGRID

The National Intelligence Grid or NATGRID is meant to bolster India's counterterrorism capabilities. The project entails combining 21 sensitive databases relating to domains, such as banks, credit cards, cell phone usage, immigration records, motor vehicle registration and income tax records into a single database for access by authorized officers from central agencies, such as the IB, Research and Analysis Wing (R&AW), CBI, Directorate of Revenue Intelligence (DRI) and Directorate of Enforcement (ED). It is essentially a data transfer tool that would give investigators a 360-degree profile of a suspect.

The project was launched in 2012 and an amount of ₹1,002.97 crore was sanctioned. The construction of NATGRID facilities including the data centre and a business continuity

---

[265]Demand for Grants 2022-23 Analysis: Home Affairs, PRS Legislative Research, https://prsindia.org/budgets/parliament/demand-for-grants-2022-23-analysis-home-affairs, accessed on 8 March 2022.

plan are said to be at advanced stage of completion.[266]

Facial Recognition

In 2021, the government approved the introduction of Automated Facial Recognition System (AFRS) across the country, allowing facial biometrics to be matched with the image of individuals whose photos and identity information are already stored in the NCRB database. It will be the world's largest government-operated facial recognition system. According to the NCRB, 'the Automated Facial Recognition System will help in automatic identification and verification of persons from digital images, photos, digital sketches, video frames and video sources by comparison of selected facial features of the images from an already existing image database.'[267] It is claimed that it will provide 'a robust system for identifying criminals, missing children/persons, unidentified dead bodies and unknown traced children/persons across the country'. The technology has raised privacy and security concerns, which would need to be addressed by the government.

Predictive Policing

The present-day policing is essentially reactive in nature. Predictive policing aims to anticipate the most probable place and time where an offence would occur, giving police officers the opportunity to be 'at the right place at the right time.' It draws from canonical theories of crime that focus on criminal events, crime prone locations and criminal opportunities.[268]

---

[266]*Ministry of Home Affairs Annual Report 2018–19*, pp. 7–8.

[267]Kunal Kislay, 'AFRS in India: The Tech Is Ready, But What About the People?', *Opinions*, 29 October 2020.

[268]Sarah Brayne, Alex Rosenblat and Danah Boyd, *Predictive Policing, Data & Civil Rights: A New Era of Policing and Justice*, available at http://www.datacivilrights.org/pubs/2015-1027/Predictive_Policing.pdf, accessed on 8 March 2022.

The underlying assumption of predictive policing is that crime is not randomly distributed across people or places and that it has patterns which are a 'function of environmental factors that create vulnerabilities for victims and spaces at certain times.'[269] There is no doubt that predictive policing has 'the potential to be a significant tool in keeping society safe but the premature use of such technology without ironing out the kinks can have dire consequences.'[270] The police would have to be careful that the data-driven decisions do not perpetuate the prevailing biases or amplify the existing inequities.

Future Challenges

Policing today is at a critical juncture. It must keep pace with the fast-evolving digital landscape, harnessing the existing and emerging technologies. Encryption, internet of things, cloud storage and 3D printing, to name only a few, are going to throw up hitherto unknown challenges. Encryption provides privacy to the common man, but is also being used by criminals and anti-national elements to cover their tracks. Internet of things, which enables devices to talk and communicate with each other, is vulnerable to hackers who can take over control of these devices. Cloud storage allows users to store their data with no knowledge on how it is spread across jurisdictional boundaries. The cloud service provider usually never informs the client about the location of the data storage, and so neither the person who owns the data nor the investigating agency has any clue about the actual location of the data. 3D printing has reached a stage where criminals can produce firearms, counterfeit currency, spurious drugs and fake parts of automobiles in the cozy comfort of their homes. Challenges to

---

[269]Cited by Amber Sinha in *Big Data in Governance in India: Case Studies,* available at https://cis-india.org/internet-governance/files/big-data-compilation, accessed on 8 March 2022.
[270]Millennium Post, *Policing in the Digital Age,* 30 November 2020.

law enforcement in these and other related areas are going to be multifaceted: getting evidence across international boundaries and jurisdictions with different privacy laws, legal assistance treaties and regulatory orders, collecting digital footprints from hundreds of devices and thereafter putting together all the evidence in a logical and coherent manner before the courts.

Needless to say, policing would have to acquire a high level of sophistication and technical expertise to be able to deal with these problems. Apart from increasing the general digital literacy of the police, we would require strong international networks to enable data sharing between governments. Procurement and technology implementation will have to be more open to the participation and involvement of private sector, and it would be desirable to have not only the views but also the cooperation of civil society groups to understand the implications to privacy and risks of algorithmic bias.

New Wings for Cyber and Social Crimes

The police need to have new wings to deal with cyber crimes and social crimes.

Cyber crimes are assuming alarming proportions. According to M.K. Narayanan, former national security advisor, 'Cyberspace has emerged as the fifth dimension of warfare, apart from land, air, sea, and outer space. With the potential to trigger an Armageddon-like event, cybersecurity threats pose the biggest challenge to humanity.'[271] According to NCRB data on *Crime in India 2020*, cyber crimes are increasing year after year. The figure stood at 27,248 in 2018, went up to 44,735 in 2019 and further increased to 50,035 in 2020. In 2020, UP reported the highest number of cyber crimes (11,097) followed by Karnataka (10,741), Maharashtra (5,496), Telangana (5,024) and Assam (3,530); 60.2 per cent of

---

[271]*Synergia Insights*, Vol. 239, November 2020.

the total cases during 2020 related to fraud, 6.6 per cent related to sexual exploitation and 4.9 per cent concerned extortion.

The UN's specialized agency for information and communication technologies—International Telecommunication Union—has ranked India on the 10th spot in the Global Cyber Security Index (GCI) 2020.[272] Interestingly, China is ranked at 33 and Pakistan at 79. There is, however, no room for complacency. The GoI has been training police and other government employees through its cyber cells across the country. Nevertheless, there is a huge lack of awareness of cyber hygiene which contributes to critical digital vulnerabilities.

The traditional daroga does not have the mental aptitude to handle these crimes in a professional manner. The police department should take students who have graduated in computer sciences from recognized institutions like the IITs. These students may, however, always be looking for better opportunities elsewhere. Under the circumstances, they could be given short service commissions of, say, five years in the department. These boys and girls could work in plain clothes and this particular wing could be placed under the state CID. The Parliamentary Standing Committee on *Police-Training, Modernisation and Reforms* (Feb. 2022) has also recommended that the states and UTs should 'recruit cyber experts/IT professionals to assist police in detecting, monitoring, preventing and investigating cyber crimes'.

The Belfer Center for Science and International Affairs of Harvard Kennedy School (USA) recently published a report titled *National Cyber Power India's Index*. One of its authors, Simon Jones, commented as follows on cyber capabilities:

> India should seek to use its forthcoming National Cyber Strategy to better articulate the cyber capabilities it

---

[272]Sandhya Sharma, 'India breaks into top 10 countries on UN's index measuring commitment to cybersecurity', *The Economic Times*, 29 June 2021.

possesses and aspires to possess, the foreign and domestic policy objectives it is seeking to fulfil through cyber means, and better articulate the roles and responsibilities of key bodies and organisations, including the Indian Armed Forces and intelligence community. India should also seek to increase its pool of cybersecurity professionals, help its citizens to understand how to keep their devices safe and secure, and improve its ability to disrupt cybercriminals and other hostile actors operating within its computer networks.[273]

The social crimes which the police are called upon to handle include offences related to beggary, prostitution, domestic violence, dowry offences, crimes against women and girl child, etc. Alex S. Vitale, author of *The End of Policing* (Verso, 2018), has argued that we need to reconsider fundamentally what it is the police should be doing at all. There has been massive expansion in the scope of policing. As stated by him:

> Policing has become more intensive, more invasive, more aggressive. Part of our misunderstanding about the nature of policing is we keep imagining that we can turn police into social workers. That we can make them nice, friendly community outreach workers. But police are violence workers. That's what distinguishes them from all other government functions. They have the legal capacity to use violence in situations where the average citizen would be arrested. So, when we turn a problem over to the police to manage, there will be violence, because those are ultimately the tools that they are most equipped to utilize: handcuffs, threats, guns,

---

[273]Nikhil Rampal, 'India is no superpower in Cyberspace, claims Harvard report', *India Today*, 22 September 2020, https://www.indiatoday. in/diu/story/india-is-no-superpower-in-cyberspace-claims-harvard-report-1724327-2020-09-22, accessed on 14 February 2022.

arrests. That's what really is at the root of policing. So if we don't want violence, we should try to figure out how to not get the police involved.[274]

A special wing needs to be created in the police for social crimes with personnel drawn from students who have graduated in social work. They could be inducted as inspectors or deputy superintendents of police.

Community policing would also go a long way in tackling these crimes. The activities of community policing are built on a robust system of police–public partnership engineered through regular interactions. In 2003, the BPR&D recommended a model of community policing with the goal of minimizing the gap between police and citizens to an extent where the former become an integral part of the community they serve and earn their acceptance and trust. Community policing programmes have been experimented in several states. Kerala has *Janamaithri Suraksha,* which has been implemented in over 200 police stations; Chhattisgarh has *Amcho Bastar, Amcho Police* (Our Bastar, Our Police); Punjab has *Saanjh* and Odisha has *Ama Police.*

Long-Term Reforms

One Police Act for the Country

Article 252 of the Constitution gives Parliament the power to legislate for two or more states by consent and it lays down that such an Act shall apply to the consenting states and to any other states by which it is adopted through a resolution passed in that behalf by the House or, where there are two Houses, by each of

---

[274]Leah Donella, 'How Much Do We Need the Police?', NPR, 3 June 2020, https://www.npr.org/sections/codeswitch/2020/06/03/457251670/how-much-do-we-need-the-police, accessed on 14 February 2022.

the Houses of the Legislature of that state. It is rather anomalous that while British India had one Police Act of 1861 for the entire country, we are confronted with a situation where every state has a different Act with sharp differences in essential features. It would be desirable that there is a central legislation and the same is *mutatis mutandis* adopted by the other states and union territories of the country. Once the GoI passes its legislation on the subject, the same, with necessary changes to suit local conditions, could be adopted by the other States/UTs. Such a step would ensure broad uniformity in the police structure across the country, which would be desirable to strengthen the federal set-up. It is true that several states have already enacted their own police acts, but then their constitutional validity has been challenged in the Supreme Court.

Police in Concurrent List

The founding fathers of the Constitution placed 'public order' and 'police' under the State List of the seventh schedule. It is interesting to place on record that during the Constituent Assembly debates on 25 November 1949, Frank Antony made the following observations on the desirability of police being in the Concurrent List:

> I ought to place on record my disappointment that certain vital subjects like Education, Health and Police should have been left entirely within the ambit of provincial autonomy...
>
> Last but not least, I should like to have seen police made central subject. Police in a province like Bombay have a deservedly good reputation. But, let us be honest. What kind of reputation or lack of reputation do the police administrations in many of the provinces enjoy? What does the man in the street think of the police regimes in many of the provinces? I know what he thinks, you know what he thinks. The police have fallen

into disrepute in many of the provinces. They are not regarded as guardians of law and order but as agencies of corruption and oppression. I should like very much to have the Police administration at least brought on to the Concurrent List.[275]

During the last nearly seven decades, the law-and-order situation in the country has undergone a sea change. There are threats to internal security which have inter-state and even international ramifications. Terrorism is sponsored from across the borders and there are outfits which have bases on our western and eastern flanks. Maoist insurgency has spread across vast areas of central India. It is simply beyond the competence of a state to handle these problems without the active involvement and support of the Centre. Even otherwise, the states are depending heavily on the Union government for the maintenance of law and order even of a routine nature. Communal riots, caste clashes, mela arrangements, inter-state disputes and similar other challenges necessitate deployment of CAPFs. It would be in the fitness of things therefore if 'police' and 'public order' are brought in the Concurrent List of the seventh schedule of the Constitution. An amendment of Clause 3 in List III, Concurrent List, would perhaps serve the purpose. It would rationalize and give *de jure* status to what prevails *de facto* on the ground.

Madhav Godbole, who was Union home secretary, has expressed himself strongly in favour of 'police' and 'public order' being shifted from the State List to the Concurrent List. Fali Nariman, a noted constitutional expert, while addressing an annual meeting of the IPF, stated that just as 'forests' were brought from the State to the Concurrent List to protect them

---

[275]Constituent Assembly of India Debates (Proceedings): Volume XI, 25 November 1949, https://www.constitutionofindia.net/constitution_assembly_debates/volume/11/1949-11-25, accessed on 14 February 2022.

from devastation, 'police' and 'public order' should also be moved to the Concurrent List in view of the state governments blatantly misusing the police for their partisan ends.

Federal Crimes

The crime scene is witnessing a tremendous change. Crime is becoming complex and multidimensional. We have today criminals without borders. The Committee on Reforms of Criminal Justice System, in this context, made the following recommendation:

> Time has come when the country has to give deep thought for a system of Federal Law and Federal Investigating Agency with an all-India Charter. It would have within its ambit crimes that affect national security and activities aimed at destabilising the country politically and economically. The creation of the Federal Agency would not preclude the State Enforcement Agencies from taking cognizance of such crimes. The State Enforcement Agencies and the Federal Agency can have concurrent jurisdiction. However, if the Federal Agency takes up the case for investigation, the State agencies' role in the investigation would automatically abate. The State agencies may also refer complicated cases to the proposed Federal Agency.[276]

The Second Administrative Reforms Commission also emphasized the need for enacting 'a new law to deal with a category of offences which have interstate and national ramifications', and recommended that the following offences may be included in the category of Federal Crimes:

1. Organized crime
2. Terrorism

---

[276]Committee on Reforms of Criminal Justice System, Volume 1, p. 211.

3. Acts threatening national security
4. Trafficking in arms and human beings
5. Sedition
6. Major crimes with inter-state ramifications
7. Assassination of (including attempts on) major public figures
8. Serious economic offences

The investigation of federal crimes could be entrusted to the NIA or the CBI.[277]

Intelligence

Intelligence is another area where drastic reforms are called for. The techniques of national security and intelligence management, according to B. Raman, have 'not received in India the attention they deserve either in the agencies themselves, or at the senior levels of the general bureaucracy or in the political leadership. The result: the agencies tend to drift from crisis to crisis, from failure to failure and from surprise to surprise.'[278]

The Intelligence Bureau (IB), which is India's premier intelligence agency, has generally given a good account of itself. When things go wrong, the reason in most of the cases is not so much the failure of intelligence as the unwillingness or the lack of political will to take appropriate action in a given situation.

It is nevertheless a fact that the IB, as also the state intelligence organizations, have been heavily politicized and this has severely affected their professional performance. It is

---

[277]The National Investigation Agency (NIA) has already been empowered to investigate offences under the UAPA, offences under Chapter VI of the Indian Penal Code and certain other offences.

[278]B. Raman, *What Ails Indian Intelligence?*, 26 June 2020, http:// ramanstrategicanalysis.blogspot.com/2010/06/what-ails-indian-intelligence.html, accessed on 14 February 2022.

common knowledge that on the eve of every general election, the IB undertakes a comprehensive exercise to help the party in power. Madhav Godbole, who was home secretary, GoI, is once reported to have remarked about a DIB that he was spending 50 per cent of his time in politicking and devoting only the remaining 50 per cent to his professional work. At the state level, the special branches are, most of the time, carrying out some instruction or the other of the ruling party to ensure its political longevity and keeping watch over the activities and plans of the opposition parties. Security of the state, in such an environment, takes the back seat. The penetration of the intelligence agencies in radical, fundamentalist organizations becomes weak in the process.

During the 26/11 terrorist attack in Mumbai, there was conspicuous failure of intelligence. The attack was spread over about 60 hours in which 166 persons (including 25 foreigners) were killed and more than 300 were injured. There were intelligence inputs about targeting Mumbai and the reports had even mentioned the names of the hotels which were to be attacked. R&AW, the country's external intelligence agency, had intercepted sensitive conversations on 18 and 24 September and on 19 November 2008. Unfortunately, the information was kicked like a football from one agency to another. There was no proper appreciation of the bits and pieces of information received. Intelligence assessment is essentially a matter of joining the dots to form a pattern. A High-Level Enquiry Committee was set up under Ram Pradhan and Vappala Balachandran, but its report was initially not placed in the public domain.[279] The report mentioned that

---

[279]It is surprising and, in retrospect, very disappointing that a National Commission of Inquiry was not constituted to look into the failures at the highest level. There are strong reasons to believe that the guilty men of 26/11 in New Delhi responsible for failing to assess the threat and taking timely action, ensured that their role was not investigated.

there were six alerts on the possibility of sea-borne attacks, 11 on the possibility of multiple and simultaneous attacks and three on the possibility of *fidayeen* attacks. The report acknowledged that 'an overall assessment and proper analysis of these reports would have revealed a strong indication that some major terrorist action was being planned against Mumbai.'[280] The Committee also said:

> The Committee is aware that several recommendations to transform management of the police were made by the National Police Commission over three decades back and confirmed by the Supreme Court. Its directions need to be addressed on priority basis.[281]

At Kargil (1999), it may be recalled that it was Gujjar herdsmen who first raised the alarm over the Pakistani Army's intrusion in the area. The Indian Army had withdrawn from some forward posts in extreme winter and that was taken advantage of by the Pakistani Army. There was no forewarning from the intelligence organizations. During the recent Chinese transgressions in Ladakh (2020) too, multiple agencies such as R&AW, National Technical Research Organisation (NTRO) and Directorate of Military Intelligence (DMI), among others, were involved in monitoring the Line of Actual Control (LAC) on the ground and in the air via satellites, but they all appear to have defaulted.[282]

---

[280]'What the High Level Inquiry Committee on the 26/11 Attacks Had to Say', *The Wire*, 26 November 2019, https://thewire.in/security/26-11-mumbai-terror-attack-inquiry-committee, accessed on 15 February 2022.
[281]Ibid.
[282]Rahul Bedi, 'Intelligence Failure on PLA Intrusions in Ladakh Brings Back Memories of Kargil', *The Wire*, 25 July 2020, https://thewire.in/security/indian-army-intelligence-pla-ladakh-kargil, accessed on 15 February 2022. Also see, Frank O'Donnell, 'China Is Taking Advantage of India's Intelligence Failures', Stimson, 28 August 2020, https://www.stimson.org/2020/china-is-taking-advantage-of-indias-intelligence-failures/, accessed on 15 February 2022.

In the US, there are Congressional committees to scrutinize the operations of intelligence organizations. The UK too has a law-codifying parliamentary oversight through the Intelligence Services Act, 1994. It is high time that we too introduce some accountability in the operations of our intelligence organizations. In the wake of the Indo-Pak confrontation over Kargil, a committee headed by a former R&AW chief, Girish Chandra 'Gary' Saxena, was appointed to suggest reforms in intelligence. Unfortunately, its report was never placed in public domain and no one knows what action, if any, was taken on its recommendations.

It has been rightly said by Balachandran that the intelligence agencies can do with 'some sunshine'.[283] Manish Tewari, Congress MP, had moved the Intelligence Services (Powers and Regulation) Bill, 2011 to place IB, R&AW and NTRO on a proper legal footing and suggested the setting up of a 'National Intelligence & Security Oversight Committee'.[284] It was a template which could have been improved upon and adopted. Unfortunately, the bill lapsed in October 2012 and since then the matter has remained buried.

The IB, which was set up through an administrative order on 23 December 1887, must be given statutory or constitutional basis. Secrecy is fine, but in a democracy, there must be safeguards to prevent the misuse of intelligence to bolster the party in power. It has been said that the allegations of widespread misuse of the Pegasus (spyware) could have

---

[283]V. Balachandran, 'Our intelligence agencies need a burst of sunshine', *The Sunday Guardian*, 17 March 2013, http://www.sunday-guardian.com/analysis/our-intelligence-agencies-need-a-burst-of-sunshine, accessed on 15 February 2022.

[284]Manish Tewari, 'State of the Union: Time for intelligence reforms?' *Deccan Chronicle*, 19 March 2016, https://www.deccanchronicle.com/opinion/op-ed/190316/state-of-the-union-time-for-intelligence-reforms.html, accessed on 15 February 2022.

been avoided 'if successive governments had not refused to change the system and hidden intelligence collection operations behind a cloak of secrecy, despite several proposals to initiate reforms'.[285]

CONCLUDING OBSERVATIONS

What is the future of Indian Police? Will it remain stuck in the quagmire of colonial model, or will it become people friendly? Has it done its best with the extremely limited resources it has and with the very severe constraints it functions under? Or, has it disappointed the people?

N.C. Saxena, an IAS officer, published an article titled 'How the IAS has let India down', in which he deplored that our country could not achieve many Millennium Development Goals (MDGs), particularly in hunger, health, nutrition, gender and sanitation.[286] His assessment was that 'most IAS officers resist change, or are indifferent to the poor'. The IPS could be faulted on similar lines. It has generally sacrificed the rule of law for the law of rulers and has been callous in its treatment of the poor, particularly the tribals.

However, taking an overall view, this would appear to be an unfair assessment of the All India Services. There is intrinsically nothing wrong with the services. It is just that their operational autonomy has been curtailed and the politicians have been blatantly misusing their powers to interfere in

[285]Vappala Balachandran, 'Misuse of Pegasus Was Enabled by Governments Ignoring Calls to Reform Intelligence Agencies', *The Wire*, 28 July 2021, https://thewire.in/rights/pegasus-misuse-intelligence-agencies-reforms-government-oversight, accessed on 15 February 2022.

[286]N.C. Saxena, 'How the IAS has let India down', *Hindustan Times*, 19 September 2019, https://www.hindustantimes.com/analysis/how-the-ias-has-let-india-down/story-3yZW0jUi2jmMMrvcg8VCMN.html, accessed on 15 February 2022.

the day-to-day functioning of the administration. Besides, Gresham's law has unfortunately started operating in the services also with officers of questionable competence and integrity quite often getting preference over those with a proven track record. Political considerations generally prevail over those of administrative propriety. The quality of politics in the country took a nosedive, particularly in the mid-'70s, when the country suffered a spell of Emergency. It has been a downhill journey since then. Politicians' treatment of All India Services' officers has undergone three phases. In the first phase, while they appreciated the honest officer, they transferred him when he became inconvenient, but sent him to places which were as prestigious. In the second phase, the politicians maltreated the officers who would not toe their line and saw to it that they were dumped in insignificant assignments. In the third and the current phase, we find officers taking a stand against the politicians being hounded; they may be suspended, framed in cases and their pension may be stopped. This political culture is causing havoc.

This is however not to deny that there has been considerable erosion in the ethical values of the present generation of officers. Corruption is rampant. What is worse, there is a nexus between the corrupt politicians, officers and criminals which is eating into the vitals of not only our society but also the administrative structure. As recorded by the Vohra Committee, 'the network of mafia is virtually running a parallel government, pushing the state apparatus into irrelevance.'[287]

A battle for reforms in the civil services and the police has been going on during the last few decades. From the IAS side, there was an attempt by a former Cabinet secretary, T.S.R. Subramanian, and about 80 other officers, majority of them

---

[287]Vohra Committee Report, Ministry of Home Affairs, p. 5.

from the IAS, who filed a PIL for civil services reforms.[288] The Supreme Court, in its judgment (31 October 2013),[289] directed the Centre and states to set up a civil services board for the management of transfers, postings, promotion and disciplinary matters relating to bureaucrats, laying down that the bureaucrats should have a fixed tenure of service, and that they should not act on verbal orders given by politicians. The struggle for police reforms has now been going on for 25 years. One can only hope and pray that these efforts for civil services and police reforms gather momentum in the years to come.

The police in India are capable of producing phenomenal results if it is given operational autonomy and there are no extraneous pressures to act or investigate on pre-determined lines. Its stellar role in putting down four major terrorist movements or insurgencies in the country deserve to be placed on record.

1. Terrorism in Punjab during the '80s was one of the most lethal terrorist movements the world has witnessed. What made it so formidable was the fact that it was aided, abetted and supported by Pakistan. Some of the finest police officers of the country happened to be posted in Punjab those days. They led from the front and were able to contain and eventually defeat the movement for the Khalistan which was threatening to disintegrate our western borders.

2. In undivided Andhra Pradesh, Greyhounds, an elite force raised by the state government,[290] vanquished

[288]The prayers made in the PIL were somewhat feeble. Considering that a formidable array of IAS officers had joined hands, they could have come up with more robust suggestions.
[289]T.S.R.Subramanian & Ors vs Union of India & Ors on 31 October 2013, https://indiankanoon.org/doc/183945465/, accessed on 15 February 2022.
[290]Greyhounds was raised by K.S. Vyas, an IPS officer, in 1989. Vyas was gunned down by Naxals while jogging in a stadium in Hyderabad on 27 January 1993.

Naxals in the Telangana area, which was their hotbed. The Ministry of Home Affairs have since recommended the Greyhounds model to other states which are also afflicted by Naxal violence.

3. In Tripura, the All Tripura Tiger Force (ATTF) and the National Liberation Front of Tripura (NLFT) posed a serious challenge to the authority of the state. However, the police launched well-calibrated operations and were able to decimate these outfits.

4. Terrorism in the Terai area of Uttar Pradesh, an area as large as Punjab and having a sizeable Sikh population, was wiped out in less than two years (1991–93).[291] Training, weaponry, motivation, leadership and emphasis on winning hearts and minds produced results within a short span of time. A remarkable feature of the operations in Terai was that there was no legacy of bitterness.

It will be no exaggeration to say that the state police and the CAPFs have been at the forefront of the country's battles in the north in Jammu and Kashmir against pro-Pak elements, in central India against the Maoist rebels, and in the Northeast against a plethora of insurgent outfits.

Defending the borders of the country has also been a huge challenge for the police. The country has land borders of 15,318 kilometres, coastline of 5,422 kilometres and island territories of 2,094 kilometres. The Border Security Force, the Indo-Tibetan Border Police, the Sashatra Seema Bal and the Assam Rifles have been playing a vital role in securing these borders.

The law-and-order problems in the country are very complex. In the *Global Peace Index 2021*, India figures at 135

---

[291]Author was the Director General of Police, UP during the period.

among 163 countries.[292] The number of policemen killed in the performance of their duties since Independence shows the enormity of the challenges which policemen face and the risks they expose themselves to in the process. It is estimated that a total of 35,780 policemen had laid down their lives till 31 August 2021—battling terrorists, extremists, separatists, secessionists, the mafia and all shades of lawless elements in different parts of the country. These figures are higher than that of Army personnel killed in action since Independence. Figures of policemen killed in other countries are significantly less.

The Indian Police's ability to manage huge crowds deserves special mention. The Kumbh Mela held in Allahabad (now Prayagraj), in 2019 witnessed a crowd of 240 million people during the 49-day bathing festival. There was virtually a sea of humanity on the important days, the crowd on *Mauni Amavasya*[293] (4 February 2019) alone was around 50 million. It was a huge challenge organizing the orderly arrival, the peaceful assembly and the safe dispersal of this crowd from the Mela area. It is a tribute to the Indian Police that there was no major mishap even though there were intelligence reports of terrorist threats. Police in other countries cannot even imagine, let alone plan, for such a mammoth crowd.

However, it must also be placed on record that there were occasions when the police cut a sorry figure and were found distressingly derelict in the enforcement of rule of law. This was most glaring on two occasions: during the Emergency (1975–77) and during the anti-Sikh riots (1984).

The COVID-19 pandemic saw the police in a new avatar. They went out of their way not only to enforce lockdown

---

[292]Global Peace Index 2021: Measuring peace in a complex world, Institute for Economics & Peace, https://www.visionofhumanity.org/wp-content/uploads/2021/06/GPI-2021-web-1.pdf, accessed on 8 March 2022. China figures at 100, USA at 122 and Russia at 154.
[293]It is the most auspicious day during the bathing festival.

but also to provide relief, distribute food and medicines, and extend any other humanitarian help which people in distress needed. The *Status of Policing in India Report: 2020-21* beautifully summed up the police's role during the pandemic in the following words:

> Police are often referred to as the most visible face of the criminal justice system. During the lockdown, however, their role expanded and they became the most visible face of the state itself. The police were the only agency ensuring not only the imposition of the lockdown but also providing basic facilities such as food and shelter to the people... With every other government agency, courts and modes of transportation shutting down, the visibility of the police was amplified during the period of home confinement.[294]

The police were hailed as 'the frontline of the frontline' and even the prime minister acknowledged that 'the human and sensitive side of policing has touched our hearts.'[295] The BBC, which is usually critical of India, lauded that there was 'growing trust between the police and public.'[296] A survey carried out by *Polstrat*[297] revealed that 69.9 per cent of people spoke of having

---

[294]'Status of Policing in India Report: Policing in the Covid-19 Pandemic 2020-2021' (Volume II), Common Cause and Lokniti–Centre for the Study Developing Societies (CSDS), https://www.commoncause.in/wotadmin/upload/SPIR%202020-2021%20Vol.%20II%20Policing%20in%20the%20Covid-19%20Pandemic.pdf, accessed on 15 February 2022.

[295]Prakash Singh, 'Police in a New Avatar', Indian Police Foundation, 8 May 2020, https://www.policefoundationindia.org/blogs/indian-police-foundation/police-in-a-new-avatar, accessed on 15 February 2022.

[296]Vikas Pandey, 'India coronavirus: How police won hearts with cakes, songs and sacrifice', BBC, 13 May 2020, https://www.bbc.com/news/world-asia-india-52586896, accessed on 15 February 2022.

[297]'COVID 19 Poll: Massive jump in trust in police forces across India', *Polstart*, 3 May 2020, https://medium.com/@news_82607/covid-19-

a lot of trust in the police. There was 60.3 per cent increase in the trust of people for the police during the period 2010–20, and the rank of police (out of the 18 institutions surveyed) jumped from 18 in 2010 to four in 2020. The quality of policing in the country would appear to have taken a leap of faith.

Be that as it may, the need for institutional reforms in the police is imperative. The police structure that we have today is essentially a legacy of the British Raj. The Police Act was legislated in the wake of the Revolt of 1857. The British wanted a police which would be subservient to them and carry out the diktat of the executive, right or wrong, legal or otherwise. The objective was to raise a force which would be 'politically useful' and uphold the imperial interests of the British Empire. It is indeed a sad reflection on our leadership that we have allowed that system to continue to this day. The only change has been that the colonial power has been replaced by the ruling party, the gora sahib by the brown sahib.

The need to have an insulated police cannot be overemphasized. C.V. Narasimhan, former director, CBI and former full-time member secretary of the NPC, expressed his views on the subject in the following words:

> An independent judiciary, which zealously ensures for every citizen all his rights under the law is the bedrock of democracy. In regard to public order it is the police who do the first investigation, and the judiciary deal only with the matter later as brought before them by the police. The independence and fairness of the judiciary will have no meaning to the citizen if the police who prepare the matter for adjudication in court are constantly subject to corrupting influences. A clean judiciary which functions alongside a politicised police is like having a clean dining

poll-massive-jump-in-trust-in-police-forces-across-india-e7966af6523d, accessed on 15 February 2022.

hall which is served from a dirty and unhygienic kitchen! A diseased household is the end result. A clean police is as important as an independent judiciary for the ultimate health of the criminal justice system.[298]

In the absence of insulation, the politicians of the country are running amuck. Two recent incidents may be briefly mentioned here. In Maharashtra, in early 2021, we had the unseemly spectacle of the ruling party using the police as an instrument of extortion to collect money from hotels and bars. In West Bengal, as brought out by the National Human Rights Commission Inquiry in July 2021, there was 'retributive violence by supporters of the ruling party against supporters of the main opposition party', which resulted in the 'disruption of life and livelihood of thousands of people and their economic strangulation'.

Police reforms, it may be emphasized, are not for the glory of the police. The very survival of the democratic structure and the sustained momentum of economic progress are at stake. The legislatures and parliament have been infiltrated with criminals and mafia dons. According to the Association for Democratic Reforms, the percentage of MPs with criminal background in the Lok Sabha in 2004 was 24 per cent; it went up to 30 per cent in 2009, 34 per cent in 2014 and was 43 per cent at the last general election in 2019.[299] The police are subjected to the indignity of paying obeisance to undesirable elements and even providing them security. People who should have been behind bars are protected by the country's elite commandos. A system which permits such aberrations is inherently faulty and has to change. Mechanisms must be put in place to safeguard the police from becoming a tool into the hands of unscrupulous

---

[298]C.V. Narasimhan, 'State Security Commission to Oversee an Imperative Need', Association of Retd Police Officers, Hyderabad, p. 6.

[299]Association for Democratic Reforms' Press Release on 25 May 2019.

politicians or oblige it to protect the criminals.

A democratic country must have democratic policing. As stated by the International Police Task Force (1996), 'in a democratic society, the police serve to protect rather than impede freedoms' and that 'the very purpose of the police is to provide a safe, orderly environment in which these freedoms can be exercised' and the police must apply the criminal law 'equally to all people without fear or favour.'[300]

The economic reforms and the resultant progress have unleashed forces which, while opening up new vistas of development, are also providing opportunities hitherto unknown to criminals. Financial irregularities have become the order of the day and we have scams and scandals. Money is being laundered in a big way. Criminals are able to spread their operations beyond the national boundaries and move with much greater ease and frequency. Drug traffickers are extending their tentacles both in the direction of the Golden Crescent and the Golden Triangle countries.

All this would need effective action—preventive as well as detective—by the law-enforcement agencies. Police, in its present form, can hardly be expected to meet the challenges of the future. It needs to be completely overhauled and modernized. Politicians should stop thinking of it as an instrument to further their narrow, partisan interests. The police should statutorily be made accountable to the people of the country and the laws of the land, and the needs and requirements of not only the police but, in fact, the entire criminal justice system should be firmly integrated with the development planning of the country.

---

[300]Cited in *Feudal Forces: Reform Delayed—Moving from Force to Service in South Asian Policing*, CHRI, 2008, p. 11, https://www.humanrightsinitiative. org/publications/police/feudal_forces_reform_delayed_moving_from_ force_to_service_in_south_asian_policing.pdf, accessed on 15 February 2022.

On the social plane, the upward mobility of the Dalits and the empowerment of women have caused considerable turbulence. There is the inevitable clash between those representing the old values and those asserting their new status, between those standing for the status quo and those insisting on change. The police, by virtue of their background and because of their accountability to the executive, generally support the entrenched vested interests. They should actually be facilitating the forces of socio-economic change and playing the role of protagonists rather than antagonists. Such a transformation is however possible only if it's working philosophy is redefined.

The life, liberty and well-being of the large masses of the Indian population are inextricably linked with reforms in the police. Former Home Minister Indrajit Gupta showed tremendous moral courage in exhorting the chief ministers 'to rise above our limited perceptions to bring about some drastic changes in the shape of reforms and restructuring of the police before we are overtaken by the unhealthy developments which appear to have been taking place all over the country.'[301]

Mahatma Gandhi's private secretary, Pyarelal Nayyar, while responding to a question as to what kind of police Gandhiji envisaged after Independence, is reported to have said that the police should be 'a body of reformers.'[302]

The country is facing formidable internal security challenges and police reforms are essential to effectively deal with them. These challenges are mainly from terrorists and fundamentalist groups in different parts of the country: separatist elements in Jammu and Kashmir, insurgent outfits

---

[301]Cited in *Workshop for the Media on Police Reforms: Police Reform: Too Important to Neglect and Too Urgent to Delay*, https://www. humanrightsinitiative.org/programs/aj/police/india/workshops/media_ on_police_reforms.pdf, accessed on 15 February 2022. Also Appendix B.
[302]SVP National Police Academy magazine, Vol. 28, No. 2, November 1978.

in the Northeast and Naxals in central India. According to an international think tank, Institute for Economics and Peace, violence cost the country 7 per cent of its GDP in 2020[303] and the impact per capita was staggering at ₹55,350. The police are the first responders to any terrorist crime or attack and are at the forefront of the campaign to contain the separatists, defeat the insurgents and neutralize the Maoists. They must therefore be professional, modern and equipped with the latest weapons. Police reforms, in the present context, are, in the words of Madhava Menon 'critical now, more than ever before'.[304]

Thus, looked at from any angle—ensuring the survival of democracy, sustaining the momentum of economic progress, being protagonists rather than antagonists of socio-economic change, giving better security to the huge mass of Indian population, meeting the technological challenges posed the new generation of criminals, or dealing with the major threats to internal security—there is no getting away from having a professional, accountable, sensitive police which gives the highest priority to upholding the rule of law and defending the country with a sense of dedication and commitment against the multifarious challenges confronting it. The Ruler's Police, which we inherited from the British, must metamorphose into the People's Police. The Force must become a Service.[305]

Police reforms have been delayed. There are, nevertheless, hopeful signs. The states, though generally non-compliant, are

---

[303]*Global Peace Index 2021: Measuring Peace in a Complex World*, Institute for Economics & Peace, p. 90. https://www.economicsandpeace.org/wp-content/uploads/2021/06/GPI-2021-web.pdf, accessed on 8 March 2022.

[304]N.R. Madhava Menon, 'Police, People and Politicians', *The Hindu*, 12 November 2002.

[305]The Preamble of the United Nations Basic Principles on the Use of Force and Firearms recognizes that 'the work of law enforcement officials is a social service'. (https://www.ohchr.org/en/professionalinterest/pages/useofforceandfirearms.aspx, accessed on 15 February 2022.)

on the defensive, claiming that they have implemented as far as possible the directions of the Supreme Court. Police reforms have caught the imagination of the people. Media raises the issue every time something goes wrong on the law-and-order front. Several NGOs across the country are campaigning for changes in police working. Political parties have started mentioning police reforms in their election manifesto, albeit grudgingly. At the highest level, the need for a SMART police has at least been recognized. We are perhaps beginning to see light at the end of the tunnel. The campaign for reforms will have to be sustained. The people of the country need to raise their voice on the subject more forcefully.

Police reforms in the country actually represent a historical process. 'There are periods in history', as Sri Aurobindo said, 'when the unseen Power that guides its destinies seems to be filled with a consuming passion for change and a strong impatience of the old.' There is already strong impatience in the country with the colonial police structure; the desire for change is also there, but it has yet to assume the characteristics of a 'consuming passion'. Hopefully, that day should not be far. The process which has been set in motion shall meanwhile move inexorably until the transformational changes which will provide the foundations for a progressive, modern India are carried out.

May all the signs of coming events be free from turmoil
And may happiness lie in that which has been done
And that which has not been done
May our past and future be peaceful
And may all be gracious unto us.

—Atharva Veda

Appendix A

LETTER FROM RAJESH PILOT, MINISTER OF STATE (INTERNAL SECURITY) TO ALL STATE GOVERNMENTS

RAJESH PILOT

MINISTER OF STATE
(INTERNAL SECURITY)
MINISTRY OF HOME AFFAIRS
INDIA
NEW DELHI-110001
27 JULY 1994

Dear

As you are aware, both the Government of India and the State Governments are greatly concerned about the public's perception that the standards of police performance are gradually getting eroded. The imperative need to improve the quality of leadership provided to the police and lift the morale of the forces has been emphasized at various fora, time and again.

2. The recently concluded Conference of Directors General of Police (6–8 July, Delhi) also deliberated on the subject in great detail. In my personal interactions with the DGsP, the impression I gathered was that small measures here and there may not really make matters much different unless a suitable mechanism/structure is put into place to evolve right leadership, boost morale and inculcate in-

built accountability. The recommendations of the National Police Commission (NPC) have been oft quoted to provide right answer to these issues.

3.   The NPC made an in-depth study of the subject and came up with important recommendations. They laid considerable emphasis on introducing a fixed tenure of office for the Chief of Police so that he could withstand extraneous influences and guide and supervise the men under his command with the advantage of continuity for a fixed tenure. Other remedial measures suggested by the NPC included the recommendation that in order to ensure fair selection of a suitable Chief of Police, the selection of the officer should be made from a panel of IPS officers of the State cadre prepared by a Committee of which the Chairman of the Union Public Service Commission should be the Chairman and the Union Home Secretary, the senior-most amongst the Heads of Central Police Organisations, the Chief Secretary of the State and the existing Chief of Police of the State should be members. I may add that apart from ensuring proper selection and security of tenure, it is essential to develop the role of the Chief of Police as a professional administrator in applying management skills to organising and directing the police effort and in making use of modern technology to facilitate police work.

4.   Related to the issue of leadership is the control and supervision of the police forces in which area also there exist large gaps and much ambiguity in the guidance provided to the police and in the system for holding the police accountable for their actions. The NPC, while observing that there is an immediate need to devise a new mechanism of control and supervision, recommended the setting up of 'State Security Commission,' which would help the State Government

discharge the superintending responsibility in an open manner within the framework of law, with due regard to healthy norms and conventions. The functions of the Commission would include, inter alia, the laying down of broad policy guidelines and directions for performance, evaluation of such performance and act as a forum of appeal for disposing of representations from police officers.

5. The NPC, while drawing attention to the deleterious effect of external affluence manifested in widespread corruption in the police forces, observed that it is important to ensure highest standards of rectitude in the functioning of the State Anti-Corruption Bureau. In line with the procedure recommended for the selection of the Chief of Police, they had suggested that the posting of the Head of the Bureau should be from a panel of IPS officers of that State cadre prepared by a Committee of which the Central Vigilance Commissioner would be the Chairman and the Secretary in the Department of Personnel and Administrative Reforms at the Centre, the Head of the Central Bureau of Investigation, the State Vigilance Commissioner and the existing Head of the State Anti-Corruption Bureau would be members.

6. I have to draw your kind attention to the above recommendations of the NPC because it is felt that these coupled with other steps would go a long way towards restoring the effectiveness and morale of the police forces in the States. While I am aware that a view might have been taken in the past on some of the recommendations of the NPC, I would urge you to have a relook at the whole issue as the situation has undergone substantial change since then warranting acceptance of the recommendations. I trust you will give it your serious consideration and take necessary steps for its implementation. I shall be thankful

for your advising us of the action proposed to be taken by you in this regard.

With regards,

Yours sincerely,

(RAJESH PILOT)

To
As per list attached.

Appendix B

LETTER FROM INDRAJIT GUPTA, UNION HOME MINISTER TO ALL STATE GOVERNMENTS AND UTS

HOME MINISTER
INDIA
NEW DELHI 110001

No.11018/5/96-PMA

3 April 1997

Dear Shri

From the utterances of the Members of Parliament as also from the feedback which I have been receiving from various other quarters, one is led to believe that there has been a general fall in the performance of the police as also a deterioration in the policing system as a whole in our country. While echoing this overall popular perception in the country, it is felt that a time has come when all of us may have to rise above our limited perceptions to bring about some drastic changes in the shape of reforms and restructuring of the police before we are overtaken by the unhealthy developments which appear to have been taking place all over the country. It is in this context that I have for long been thinking of addressing you so that we can break out of our colonial system of policing and bring about certain reforms and structural changes in consonance with the developments which have taken place during the last 50 years or so in the administration of criminal justice in general and police functioning and practices in particular.

2. The popular perception all over the country appears to be that many of the deficiencies in the functioning of the police in our country have arisen largely due to an overdose of unhealthy and petty political interference at various levels starting from transfer and posting of policemen of different ranks, misuse of police for partisan purposes and political patronage quite often extended to corrupt police personnel. This is the general perception of the people and we all should share our quota of blame in this regard irrespective of our party affiliations. Added to this malady is the prevailing system of inadequate public accountability of police performance, extremely poor level of police–public relationship, increasing levels of police misconduct, poor state of police leadership and discipline and virtual absence of an effective public grievances redressal mechanism. In fact, within the police forces also there is strong resentment against political and other extraneous interference or pressure in the discharge of their lawful professional duties.

3. At the same time, it should also be recognised by us that quite often it is the police, including the para-military forces, which have stood between lawlessness verging on anarchy and functioning of our democracy. It is also a fact that, besides the armed forces, it is the police and the Central Paramilitary Organisations (BSF, CRPF, CISF, ITBP, etc.) whose personnel are laying down their lives in our continuing battle against the secessionist and terrorist forces in the various parts of our country. It is, therefore, of great national importance that we rise above any narrow and partisan considerations to insulate the police from the growing tendency of partisan or political interference in the discharge of its lawful functions of prevention and control of crime including investigation of cases and maintenance of public order. Unless this task is taken up

by us all, we at the Centre or in the States, may soon find ourselves to be incapable of maintaining our democratic institutions to which we are all committed.

4. It is with this sincere commitment in view that I address my colleagues for accomplishing a very difficult but nationally significant task in the matter of some urgently needed reform and restructuring of the police in our country. The details of my thinking and considered suggestions on this are included in the enclosed Note.

5. It is a sad commentary on our professed commitment to the people to provide them with a professionally competent and reasonably clean police administration that we have so far not even made any serious attempt to implement many of the basic and salutary recommendations of the National Police Commission to bring about the required changes in police performance and behaviour pattern. On the contrary, quite often the recommendations of the NPC for police reforms have been misrepresented, perhaps deliberately, as amounting to giving unbridled power to the police. In reality, however, proper implementation of the recommendations will amount to not only curbing many of the existing powers of misuse by the police but also by those who are the existing controllers of the police, viz., the political executives and the bureaucracy. The proposed reforms will reduce to the minimum the possible misuse of powers both by the policemen themselves and also by their controllers by introducing more effective systems of checks and balances and also by ensuring discharge of police functions strictly in accordance with law and professional requirements without fear or favour. It will also ensure greater transparency, accountability and responsiveness to public criticism of police functioning.

6. If recent developments are any indication, judicial intervention in bringing to book many of the allegedly

corrupt politicians and other public servants has been hailed by a wide cross-section of the people as a step in the right direction. I have a feeling that if the political executives do not take the desired measures even now to bring about [the] suggested reforms and restructuring of the police, the day may not be far off when the judiciary may intervene decisively to force such socially desirable changes down the throat of the political executives.

7. In the end I would earnestly request you to kindly take a hard look at the reality around us and do all that is needed and expected from us all in bringing about the long awaited basic changes in the functioning of the police including the police system in keeping with the legitimate aspirations of the common people.

With regards,

Yours sincerely,

Sd/-
(INDRAJIT GUPTA)
UNION HOME MINISTER

Encl: Note on police reforms
and restructuring

3 April 1997
NEW DELHI

To
1. Chief Ministers of all State Governments and UTs.
2. Lt. Governors/Administrators of UTs of Andaman & Nicobar Islands, Chandigarh, Dadra & Nagar Haveli, Daman & Diu, Lakshadweep.

Appendix C

SUPREME COURT'S JUDGMENT ON POLICE REFORMS CASE (22 SEPTEMBER 2006)

IN THE SUPREME COURT OF INDIA
Writ Petition (Civil) No. 310 of 1996
Decided On: 22.09.2006

Appellants: Prakash Singh and Ors. Vs. Respondent:
Union of India (UOI) and Ors
Hon'ble Judges:
Y.K. Sabharwal, C.J., C.K. Thakker and
P.K. Balasubramanyan, JJ.

JUDGMENT

Y.K. Sabharwal, C.J.

1. Considering the far reaching changes that had taken place in the country after the enactment of the Indian Police Act, 1861 and absence of any comprehensive review at the national level of the police system after independence despite radical changes in the political, social and economic situation in the country, the Government of India, on 15 November, 1977, appointed a National Police Commission (hereinafter referred to as 'the Commission'). The commission was appointed for fresh examination of the role and performance of the police both as a law enforcing agency and as an institution to protect the rights

of the citizens enshrined in the Constitution.

2. The terms and reference of the Commission were wide ranging. The terms of reference, inter alia, required the Commission to redefine the role, duties, powers and responsibilities of the police with special reference to prevention and control of crime and maintenance of public order, evaluate the performance of the system, identify the basic weaknesses or inadequacies, examine if any changes necessary in the method of administration, disciplinary control and accountability, inquire into the system of investigation and prosecution, the reasons for delay and failure and suggest how the system may be modified or changed and made efficient, scientific and consistent with human dignity, examine the nature and extent of the special responsibilities of the police towards the weaker sections of the community and suggest steps and to ensure prompt action on their complaints for the safeguard of their rights and interests. The Commission was required to recommend measures and institutional arrangements to prevent misuse of powers by the police, by administrative or executive instructions, political or other pressures or oral orders of any type, which are contrary to law, for the quick and impartial inquiry of public complaints made against the police about any misuse of police powers. The Chairman of the Commission was a renowned and highly reputed former Governor. A retired High Court Judge, two former Inspector Generals of Police and a Professor of TATA Institute of Social Sciences were members with the Director, CBI as a full time Member Secretary.

3. The Commission examined all issues in depth, in period of about three and a half years during which it conducted extensive exercise through analytical studies and research of variety of steps combined with an assessment and

appreciation of actual field conditions. Various study groups comprising of prominent public men, Senior Administrators, Police Officers and eminent academicians were set up. Various seminars held, research studies conducted, meetings and discussions held with the Governors, Chief Ministers, Inspector Generals of Police, State Inspector Generals of Police and Heads of Police organizations. The Commission submitted its first report in February 1979, second in August 1979, three reports each in the years 1980 and 1981 including the final report in May 1981.

4. In its first report, the Commission first dealt with the modalities for inquiry into complaints of police misconduct in a manner which will carry credibility and satisfaction to the public regarding their fairness and impartiality and rectification of serious deficiencies which militate against their functioning efficiently to public satisfaction and advised the Government for expeditious examination of recommendations for immediate implementation. The Commission observed that increasing crime, rising population, growing pressure of living accommodation, particularly, in urban areas, violent outbursts in the wake of demonstrations and agitations arising from labour disputes, the agrarian unrest, problems and difficulties of students, political activities including the cult of extremists, enforcement of economic and social legislation etc. have all added new dimensions to police tasks in the country and tended to bring the police in confrontation with the public much more frequently than ever before. The basic and fundamental problem regarding police taken note of was as to how to make them functional as an efficient and impartial law-enforcement agency fully motivated and guided by the objectives of service to the public at large,

upholding the constitutional rights and liberty of the people. Various recommendations were made.

In the second report, it was noticed that the crux of the police reform is to secure professional independence for the police to function truly and efficiently as an impartial agent of the law of the land and, at the same time, to enable the Government to oversee the police performance to ensure its conformity to the law. A supervisory mechanism without scope for illegal, irregular or mala fide interference with police functions has to be devised. It was earnestly hoped that the Government would examine and publish the report expeditiously so that the process for implementation of various recommendations made therein could start right away. The report, inter alia, noticed the phenomenon of frequent and indiscriminate transfers ordered on political considerations as also other unhealthy influences and pressures brought to bear on police and, inter alia, recommended for the Chief of Police in a State, statutory tenure of office by including it in a specific provision in the Police Act itself and also recommended the preparation of a panel of IPS officers for posting as Chiefs of Police in States. The report also recommended the constitution of Statutory Commission in each State the function of which shall include laying down broad policy guidelines and directions for the performance of preventive task and service-oriented functions by the police and also functioning as a forum of appeal for disposing of representations from any Police Officer of the rank of Superintendent of Police and above, regarding his being subjected to illegal or irregular orders in the performance of his duties.

With the 8th and final report, certain basic reforms for the effective functioning of the police to enable it to promote the dynamic role of law and to render impartial service to the people were recommended and a draft new Police Act incorporating the recommendations was annexed as an appendix.

5. When the recommendations of National Police Commission were not implemented, for whatever reasons or compulsions, and they met the same fate as the recommendations of many other Commissions, this petition under Article 32 of the Constitution of India was filed about 10 years back, inter alia, praying for issue of directions to Government of India to frame a new Police Act on the lines of the model Act drafted by the Commission in order to ensure that the police is made accountable essentially and primarily to the law of the land and the people. The first writ petitioner is known for his outstanding contribution as a Police Officer and in recognition of his outstanding contribution, he was awarded the 'Padma Shri' in 1991. He is a retired officer of Indian Police Service and served in various states for three and a half decades. He was Director General of Police of Assam and Uttar Pradesh besides the Border Security Force. The second petitioner also held various high positions in police. The third petitioner—Common Cause—is an organization which has brought before this Court and High Courts various issues of public interest. The first two petitioners have personal knowledge of the working of the police and also problems of the people. It has been averred in the petition that the violation of fundamental and human rights of the citizens are generally in the nature of non-enforcement and discriminatory application of the laws so that those having clout are not held accountable even for blatant violations of laws and, in any case, not brought to justice for the direct violations of the rights of citizens in the form of unauthorized detentions, torture, harassment, fabrication of evidence,

malicious prosecutions, etc. The petition sets out certain glaring examples of police inaction. According to the petitioners, the present distortions and aberrations in the functioning of the police have their roots in the Police Act of 1861, structure and organization of police having basically remained unchanged all these years.

6. The petition sets out the historical background giving reasons why the police functioning has caused so much disenchantment and dissatisfaction. It also sets out recommendations of various Committees which were never implemented. Since the misuse and abuse of police has reduced it to the status of a mere tool in the hands of unscrupulous masters and in the process, it has caused serious violations of the rights of the people, it is contended that there is [the] immediate need to redefine the scope and functions of police, and provide for its accountability to the law of the land, and implement the core recommendations of the National Police Commission. The petition refers to a research paper 'Political and Administrative Manipulation of the Police' published in 1979 by Bureau of Police Research and Development, warning that excessive control of the political executive and its principal advisers over the police has the inherent danger of making the police a tool for subverting the process of law, promoting the growth of authoritarianism, and shaking the very foundations of democracy.

The commitment, devotion and accountability of the police has to be only to the rule of law. The supervision and control have to be such that it ensures that the police serve the people without any regard, whatsoever, to the status and position of any person while investigating a crime or taking preventive measures. Its approach has to be service oriented, its role has to be defined so that in appropriate cases, where on account of acts of omission and commission of police, the rule of law becomes a casualty, the guilty Police Officers are brought to book and appropriate action taken without any delay.

7. The petitioners seek that [the] Union of India be directed to redefine the role and functions of the police and frame a new Police Act on the lines of the model Act drafted by the National Police Commission in order to ensure that the police is made accountable essentially and primarily to the law of the land and the people. Directions are also sought against the Union of India and State Governments to constitute various Commissions and Boards laying down the policies and ensuring that police perform their duties and functions free from any pressure and also for separation of investigation work from that of law and order. The notice of the petition has also been served on State Governments and Union Territories. We have heard Mr Prashant Bhushan for the petitioners, Mr G.E. Vahanvati, learned Solicitor General for the Union of India, Ms. Indu Malhotra for the National Human Rights Commission and Ms. Swati Mehta for the Common Welfare Initiatives. For most of the State Governments/ Union Territories oral submissions were not made. None of the State Governments/Union Territories urged that any of the suggestion put forth by the petitioners and Solicitor General of India may not be accepted.

Besides the report submitted to the Government of India by [the] National Police Commission (1977–81), various other high-powered Committees and Commissions have examined the issue of police reforms, viz. (i) National Human Rights Commission (ii) Law Commission (iii) Ribeiro Committee (iv) Padmanabhaiah Committee and (v) Malimath Committee on Reforms of Criminal Justice System.

8. In addition to above, the Government of India in terms of Office Memorandum dated 20 September 2005 constituted a Committee comprising Shri Soli Sorabjee, former Attorney General and five others to draft a new Police Act in view of the changing role of police due to various socio-economic and political changes which have taken place in the country and the challenges posed by modern-day global terrorism, extremism, rapid urbanization as well as fast-evolving aspirations of a modern democratic society. The Sorabjee Committee has prepared a draft outline for a new Police Act (9 September 2006). About one decade back, viz. on 3 August 1997, a letter was sent by a Union Home Minister to the State Governments revealing a distressing situation and expressing the view that if the rule of law has to prevail, it must be cured. Despite strong expression of opinions by various Commissions, Committees and even a Home Minister of the country, the position has not improved as these opinions have remained only on paper, without any action. In fact, position has deteriorated further. The National Human Rights Commission in its report dated 31 May 2002, inter alia, noted that:

'Police Reform:

28(i) The Commission drew attention in its 1 April 2002 proceedings to the need to act decisively on the deeper question of Police Reform, on which recommendations of the National Police Commission (NPC) and of the National Human Rights Commission have been pending despite efforts to have them acted upon. The Commission added that [the] recent event in Gujarat and, indeed, in other states of the country, underlined the need to proceed without delay to implement the reforms that have already been recommended in order to preserve the integrity of the investigating process and to insulate it from extraneous influences.'

9. In the above noted letter dated 3 April 1997 sent to all the State Governments, the Home Minister while echoing the overall popular perception that there has been a general fall in the performance of the police as also a deterioration in the policing system as a whole in the country, expressed that time had come to rise above limited perceptions to bring about some drastic changes in the shape of reforms and restructuring of the police before the country is overtaken by unhealthy developments. It was expressed that the popular perception all over the country appears to be that many of the deficiencies in the functioning of the police had arisen largely due to an overdose of unhealthy and petty political interference at various levels starting from transfer and posting of policemen of different ranks, misuse of police for partisan purposes and political patronage quite often extended to corrupt police personnel. The Union Home Minister expressed the view that rising above narrow and partisan considerations, it is of great national importance to insulate the police from the growing tendency of partisan or political interference in the discharge of its lawful functions of prevention and control of crime including investigation of cases and maintenance of public order. Besides the Home Minister, all the Commissions and Committees noted above, have broadly come to the same conclusion on the issue of urgent need for police reforms. There is convergence of views on the need to have (a) State Security Commission at State level; (b) transparent procedure for the appointment of Police Chief and the desirability of giving him a minimum fixed tenure; (c) separation of investigation work from law and order; and (d) a new Police Act which should reflect the democratic aspirations of the people. It has been

contended that a statutory State Security Commission with its recommendations binding on the Government should have been established long before. The apprehension expressed is that any Commission without giving its report binding effect would be ineffective.

10. More than 25 years back, i.e. in August 1979, the Police Commission Report recommended that the investigation task should be beyond any kind of intervention by the executive or non-executive. For separation of investigation work from law and order even the Law Commission of India, in its 154th Report, had recommended such separation to ensure speedier investigation, better expertise and improved rapport with the people without of course any water-tight compartmentalization in view of both functions being closely inter-related at the ground level. The Sorabjee Committee has also recommended establishment of a State Bureau of Criminal Investigation by the State Governments under the charge of a Director who shall report to the Director General of Police. In most of the reports, for appointment and posting, constitution of a Police Establishment Board has been recommended comprising of the Director General of Police of the State and four other senior officers. It has been further recommended that there should be a Public Complaints Authority at the district level to examine the complaints from the public on police excesses, arbitrary arrests and detentions, false implications in criminal cases, custodial violence etc. and for making necessary recommendations.

Undoubtedly and undisputedly, the Commission did commendable work and after in depth study, made very useful recommendations. After waiting for nearly 15 years, this petition was filed. More than 10 years have elapsed since this petition was filed. Even during this period, on more or less similar lines, recommendations for police reforms have been made by other high powered committees as above noticed. The Sorabjee Committee has also prepared a draft report. We have no doubt that the said Committee would also make very useful recommendations and come out with a model new Police Act for consideration of the Central and the State Governments. We have also no doubt that the Sorabjee Committee Report and the new Act will receive due attention of the Central Government which may recommend to the State Governments to consider passing of State Acts on the suggested lines. We expect that the State Governments would give it due consideration and would pass suitable legislations on recommended lines, the police being a State subject under the Constitution of India. The question, however, is whether this Court should further wait for Governments to take suitable steps for police reforms. The answer has to be in the negative.

11. Having regard to (i) the gravity of the problem; (ii) the urgent need for preservation and strengthening of rule of law; (iii) pendency of even this petition for last over 10 years; (iv) the fact that various Commissions and Committees have made recommendations on similar lines for introducing reforms in the police set-up in the country; and (v) total uncertainty as to when police reforms would be introduced, we think that there cannot be any further wait, and the stage has come for issue of appropriate directions for immediate compliance so as to be operative till such time a new model Police Act is prepared by the Central Government and/or the State Governments pass the requisite legislations. It may further be noted that the quality of Criminal Justice System in the country, to a large extent, depends upon the working of the police force. Thus, having regard to the larger public interest, it is absolutely necessary to issue the requisite

directions. Nearly 10 years back, in *Vineet Narain and Ors. v. Union of India and Anr. AIR 1998 SC 889*, this Court noticed the urgent need for the State Governments to set up the requisite mechanism and directed the Central Government to pursue the matter of police reforms with the State Governments and ensure the setting up of a mechanism for selection/appointment, tenure, transfer and posting of not merely the Chief of the State Police but also all police officers of the rank of Superintendents of Police and above. The Court expressed its shock that in some states the tenure of a Superintendent of Police is for a few months and transfers are made for whimsical reasons which has not only demoralizing effect on the police force but is also alien to the envisaged constitutional machinery. It was observed that apart from demoralizing the police force, it has also the adverse effect of politicizing the personnel and, therefore, it is essential that prompt measures are taken by the Central Government.

12. The Court then observed that no action within the constitutional scheme found necessary to remedy the situation is too stringent in these circumstances. More than four years have also lapsed since the report above noted was submitted by the National Human Rights Commission to the Government of India. The preparation of a model Police Act by the Central Government and enactment of new Police Acts by State Governments providing therein for the composition of State Security Commission are things we can only hope for the present. Similarly, we can only express our hope that all State Governments would rise to the occasion and enact a new Police Act wholly insulating the police from any pressure whatsoever thereby placing in position an important measure for securing the rights of the citizens under the Constitution for the rule of law, treating everyone equal and being partisan to none,

which will also help in securing an efficient and better criminal justice delivery system. It is not possible or proper to leave this matter only with an expression of this hope and to await developments further. It is essential to lay down guidelines to be operative till the new legislation is enacted by the State Governments.

13. Article 32 read with Article 142 of the Constitution empowers this Court to issue such directions, as may be necessary for doing complete justice in any cause or matter. All authorities are mandated by Article 144 to act in aid of the orders passed by this Court. The decision in *Vineet Narain's case* (supra) notes various decisions of this Court where guidelines and directions to be observed were issued in absence of legislation and implemented till legislatures pass appropriate legislations.

14. With the assistance of learned Counsel for the parties, we have perused the various reports. In discharge of our constitutional duties and obligations having regard to the aforenoted position, we issue the following directions to the Central Government, State Governments and Union Territories for compliance till framing of the appropriate legislations:

State Security Commission:

(1) The State Governments are directed to constitute a State Security Commission in every State to ensure that the State Government does not exercise unwarranted influence or pressure on the State police and for laying down the broad policy guidelines so that the State police always acts according to the laws of the land and the Constitution of the country. This watchdog body shall be headed by the Chief Minister or Home Minister as Chairman and have the DGP of the State as its ex-officio Secretary. The other members of the Commission shall be chosen in

such a manner that it is able to function independent of Government control. For this purpose, the State may choose any of the models recommended by the National Human Rights Commission, the Ribeiro Committee or the Sorabjee Committee, which are as under:

NHRC	Ribeiro Committee	Sorabjee Committee
1. Chief Minister/HM as Chairman	1. Minister I/C Police as Chairman	1. Minister I/C Police (ex-officio Chairperson)
2. Lok Ayukta or, in his absence, a retired Judge of High Court to be nominated by Chief Justice or a Member of State Human Rights Commission	2. Leader of Opposition	2. Leader of Opposition
3. A sitting or retired Judge nominated by Chief Justice of High Court	3. Judge, sitting or retired, nominated by Chief Justice of High Court	3. Chief Secretary
4. Chief Secretary	4. Chief Secretary	4. DGP (ex-officio Secretary)
5. Leader of Opposition in Lower House	5. Three non-political citizens of proven merit and integrity	5. Five independent Members
6. DGP as ex-officio Secretary	6. DG Police as Secretary	

The recommendations of this Commission shall be binding on the State Government. The functions of the State Security Commission would include laying down the broad policies and giving directions for the performance of the preventive tasks and service-oriented functions of the police, evaluation of the performance of the State police and preparing a report thereon for being placed before the State legislature.

Selection and Minimum Tenure of DGP:

(2) The Director General of Police of the State shall be selected by the State Government from amongst the three senior-most officers of the Department who have been empanelled for promotion to that rank by the Union Public Service Commission on the basis of their length of service, very good record and range of experience for heading the police force. And, once he has been selected for the job, he should have a minimum tenure of at least two years irrespective of his date of superannuation. The DGP may, however, be relieved of his responsibilities by the State Government acting in consultation with the State Security Commission consequent upon any action taken against him under the All India Services (Discipline and Appeal) Rules or following his conviction in a court of law in a criminal offence or in a case of corruption, or if he is otherwise incapacitated from discharging his duties.

Minimum Tenure of I.G. of Police & other officers:

(3) Police Officers on operational duties in the field like the Inspector General of Police in-charge Zone, Deputy Inspector General of Police in-charge Range, Superintendent of Police in-charge district and Station House Officer in-charge of a Police Station shall also have a prescribed minimum tenure of two years unless it is found necessary to remove them prematurely following disciplinary proceedings against them or their conviction in a criminal offence or in a case of corruption or if the incumbent is otherwise incapacitated from discharging

his responsibilities. This would be subject to promotion and retirement of the officer.

Separation of Investigation:

(4) The investigating police shall be separated from the law-and-order police to ensure speedier investigation, better expertise and improved rapport with the people. It must, however, be ensured that there is full coordination between the two wings. The separation, to start with, may be effected in towns/urban areas which have a population of ten lakhs or more, and gradually extended to smaller towns/urban areas also.

Police Establishment Board:

(5) There shall be a Police Establishment Board in each State which shall decide all transfers, postings, promotions and other service-related matters of officers of and below the rank of Deputy Superintendent of Police. The Establishment Board shall be a departmental body comprising the Director General of Police and four other senior officers of the Department. The State Government may interfere with decision of the Board in exceptional cases only after recording its reasons for doing so. The Board shall also be authorized to make appropriate recommendations to the State Government regarding the posting and transfers of officers of and above the rank of Superintendent of Police, and the Government is expected to give due weight to these recommendations and shall normally accept it. It shall also function as a forum of appeal for disposing of representations from officers of the rank of Superintendent of Police and above regarding their promotion/transfer/disciplinary proceedings or their being subjected to illegal or irregular orders and generally reviewing the functioning of the police in the State.

Police Complaints Authority:

(6) There shall be a Police Complaints Authority at the district level to look into complaints against police officers of and up to the rank of Deputy Superintendent of Police. Similarly, there should be another Police Complaints Authority at the State level to look into complaints against officers of the rank of Superintendent of Police and above. The district-level Authority may be headed by a retired District Judge while the State-level Authority may be headed by a retired Judge of the High Court/Supreme Court. The head of the State-level Complaints Authority shall be chosen by the State Government out of a panel of names proposed by the Chief Justice; the head of the district-level Complaints Authority may also be chosen out of a panel of names proposed by the Chief Justice or a Judge of the High Court nominated by him. These authorities may be assisted by three to five members depending upon the volume of complaints in different states/districts, and they shall be selected by the State Government from a panel prepared by the State Human Rights Commission/Lok Ayukta/State Public Service Commission. The panel may include members from amongst retired civil servants, police officers or officers from any other department, or from the civil society. They would work whole time for the Authority and would have to be suitably remunerated for the services rendered by them. The Authority may also need the services of regular staff to conduct field inquiries. For this purpose, they may utilize the services of retired investigators from the CID, Intelligence, Vigilance or any other organization. The State-level Complaints Authority would take cognizance of only allegations of serious misconduct by the police personnel, which would include incidents involving death, grievous hurt or rape in police custody. The

district-level Complaints Authority would, apart from the above cases, may also inquire into allegations of extortion, land/house grabbing or any incident involving serious abuse of authority. The recommendations of the Complaints Authority, both at the district and state levels, for any action, departmental or criminal, against a delinquent police officer shall be binding on the concerned authority.

National Security Commission:

(7) The Central Government shall also set up a National Security Commission at the Union level to prepare a panel for being placed before the appropriate Appointing Authority, for selection and placement of Chiefs of the Central Police Organisations (CPO), who should also be given a minimum tenure of two years. The Commission would also review from time to time measures to upgrade the effectiveness of these forces, improve the service conditions of its personnel, ensure that there is proper coordination between them and that the forces are generally utilized for the purposes they were raised and make recommendations on that behalf. The National Security Commission could be headed by the Union Home Minister and comprise heads of the CPOs and a couple of security experts as members with the Union Home Secretary as its Secretary.

The aforesaid directions shall be complied with by the Central Government, State Governments or Union Territories, as the case may be, on or before 31 December 2006 so that the bodies afore-noted became operational on the onset of the new year. The Cabinet Secretary, Government of India and the Chief Secretaries of State Governments/Union Territories are directed to file affidavits of compliance by 3 January 2007.

15. Before parting, we may note another suggestion of Mr Prashant Bhushan that directions be also issued for dealing with the cases arising out of threats emanating from international terrorism or organized crimes like drug trafficking, money laundering, smuggling of weapons from across the borders, counterfeiting of currency or the activities of mafia groups with transnational links to be treated as measures taken for the defence of India as mentioned in Entry I of the Union List in the Seventh Schedule of the Constitution of India and as internal security measures as contemplated under Article 355 as these threats and activities aim at destabilizing the country and subverting the economy and thereby weakening its defence. The suggestion is that the investigation of above cases involving inter-state or international ramifications deserves to be entrusted to the Central Bureau of Investigation.

16. The suggestion, on the face of it, seems quite useful. But, unlike the aforesaid aspects which were extensively studied and examined by various experts and reports submitted and about which for that reason, we had no difficulty in issuing directions, there has not been much study or material before us, on the basis whereof we could safely issue the direction as suggested. For considering this suggestion, it is necessary to enlist the views of expert bodies. We, therefore, request the National Human Rights Commission, the Sorabjee Committee and the Bureau of Police Research and Development to examine the aforesaid suggestion of Mr Bhushan and assist this Court by filing their considered views within four months. The Central Government is also directed to examine this suggestion and submit its views within that time.

Further suggestion regarding monitoring of the aforesaid directions that have been issued either by the

National Human Rights Commission or the Police Bureau would be considered on filing of compliance affidavits whereupon the matter shall be listed before the Court.

Y.K. Sabharwal, CJI
C.K. Thakker
P.K. Balasubramanyan

New Delhi
22 September 2006

Appendix D

AN OPEN LETTER TO ALL THE POLICE OFFICERS OF THE COUNTRY

Dear Friends,

I have been thinking of writing to all the police officers of the country for quite some time, particularly the Superintendents of Police, in the context of Supreme Court directions on Police Reforms.

The letter got delayed because I was not sure how to go about it. When I learnt about the G-files and was told that it is distributed to all the Superintendents of Police of the country, I thought this was the best medium to make use of.

You are all aware of the Supreme Court directions. However, very briefly, these visualize three new institutions at the State level: the setting up of the State Security Commission to insulate the police from political pressures; the Police Establishment Board to give autonomy to police in personnel matters; and the Police Complaints Authority to strengthen the accountability mechanism. Besides, the Apex Court has laid down a transparent procedure for the selection of DGP, prescribed a minimum tenure for all the field officers, and directed that the investigation and law-and-order functions be separated in the bigger towns.

Quite a few states (10 of them, to be precise) have fully complied with the directions. Some states have done partial compliance. Some have passed laws which are not necessarily in conformity with the Supreme Court directions. Some have adopted a defiant posture; a contempt application has already been filed against them.

The Court battle will go on. Meanwhile, we should see that an atmosphere in favour of Police Reforms is built up. For this purpose, we need to mobilize the support of NGOs and other significant segments of society, particularly the media.

But there is another area where all of you must contribute. You have to demonstrate not only your willingness but keenness to change. There are many aspects of police functioning which could be improved by your personal initiative and interest. You should do whatever is possible within the existing framework. These may appear small matters to you, but from the point of view of the people, they are very important. I propose to outline some of these issues which deserve your special attention:

1. Reception: A complainant who approaches the police for any kind of help or redress should be properly received. His problem should be listened to with patience and understanding. The matter may or may not relate to the police. It may or may not be within the competence of the police officer concerned to take appropriate action in the matter. But he could always give a patient hearing to the complainant and do whatever he possibly can in his powers.

2. Behaviour: There are always complaints about police behaviour, that it is uncouth, unsympathetic and even brutish. Why can't we give lessons to the lower functionaries to behave politely, courteously and with compassion? These traits can be inculcated. Training institutions could emphasize this. Our own officers, during their tours, could drill this into the minds of the policemen. If the behaviour is sympathetic, the complainant is not hurt to that extent even if the

grievance remains unaddressed or the case is not worked out.

3. Reporting: Non-registration of cases continues to be a serious problem. I am conscious of the fact that people tend to lodge frivolous complaints. These could be quickly verified. In fact, in many cases, through experience you can make out whether the complaint is genuine or fake. In any case, there is a lot of scope for improvement in the registration of cases. You should have the moral courage to justify the increase in crime figures to the senior officers and the politicians.

4. Integrity: There are frequent complaints of policemen demanding money or even extorting that from the common man. Better supervision followed by strict action should bring down these complaints. Of course, the officers' conduct themselves will have to be above board. It may not be possible to eliminate corruption but you could certainly contain it.

5. Women/Tribals/SCs/Poor People: These sections of people deserve your special consideration. Any high-handedness in dealing with them brings the police into disrepute. Incidents are played up by the media and the image of the force is tarnished.

6. Uphold the rule of law: This should be your paramount consideration. Deviating from this for short-sighted gains would invariably land you in trouble, if not today, at some date later on. A large number of police officers have suffered for complying with the illegal directions of the superiors. Two examples should suffice. The officers who abused their authority while combating terrorism in Punjab continue to be hounded to this day. Second, the officers who committed irregularities in the recruitment of constables in UP were suspended *en masse*. What I want to emphasize is that even if

you have to pay a price today for not doing something which is wrong or illegal, you should be willing to pay that today and retain your self-respect and honour rather than risk humiliation or even prosecution at a later date.

You would see that none of the above suggestions require any support or orders from above. They do not involve any financial implications either. It is just a question of deciding to observe and enforce certain norms of behaviour and rules of functioning. All I want to emphasize is that the policemen should be polite and courteous, appear helpful and that their behaviour, particularly towards the weaker sections, should be marked by a humane approach.

Whatever contribution you would make in this direction would go a long way in generating public opinion in favour of Police Reforms. Even otherwise, it would change the perception of people about the police. The police image would be refurbished.

We have to show that the police *is* willing to change, that it *is* in fact keen to change and that we shall henceforth have a people-friendly police accountable primarily to the laws of the land and the Constitution of the country. What was essentially a Force is now a Service. The Ruler's Police has metamorphosed into the People's Police.

(The writer is a former police chief of UP and DG BSF.
He was awarded the Padma Shri.)

Note: Copies of the letter were sent to the DGPs of all the states for being disseminated to all the SPs in-charge districts. The letter was also published in *G-files* Vol. I, Issue 7 of October 2007, copies of which were sent to all the districts of the country.

Appendix E

FINAL REPORT OF JUSTICE K.T. THOMAS COMMITTEE CONSTITUTED BY THE SUPREME COURT

BEFORE THE SUPREME COURT OF INDIA
{In Writ Petition (Civil) No.310/1996, *Prakash Singh & others v. Union of India & others*}

Part V
Findings and Conclusions

18. Insofar as the implementation of the six specific Directives of the Supreme Court is concerned, the Committee has no hesitation in concluding that practically no State has fully complied with those Directives so far, in letter and spirit, despite the lapse of almost four years since the date of the original judgment. In the States, where new police legislations have not been enacted, the directions are purported to have been complied with by issuing executive orders but the contents of such executive orders clearly reflect dilution, in varying degrees, of the spirit, if not the letter, of the Court directives.

19. This is reflected by Annexure I which gives a snapshot of the actual levels of compliance in respect of each of the Supreme Court directives, by the States which have adopted the mechanism of issuing executive orders. Annexure II, which contains the Committee's assessment

of the relevant provisions of the new police legislations enacted by 12 States, reflects the same story.

20. In the executive orders issued by many States as well as in the new police legislations passed by some States, the composition of the State Security Commission (Directive No. 1) reflects deviation by way of exclusion of either the Leader of the Opposition or the judicial element or both. Even in the matter of the ratio between the official and non-official members, we noticed the numerical majority in many cases being kept in favour of officials over non-officials.

21. Regarding the selection of DGP (Directive No. 2), notwithstanding the afore-mentioned difficulty in involving the UPSC for empanelment of officers, most of the States have been sticking to the earlier-existing procedure of selection, without even laying down any merit-based, transparent criteria for the same. As for the tenure of DGP, most States have side-stepped the core of the Supreme Court directive.

22. The Committee observed that there was near uniformity among all the States in not following Directive No. 3, which relates to provision for a fixed tenure for certain categories of police officers, in the manner envisaged by the Supreme Court.

23. As for Directive No. 4 (separation of investigation from law and order), provision has, albeit, been made in the executive orders, in most of the States, but those remain only on paper so far. No concrete steps seem to have been taken to implement the directive on the ground level. Indeed, such separation would involve some augmentation of police manpower and this has been projected as a 'difficulty' by some state governments. Some others have, on the other hand, taken steps to sanction additional manpower and promised that the

separation would be effectively implemented once the new manpower is in place after recruitment and training. For details, see Annexures I & II.

24. The Police Establishment Boards (Directive No. 5) have been created in most of the States but their effectiveness has been persistently questioned by the civil society groups in their representations made before the Committee. The ground-situation of transfers in the four States where sample checks were made by the Committee (UP, Maharashtra, Karnataka and West Bengal) was found to be suggestive of uncertainty of tenures in the transfers and postings of police officers (For details, see Annexures III, IV and V).

25. The Police Complaints Authorities (Directive No. 6) have not been created in most of the States so far (for details see Annexure I). Civil society groups have represented that even in the States which have claimed compliance to this directive, the said Authorities have yet to be put in place at the ground level.

26. Further, the Committee has noticed that some state governments (for example, Tamil Nadu) have introduced legislative Bills, purportedly in compliance of the Supreme Court's directives, but while the Bills have yet to be passed by their Legislatures, in the executive orders issued by the state governments in the interregnum, the provisions of even the proposed Bills have been diluted. Pending passage of the Bills by the Legislature, the state governments may be asked by the Supreme Court to modify such executive orders to bring the same in accordance with their own proposed Bills, without further delay.

27. For checking of ground realities of implementation of the directives, the Committee, as stated earlier, took up the task in respect of four States located in four different geographical zones. The reports on this sample verification

are placed in Annexure III (UP and Maharashtra), Annexure IV (Karnataka), and Annexure V (West Bengal). It can be seen from these Annexures that the level of compliance of the Supreme Court directives in these States is ranging from total non-compliance to partial or marginal compliance to mere paper implementation. The Supreme Court, to begin with, may, therefore, initiate action as deemed appropriate, against these States.

28. As for the remaining States, it is for the Supreme Court to decide on the course and modalities of such verification, to assess the exact level of compliance of the directives by them, before deciding on the action to be taken in respect of them.

29. In the end, the Committee, while reiterating its earlier observation about the indifferent response of most of the state governments, in spite of the letters and reminders addressed to the Chief Ministers personally by the Chairman, would like to express its dismay over the total indifference to the issue of reforms in the functioning of Police being exhibited by the States.

30. Proper functioning of police forces is crucial for the Rule of Law to prevail in any society. It is also a critical requisite for ensuring the Fundamental Rights of the people enshrined and guaranteed under our Constitution. The indifference of the state governments to the issue of police reforms and non-compliance of the Directives of the Supreme Court in this regard, despite the tenacious efforts made by the Committee within the boundaries of its limited mandate, have to be viewed in that perspective.

(Justice K.T. Thomas)
Chairman

(Kamal Kumar)   (Dharmendra Sharma)
Member   Member

Appendix F

IP TO IPS

From the Indian Police

To

The Indian Police Service

With the dawn of Independence
On the midnight of August 14, 1947
Indian officers of the Indian Police assumed leadership of
the Police in India from the departing British officers
With a commitment and total dedication to
Defend the Honour, Security and Integerity of India
Serve with loyalty the Government & the Constitution of India
Adhere to the Rule of Law
Preserve Public safety and order
The officers of the Indian Police became the nucleus and
the moving spirit of the newly formed Indian Police Service
for meeting the many challenges before the Nation
We, the surviving members, Salute the memory of the
INDIAN POLICE
We felicitate and congratulate the succeeding
INDIAN POLICE SERVICE
for carrying forward these ideals and nursing to fullness
the high traditions of the Service

V. G. KANETKAR	P. G. BHATTACHARYA	P. K. SEN	K. F. RUSTAMJI
S. B. SHETTY	N. RAMA IYER	TRILOKI NATH	A. G. RAJADHAKSHA
F. V. ARUL	R. N. KAO	B. CHATTERJEE	E. S. MODAK
A. K. DAVE	ASHWINI KUMAR	R. K. GUPTA	K. SANKARAN NAIR

Appendix G

PROFILE OF INDIAN POLICE[306]

1.	Total strength of State Police	2.62 million (S)
		2.09 million (A)
2.	Total strength of Central Armed Police Forces	1.10 million (S)
		0.98 million (A)
3.	Total number of police stations	16,955
4.	Total number of police outposts	8,948
5.	Police per hundred thousand population	195.39 (S)
		155.78 (A)
6.	Population per policeman	511.81
7.	Area per policeman	1,25 sq. km
8.	Policemen per 100 sq. km area	79.80
9.	Women police total strength	2,15,504 (10.30 % of total)
10.	IPS Officers	4,982 (S)
		4,074 (A)

(Note: 'S' is Sanctioned, 'A' is Actual)

---

[306]Source: *Data on Police Organisations* (As on 1 January 2020), Bureau of Police Research and Development, Ministry of Home Affairs, Govt of India.

Appendix H

WHEN GOD CREATED POLICE OFFICERS

When the Lord was creating police officers, He was into His sixth day of overtime when an angel appeared and said, 'You're doing a lot of fiddling around on this one, Lord?'

And the Lord said, 'Have you read the specification on this order? A police officer has to be able to run five miles through alleys in the dark, scale walls, enter homes the health inspector wouldn't touch, and all the while, not wrinkle his uniform.

'He has to be able to sit in an unmarked car all day on surveillance, guard a murder scene that night, canvass the neighbourhood for witnesses and still testify in court the next day.

'He has to be in good physical condition at all times, running on coffee and half-eaten meals. And he's meant to have six pairs of hands.'

The angel shook her head slowly and said, 'Six pairs of hands? No way!'

'It's not the hands that are causing me problems,' said the Lord, 'it's the three pairs of eyes a police officer has to have.'

'That's on the standard model?' asked the angel, surprised.

The Lord nodded. 'One pair that sees through a bulge in a pocket before he asks, "May I see what's in there, sir?" (When he already knows and wishes he'd taken that accounting job.) Another pair here in the side of his head for his partners' safety. And another pair of eyes in front that can look reassuringly at a bleeding victim and say, "You'll be all right, ma'am," when he knows it isn't so.'

'Lord,' said the angel, touching his sleeve, 'rest and work on this tomorrow then.'

'I can't,' said the Lord, 'I already have a model that can talk a large, out-of-control drunk into a patrol car without incident and feed a family of five on a civil service pay cheque.'

The angel circled the model of the officer very slowly. 'Can it think?' she asked.

'You bet,' said the Lord. 'It can tell you the elements of a hundred different crimes; detain, investigate, search and arrest a violent thug on the street in less time than it takes five learned judges to debate the legality of the stop...and still keeps its sense of humour.

'This officer also has phenomenal personal control. He can deal with crime scenes that you'd find painted in hell, coax a confession from a child abuser, comfort a murder victim's family and then read in the daily paper how law enforcement isn't sensitive to the rights of criminal suspects.'

Finally, the angel bent over and ran her finger across the cheek of the police officer. 'There's a leak,' she pronounced. 'I did say that You were trying to put too much into this model.'

'That's not a leak,' said the Lord, 'it's a tear.'

'What's the tear for?' asked the angel.

'It's for bottled-up emotions, for fallen colleagues.'

'You're a genius!' said the angel.

The Lord looked sombre. 'I didn't put it there,' he said.

(Author unknown)

INDEX

www.ingramcontent.com/pod-product-compliance
Lightning Source LLC
Chambersburg PA
CBHW020450270326
41926CB00008B/557